beyond
THE BRAND

WHY ENGAGING THE RIGHT CUSTOMERS IS ESSENTIAL TO WINNING IN BUSINESS

JOHN WINSOR

Dearborn™
Trade Publishing
A **Kaplan Professional** Company

This publication is designed to provide accurate and authoritative information in regard to the subject matter covered. It is sold with the understanding that the publisher is not engaged in rendering legal, accounting, or other professional service. If legal advice or other expert assistance is required, the services of a competent professional should be sought.

Vice President and Publisher: Cynthia A. Zigmund
Acquisitions Editor: Michael Cunningham
Senior Project Editor: Trey Thoelcke
Interior Design: Lucy Jenkins
Cover Design: Jody Billert
Typesetting: Elizabeth Pitts

Published by Dearborn Trade Publishing
A Kaplan Professional Company

Printed in the United States of America

04 05 06 10 9 8 7 6 5 4 3 2 1

Library of Congress Cataloging-in-Publication Data

Winsor, John, 1959-
    Beyond the brand : why engaging the right customers is essential to winning in business / John Winsor.
        p.   cm.
    Includes bibliographical references and index.
    ISBN 0-7931-8836-9
    1. Product management. 2. Brand loyalty. I. Title.
    HF5415.15.W565   2004
    658.8−dc22

                                                                2004009565

Dearborn Trade books are available at special quantity discounts to use for sales promotions, employee premiums, or educational purposes. Please call our Special Sales Department to order or for more information at 800-245-2665, e-mail trade@dearborn.com, or write to Dearborn Trade Publishing, 30 South Wacker Drive, Suite 2500, Chicago, IL 60606-7481.

To Barbara Perry, Ph.D., for her guidance, mentoring, and, most of all, friendship.

For Bridget, Charlie, and Harry: the best teachers.

Contents

P *r e f a c e*

*Let us make a special effort to stop communicating
with each other, so we can have some conversation.*
JUDITH MARTIN (MISS MANNERS)[1]

Does the following situation sound familiar? You arrive at a much-anticipated party. Once there, you notice several interesting-looking people at various spots in the room holding court with small crowds gathered around them. As you approach one of these groups, you notice that the woman in the center is well dressed, funny, and engaging. Each story she tells about herself seems more interesting than the last. Yet, after a few minutes, you begin to realize that she's not really engaging in a dialogue with those around her; aside from a few deft acknowledgments of others' questions or interjections, she's just plowing ahead with her own monologue. It isn't long before many in her audience start to get bored and leave—and you are definitely one of them.

This woman's behavior is not much different from that of many companies in today's consumer environment. Subscribing to the illusion that they can control their world, companies use branding tools to give them that distinctive "look" and "voice," focusing on how their brands will be perceived and how they can make people fall in love with them. As often as not, however, branding merely becomes a one-way conversation between the company and its customers. Such a conversation can be limiting, if not destructive.

Branding is a wonderful tool that has gone a long way to help companies engage in a conversation with their customers, but the time has come to evolve beyond the brand. The word *brand* has become such an integral part of the modern business lexicon that everyone seems to know intuitively what it means, yet if you asked ten people, you would get ten slightly different answers. So, what is a brand? The *Webster's II New Riverside Dictionary*[2] defines a brand as:

> — *n.* 1. a. A trademark or distinctive name identifying a product or a manufacturer. b. The make of a product thus marked. 2. A type: kind. 3. A mark showing identity or ownership, burned on an animal's hide. 4. A mark once burned on the skin of criminals. —*v.* To mark with or as if with a brand.

While dictionary definitions are a good place to start, they never seem to capture the latest cultural meaning of a term or phrase, especially one as well worn as *brand*.

The word *brand* has evolved to mean everything that personifies a company or product. It means much more than a logo or a great advertising campaign. It is further defined by every new product created, every press release that the company issues, and every customer service person's voice.

While this seems to be a common understanding of *brand,* it leaves out one important element—the customer. In reality, people outside the company, both customers and noncustomers, define the brand in their own minds and in the conversations they have with each other. A brand is not only owned by a corporation and its shareholders; it is owned by all of the stakeholders, people both inside and outside the company. John Philip Jones, veteran of the ad industry, author of the book *What's in a Name?,* and professor of advertising at Syracuse University, argues that a brand is a set of qualities that are not located in the product itself but that consumers perceive as real and value enough to buy. In his definition, a brand exists only insofar as people are willing to believe in it, and once their trust is lost, the brand withers away.[3] A brand, in other words, is created through communication; it is the joint construction of company and consumer who, together, co-create the brand's meaning throughout their mutual relationship.

Therefore, the health of a brand does not lie merely in finding the right way to position your voice and in chasing short-term profits.

Healthy brands come about through creating two-way relationships that are long-term and sustainable. To do this, companies must begin to engage with consumers as people and with marketplaces as communities.

One of the major factors contributing to the current state of brands and branding is the application of a top-down philosophy to better understand people. While top-down tools might work well in finance or manufacturing, they lose their effectiveness when applied to the humanistic world of branding and product development. Instead of focusing on using top-down, inside-out tools to engage with people outside the company, especially customers, new bottom-up, outside-in tools must be developed to listen to the right customers.

While using top-down communication may seem fast and efficient, it is not. Today, we all want things done quickly. We expect to lose ten pounds in a week, learn French in a month, or buy music in an instant on the Internet. The reality is that we're stuck on a treadmill, with more things on our to-do list than we could ever accomplish. Businesses suffer from this same problem of having too many things to do. For many people inside businesses, there is not enough time in the day to answer e-mails, attend meetings, and still have the time to interact directly with customers in their dynamic world. But does this top-down, superfast flow of communication always tell a business everything it needs to know about a community and, most importantly, about its customers? Is top-down communication sufficient in a highly dynamic business environment?

To respond to this dynamism, companies now call upon the help of outside resources in many areas. Independent sales representatives, advertising agencies, PR firms, research companies, call centers, and distribution centers are often utilized with substantial *financial* savings to a company. However, the *real* cost of these activities is an increased layer of insulation between a company's executives—its strategic decision makers—and the customer. This increased isolation is detrimental in our highly dynamic world. While consumer research methodologies developed and used over the past 40 years worked well in their time, their effectiveness is rapidly diminishing. Today, to be successful, you must know your customer more intimately. This means finding ways to pierce the layers of insulation that have grown between you and your customer.

Many companies are awash in market information but don't really know their customers on any personal level. Technology has provided the tools to know what people buy and where they buy it in excruciating detail, yet all of this data cannot answer the question of *why* people consume the products they do. You can talk a lot about customer service and the importance of customers in your business, but unless you are out there, engaged in a real dialogue with the right people, it's impossible to know them well enough to deliver the products they really want.

Today, people expect to be more involved in the purchases they make, forcing companies to seek out those who can help them create relevant products. Customers are demanding that companies employ a bottom-up strategy, not only listening to them but also giving them the ability to co-create the products they buy. The act of co-creation lies along a spectrum. For some people, co-creation means personalization and customization; for others, it is feeling that a customer service representative took their concerns seriously and responded to them.

An example of a technology that has provided the foundation for co-creation is digital music. Apple's iPod mp3 player has changed the way that music customers listen to their music. Instead of making customers buy and play CDs that might contain a few songs that they love but more they don't, the iPod has allowed for the co-creation process of creating and sharing play lists—lists constructed by the customers themselves of purchased digital songs.

Some products are so technical, especially in the technology sector, they need to be created in the confines of an advanced R&D facility. Even though such disruptive products and services outstrip the current imaginations of their potential customers, they cannot be created in a vacuum. Even these products need to be based on inspiration that is found in the context of the customers' lives. In this case, one could say it is not the customers themselves but their culture and their needs, values, and concerns that act as factors in the process of co-creation. Allowing for co-creation can drive long-term customer loyalty, helping to drive long-term profits.

When I started Radar Communications, Nike was our first customer. Mark Parker, Nike's president, hired us to help Nike listen to the conversations happening in the marketplace, which could directly affect Nike. Mark has always made it a priority to stay connected to insightful and intuitive people, not only in sports but in popular culture as well. He understood that he, personally, was several layers removed from working with customers on a day-to-day basis. He also believed that information from Nike's customers would inevitably get caught in a classic game of "telephone;" it was only human nature for a story to be changed along the way. Mark estimated that everyone who touched customer information subconsciously altered it 2 to 3 percent. Hence, by the time he got the information, it could be radically different from the original message.

Mark wanted to know what the real issues were for his current and potential customers so that he could help create the right products for them.[4] The idea was to get the voice of the customer integrated deeply into the strategic core of the company and use this shared meaning to move the company forward in a more effective way. Working with Mark inspired me to start helping companies learn how to bring the voices of the many (consumers) to the ears of the few—their internal teams.

Indeed, this has become Radar's central mission: We help companies listen to and learn from the key voices in their communities by using organic, bottom-up tools of gaining knowledge about people, instead of relying on the typical bureaucratic, top-down methods of consumer research. The goal is to help companies gain a deeper understanding of the dynamic environment in which they must evolve, enabling them to anticipate change rather than react to it.

One of the bottom-up tools we use is anthrojournalism. This tool combines anthropological and journalistic methods and allows us to use the above-mentioned key voices. These key voices (we call them our "reporters"), telling their own stories, guide us in the exploration of the context of their lives and offer compelling ways for their stories to inspire innovation in marketing and product design for our clients.

The idea has been a resounding success. In four-and-a-half years, our company has grown significantly. Radar has become a leader in helping companies listen to their customers by using unique bottom-up tools. We facilitate the co-creation of real innovation in product development and marketing efforts with our clients' customers.

This book is the distillation of the ideas and knowledge I have gleaned from years of working, listening, observing, and participating in the dynamic marketplace. In it, I want to share some inspiring insights and stories that may encourage you and your company to go out and learn more about your own customers, developing your own bottom-up strategy for co-creation. The tools that I share have been developed over the past 20 years and have helped dozens of Fortune 500 companies develop new bottom-up strategies for co-creation with the key voices of their communities.

While change always feels overwhelming, it's good to look around for examples and inspiration. I've been impressed by the evolution that Samuel J. Palmisano, the chairman and chief executive of IBM, has implemented by focusing on involving customers in product co-creation from the bottom up, beyond the IBM brand. When Palmisano took over from Louis V. Gerstner, Jr. in 2002, he understood that either you innovate or your products become commodities. To develop innovation, Palmisano created what he called an "on-demand" strategy, with the goal of creating a deeper connection with IBM's customers. The company's on-demand strategy focuses on adapting products, with key customers' help, to solve more complicated problems. Such a strategy presupposes that IBM not only understands the customers' needs but also engages them in an ongoing dialogue. Palmisano's plan leveraged not only IBM's software expertise but also its consulting knowledge gained from the acquisition of PwC Consulting.

At IBM's 2003 annual worldwide management meeting, there was a discussion of how to develop the on-demand vision. Unfortunately, it centered on what internal strategies would be necessary. Palmisano cut the discussion short and announced that everyone in the room needed to go out and talk to their customers, the companies that IBM works with, about their most difficult business problems. He suggested that if the management group got out of the office and actually solved problems with their customers, they'd understand what to do.

A year later, the company is organized around 12 industry groups and has developed a team approach to include the clients in the co-creation process of developing technological solutions that fit the customers' demands. IBM now sees its evolving values as customer relationships, innovation, and trust. Palmisano understands that IBM's customers don't buy technology products as much as they invest in a relationship with a trusted technology supplier.[5] If IBM, with 303,000 employees working in 125 countries, can develop a bottom-up, co-creation process with their customers, anybody can. With such progressive thinking, the day may soon come when companies elevate listening to a strategic level by creating the position of chief intelligence officer.[6]

This book is organized in the following way. In the first few chapters I examine several important trends in business and in the culture at large that have changed the rules of the game for all companies in our dynamic world. These issues include the illusion of control, the adventures of modern branding, and the power of the people.

In the second section of the book, I outline seven steps for developing bottom-up strategies, which will allow your company to thrive in today's dynamic consumer environment (see Figure 0.1). This strategy means focusing on developing a renewed sense of wonder. It also means getting to know your customers and suppliers as people.

Ultimately, a bottom-up strategy provides companies with the flexibility to be extraordinary. It can act as a map of how to become more engaged in your community. Following are the seven steps toward developing such a strategy, which I will discuss and explain in detail in the second part of the book:

1. Focus on key voices
2. Get the story

3. Listen
4. Find inspiration
5. Hone your intuition
6. Find the center of gravity
7. Tell the story

These steps are tools that you can incorporate into every interaction you have with not only your key customers but any customer, welcoming the power of the people into your business to help you co-create.

There is one caveat, however: Just like everything else in life, developing a bottom-up way of thinking, communicating, and strategizing does take a lot of practice.

In 1998, I sold the consumer magazines that I had owned for ten years and took an extended sabbatical. I went to Mexico to learn how to surf. Surfing has taught me that there is no substitution for repetitive practice. Many of the lessons I've learned from the sport of surfing are at the core of this book. Surfing is one of the iconic alternative sports, representing not only the youth culture but also the beach culture. Many companies have used surfing to leverage their brands into household names in every town across the country. Everybody loves the image of surfing. Yet, I've discovered that very few people actually surf. Why is that? There is one simple answer: Surfing is hard. I have a personal theory about surfing. It takes riding a thousand waves to become a surfer. It doesn't matter if you catch 20 waves a day for 50 days or 1 wave a day for 1,000 days; you just can't get around the experience of learning the hard way.

Just as in surfing, there is no substitution for 1,000 waves or, in this case, 1,000 personal interactions with your customer. I know it seems like an overwhelming number, but there is just no way around it. Mastering the seven steps above takes lots of practice. And practice will give you the chance to develop your own style of engaging in a bottom-up strategy with your customers and the marketplace, offering you the opportunity to drive real innovation.

FIGURE 0.1 *Developing a Bottom-Up Strategy*

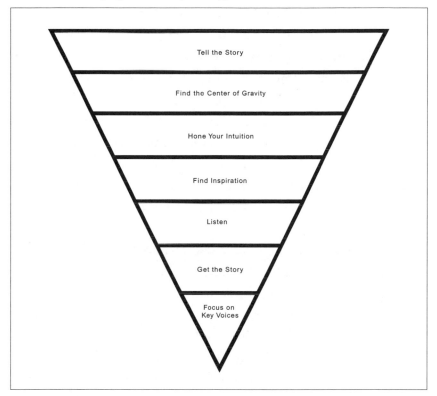

To make the book more practical and interactive, I've dedicated the last chapter to a large case study on "Millennials," young people between the ages of 11 and 21, that we completed in the fall of 2003. This section will help you understand the way in which many of the principles and tools I talk about throughout the book have been used in the context of the real world. I've also made this chapter interactive by integrating it in the book's Web page (http://www.beyond-the-brand.com), so that you can actually experience people telling their stories firsthand, via video.

Throughout the writing of this book, I have been inspired by the dialogue that I have shared with the many wonderful people, both clients and Radar team members, with whom I've had the good fortune to work. In the spirit of this dialogue, think about what information in this book resonates with you. Have you done things that have helped you co-create innovation with your customers?

Thriving in this new, bottom-up economy is a journey. There are no quick answers, just wonderful learning experiences. A journey always seems to start best when you have a bit of inspiration hidden in your pocket. To illustrate this, I'd like to offer you a piece of prose by Ranier Marie Rilke that has inspired me along this journey of writing *Beyond the Brand.*

Only someone who is ready for everything, who doesn't exclude any experience, even the most incomprehensible, will himself sound the depths of his own being. For, if we imagine this being of the individual as a larger or smaller room, it is obvious that most people come to know only one corner of their room, one spot near the window, one narrow strip on which they keep walking back and forth. In this way they have a certain security. And yet, how much more human is the dangerous insecurity that drives those prisoners in Poe's stories to feel out the shapes of their horrible dungeons and not be strangers to the unspeakable terror of their cells. We, however, are not prisoners. No traps or snares have been set around us, and there is nothing that should frighten or upset us.[7]

Enjoy the journey. I hope it proves to be full of inspirational challenges and profitable learning for both you and your company.

The journey of writing *Beyond the Brand* has been taken, encouraged, and supported by so many. There are three people, however, without whose dedication to a deep dialogue this book would never have happened. Thanks to Annie Weber, Nadezhda Kaneva, and Lou Patterson for all of their guidance and long hours. My agent, Rob McQuilkin, and everyone at Dearborn Trade Publishing, especially Michael Cunningham, have provided much thoughtful support. The team at Radar Communications provides me with constant challenge, stimulation, support, and laughter. My special thanks go to Daemon Filson and Dave Kingsbury for helping me begin this wonderful Radar journey out in the garage; without everyone's continued hard work, this would have never been possible. Thank you Dede Aeschliman, Connie Cignetti, Berto de la Roca, Kirsten Gunnerud, Josh Harrod, Carol Kauder, Troy Mault, Bryan McCarthy, Kyle McCuistion, Kim Morris, Dagny Scott-Barrios, Jim Sincock, Summer Stewart, Tara Thrasher, Jeb Tilly, Stacy Valencia, and Scott Webber.

Because most books are a compilation of ideas and inspirations that have been discussed over the past couple of decades, many voices have influenced the book. Clients, business associates, and friends have provided me with constant inspiration and encouragement. They include: Marie-Helene Ambard, Greg Bagni, Antony Barton, Henry Beer, Graceann Bennett, Jan Berie, Sandy Bodecker, Scott Bowers, Shirley Bunger, Jaycie Chitwood-Mason, Kevin Cooney, Janet Cordell, Chris Cowart, Adam Devito, John Eberle, Mark Edmiston, Becky Folds, Greg Foweraker, Byron Freney, Ken Gart, David Hackworthy, Clay Hall, Brad

Harrington, Tinker Hatfield, Karen Havis, Clyde Heppner, Karen Hofmann, Lauren Holden, Michael Jager, Steve Jenkins, Mike Kallenberger, John Kastenholz, David Kemp, Susan Kennedy, Nancy Kosciolek, Marta LaRock, Kyle Lefkoff, Brad Little, Jeff Mason, Beth McConahey, Ross McDonald, Steve McDonald, Peter Metcalf, Bob Meyers, Robin Mitchell, Molly Mulcahy, Cara Newkirk, David Nottoli, Amie Owens, Mark Parker, Shawn Parr, Laura Peach, Michael Perman, Lisa Purcell, Trip Randall, Don Remlinger, Kirk Richardson, Bill Roberts, Peter Ruppe, Karin Sachs, Lisa Saxon Reed, Donatella Scanniello, John Simmons, Ellen Sizemore, Marsha Skidmore, Scott Soden, Tammi Taylor, Irene Tengwall, Jackie Thomas, Scott Tinley, Vesna Vidojevski, Emma Whitmore, Karen Wood, and Alison Zelen.

A special thank you goes out to the Sayulita crew for their diligence, support, and patience during the creation of this book. Thank you Amy Beidleman, Neal Beidleman, Paul Fuller, Mary Gorman, Cheri Hasburgh, Patrick Hasburgh, Kerry Kirkpatrick, John Krakauer, Charlie LaVenture, Sally LaVenture, Mike Pilling, Chris Van Dyke, and John B. Winsor.

Part One

WHAT JUST HAPPENED?

1

THE ILLUSION OF CONTROL

"The most erroneous stories are those we think we know best—and therefore never scrutinize or question."
STEPHEN JAY GOULD[1]

Businesses have long lived under the pretense that the world in which we live is controllable. Even the language of business—*plan, budget, target*—contributes to this illusion. How did this come to be? Encouraged by the promises of the scientific revolution, businesses operated under the belief that, with the right systems and controls, anything could be accomplished. After all, wasn't this the same age that put a man on the moon?

In reality, companies are a lot like frogs. Do you know the best way to cook a frog? The frog gets cooked when the water it sits in starts out cool and the temperature changes only one degree at a time. The frog does not have the subtle sensory skills to see and feel its environment change. This same thing often happens to established companies. The external environment may change only slowly—but if companies fail to notice that change, they're dead in the water.

Entrepreneurial companies have an easier time adapting, because they have more mobility and can react to changes more quickly. These companies act more like a live frog put into boiling water. They can immediately feel the radical difference in the environment and jump out of harm's way.

Established companies that have been historically successful have a very difficult time jumping at all, even out of boiling water. Even when they do recognize a temperature difference, they are rendered immobile by their stubborn dependence on existing systems. Instead, they choose to remain under the delusion that they can control the temperature of the water.

The events of the past couple of years have challenged this notion of control in significant ways. We've become perfectly accustomed to media stories about some of the most successful companies in the world fighting for their very survival. In half a decade, the environment in which these businesses were able to prosper for the past half-century or more has changed beyond recognition.

A few external forces will continue to radically affect the environment in which we live. Between the effects of global cultural shifts, radical changes in the macroeconomic environment, disruptive technologies, the rising power of retailers, the culture of fear, and the role of chance, the business environment will never be the same.

GLOBAL CULTURAL SHIFTS

There is no doubt that our world is much smaller than even a decade ago, and the power of globalization to shift the cultural tectonic plates so rapidly has been surprising. We have seen global events in the past few years that have clearly highlighted cultures, once isolated and dealing with one another only on an infrequent basis, suddenly coming into direct conflict. If anything is to be learned from this age of terrorism, it is that, while we have understood the *idea* of globalization, we have not fully realized the consequences of this realignment. Not only has globalization fueled a growing conflict between Western capitalism and the rest of the world, it has also fueled an antiglobalization movement within our civilization.

The Economist Magazine commented on one facet of the antiglobalization movement by saying: "Standing in opposition to brands is no longer merely an antiestablishment badge for youth; it is a full-fledged social movement."[2] The reality is that many people have begun to feel that marketing is mere propaganda. Their attitudes further fuel the antiglobalization movement and reinforce customers' skepticism toward modern branding efforts.

Kalle Lasn, founder of *Adbusters Magazine* and a leader in the antiglobalization movement, sees it this way: "The old political battles that have consumed humankind during most of the twentieth century—black versus white, Left versus Right, male versus female—will fade into the background. The only battle worth fighting and winning, the only one that can set us free, is The People versus The Corporate Cool Machine. We will strike by organizing resistance against the power trust that owns and manages the brand. America™ has splashed its logo everywhere. And now resistance to that brand is about to begin on an unprecedented scale. We will uncool its fashions and celebrities, its icons, signs, and spectacles. We will jam its image factory until the day it comes to a sudden, shattering halt. And then, on the ruins of the old consumer culture, we will build a new one with a noncommercial heart and soul."[3]

What started out as a voice in the woods has become a conversation on every street corner around the world. A counterculture has formed around this idea that the branding efforts behind many global consumer goods have contributed to a destructive consumer culture. Many have joined the call for change, including Kalle Lasn of *Adbusters Magazine;* historian Tom Frank, author of *The Conquest of Cool: Business Culture, Counterculture, and the Rise of Hip Consumerism;* the alternative culture journal the *Baffler;* Eric Schlosser with his best-selling *Fast Food Nation;* the Center for a New American Dream; and the *Utne Reader.* No other person, however, has brought more attention to the antibranding/globalization movement than Naomi Klein in her book, *No Logo: Taking Aim at the Brand Bullies.* Klein has rallied those opposed to unchecked globalization by trying to link global companies' branding efforts to the central concerns of environmental issues, human rights, and cultural degradation.[4] All of this activity suggests that the anti-branding/globalization movement is quickly becoming a dominant mantra of America's counterculture. This cultural jamming will only be used more frequently to attack the disconnection between brand promises and corporate actions.

After spending a fair amount of time thinking about this problem and dissecting it for our clients at Radar, it becomes obvious that most companies have not maliciously pursued destructive policies. Instead, they have lost touch with their customers and the worlds in which they live, while most managers have been focused primarily on satisfying their shareholders' needs. While this approach may be fine in the short run, the reality is that, without customers who are passionate about a company's products, there won't be any shareholders to worry about. In essence, the long-term relationship with customers must become a short-term focus for companies in our highly connected world.

DISRUPTIVE TECHNOLOGY

Adding to this economic uncertainty is the reality of disruptive technologies, which can affect every company and industry. In this context, *disruptive* might mean something new, different, or just distracting to companies attempting to do things the "usual" way. Every age has been forced to react to its version of disruptive technology: "Those who do not learn from history are doomed to repeat it," said philosopher George Santayana.[5] Disruptive innovations have toppled established companies, not because those companies were unaware of the technology, but because they believed this new technology would not seriously threaten their current methods, practices, or products in the minds of their customers.

Technologies we now take for granted were hugely influential—and disruptive in many ways—to industries and companies in their time. While various contributions to productivity, efficiency, and overall impact on the marketplace are now seen as positive, their presence initially meant that companies had to completely rethink their existing strategies. While it was impossible to ignore new technology, the idea of embracing it—and, therefore, taking the time to learn how to use it—was daunting to many companies in a variety of industries.

The telephone is probably the most profound contribution to information technology in the past century; it made possible the centralization of management of today's largest corporations. Other technologies that proved highly disruptive at first but eventually led to huge leaps of innovation and change include the steam engine, railroads, the internal combustion engine, electricity, radio, television and movies, plastics, air travel, and microelectronics.

In its essence, disruptive technology brings radical change through the introduction of a new way of doing things at a much lower cost. Typically, start-up companies become industry leaders by being flexible enough to evolve their business models, taking advantage of changes and opportunities brought about by disruptive technology. Leading companies don't fail because these new, radical technologies exist. More likely, they fail because of the way they react (or fail to react) to them. They don't pay attention to these disruptions or view them as opportunities, because they are so heavily invested in their own historically successful systems that change is too difficult.

Information technology, which facilitates the delivery of important information, will continue to transform the economy in the foreseeable future. This and other technologies will continue to globalize every industry. Those companies that become nimble at organizing and understanding more information—especially market and customer information—will continue to outpace their competitors. The biggest threat to companies is not disruptive technology or global competition but complacency. By refusing to address or explore new technologies, companies will be blindsided by the continuing pace of change and left behind by forward-thinking competitors.

Established companies must figure out how to compete with start-up companies by finding ways to create their own disruptive technologies, even if doing so might threaten all or some of the company's current products and processes. It's "destroy yourself or be destroyed by someone else." This means that executives must accept the fact that they may fail when exploring new opportunities. Companies must actively integrate and accept failure as part of their culture, welcoming it as a valuable motivator and learning opportunity.

Case Study: Apple Supercomputer

An example of radical thinking that produced disruptive technological change happened in 2003 at Virginia Polytechnic Institute. The school was in the market for a supercomputer that could run the more sophisticated engineering models that students were creating. Like most customers in every industry, the school wanted the best machine, which typically would cost between $100 million and $250 million, but had an actual budget of under $10 million. So, in the fall of 2003, Virginia Tech decided to take the radical step of *building* a supercomputer. The school started by going to Apple Computers and buying 1,100 PCs—as parts. The resulting homemade supercomputer was assembled from off-the-shelf personal computers in less than one month, at a cost of slightly over $5 million. The computer was built by faculty, technicians, and students at Virginia Tech and is now shaking up the world of high-performance computing. The 1,100 Apple Macintosh G5 computers, powered by 2,200 IBM 64-bit microprocessors, have been connected to produce one very fast machine—on its first speed test it was able to compute at 7.41 trillion operations a second. It is about to be ranked as one of the fastest machines in the world; only three other computers in the world are faster. The current world leader for speed is the Japanese Earth Simulator, which was built using 5,120 custom processors that have special circuitry for performing at 35.8 trillion operations a second, at an estimated cost of $250 million. The second fastest machine is the custom-built Los Alamos National Laboratory computer, which cost an estimated $100 million.[6]

The Virginia Tech computer has turned the supercomputer industry on its ear by producing a world-class computer from parts that can be bought at Comp USA, at a cost that is one-tenth that of most supercomputers.

Every business faces these kinds of radical changes from disruptive technology brought to market by both competitors and customers. These dynamic changes demand that businesses focus on knowing their customers and the markets in which they work more intimately. It also means that you must take more risks in satisfying your customers' needs, even if that means being personally disruptive to your current methods or products.

THE RISING POWER OF RETAILERS

At Radar, one of the topics of conversation that keeps coming up with all of our clients is the schism in retail. While a few specialty retailers are still in existence, there are virtually no midsize retailers. Instead, the retail environment has consolidated in every industry, giving a handful of companies more control. Today, these large retailers are not only asking for low prices but also demanding exclusive product designs and aesthetics. While companies like Sears played this powerful role a century ago, the consolidation of power has only increased. The growth of consolidated retailers may cause only minor problems for large companies, but it is extremely troubling for smaller and midsized firms. Some of our clients worry that there isn't room for everybody in the already crowded marketplace. The only way to overcome this fear is by developing a bottom-up strategy to co-create with customers and drive innovation fearlessly. Only by owning the relationship with the customer do brands have an opportunity to reverse this trend of increasing retail power.

Case Study: Wal-Mart

Technology isn't the only thing that can prove disruptive to companies; often the competition has companies scrambling to stay on top. Currently, all eyes are on Wal-Mart as a leading—and threatening—retailer; Wal-Mart produced $245 billion in revenues in 2002, making it the world's largest company. Contributing to these massive revenues, 138 million shoppers (half the U.S. population) visited Wal-Mart's 4,750 stores every week in 2002, with 82 percent of all households in America making at least one purchase there.

Wal-Mart draws its high volume of customers through what they call their "everyday low prices." Experts have estimated that Wal-Mart saved these customers $20 billion last year—making it abundantly clear why customers consistently choose to shop there. Wal-Mart has discovered what drives customers to its doors and continues to take the necessary steps to keep them coming back. This pricing pressure, on the other hand, has caused manufacturers to cut their costs to the point where the only way to hit Wal-Mart's mandate is to ship their manufacturing overseas to save on labor costs.

While the company has focused deeply on cutting costs, Wal-Mart has grown horizontally as well. It now controls many categories. It sells 30 percent of all household goods such as toothpaste, shampoo, and paper towels; many people believe that the number could reach 50 percent by 2010. It also accounts for 15 to 20 percent of all sales of CDs, videos, DVDs, and single copy magazines.

Wal-Mart also has a large effect on society as a whole, employing over 1.4 million employees. Such power affects wages and working conditions worldwide. Because Wal-Mart is not unionized, its labor costs are 20 percent less than for its unionized competitors. In 2001, its sales clerks made less, on average, than the federal poverty level. If Wal-Mart can maintain its current growth rate of 15 percent, its revenues could surpass $600 billion in 2011.[7]

This all happened because Wal-Mart is extremely close to its customers and does whatever it takes to deliver on the promise of "everyday low prices." Some of these shoppers, however, may have forgotten that there is a difference between the price of something and the cost. Wal-Mart's focus on price underscores something that people are only starting to realize about globalization: Cheaper prices have consequences. We want it all. Not only do we expect good working and living conditions and the best health care in the world, but we also want a clean environment. And all of these things cost money.

The Rise of the Private Label Brand

Compounding the issues surrounding the rise in power of specific retailers is the increased leverage some have gained from their own private label (in-store) brands. The power of these brands is beginning to dominate the market. If you are not the first or second product in your category, watch out—you've got a new threat. Currently, 25 percent of the products sold in the United States are private label (at Wal-Mart, their private label brands make up 40 percent of all products sold).

One of the main drivers behind this growth is retailers' desire to have more control over their relationships with customers. Globalization has made it easier for retailers to go directly to their suppliers in the Far East, substantially lowering costs for their customers and dramatically increasing their own profits. Given this new dynamic, it is easy for a brand to get blindsided, as its big customers control relationships with their eventual customers, edging the brands right out of the game.

While private label brands have typically been known for their lower quality and price, some retailers are starting to play at the high end of markets, as well. Many department store retailers have discovered an opportunity to deliver more differentiated merchandise. Retailers such as

Saks and Federated Department Stores are trying to boost their private labels in both quality and price. For instance, Federated dressed the star of ABC's *The Bachelor* in Alfani, its popular private label line of men's clothing. Likewise, Target has hooked up with Isaac Mizrahi to design a line of women's clothing. One of the reasons for the growth of high-end private label products is that consumers aren't swayed by traditional name brands as much today. In a recent poll by Brand Keys, a market research firm, nearly 61 percent of consumers said that high-end apparel logos and labels are less important to them now than a few years ago. In response to this way of thinking, Federated has said that it will increase the percentage of private label brands it sells to 20 percent or more, from about 16 percent currently.

The reality is that private label brands will continue to compete with their independent counterparts. If your brand is not a market leader, then your product could be in serious trouble in the next decade. The private label issue is only another example of the consolidation of retail power and the more competitive nature of a brand's own retail partners. Again, the only way to deal with such drastic change is to recenter the brand around its customers, owning that essential relationship.

THE CULTURE OF FEAR

In Michael Moore's 2002 movie, *Bowling for Columbine,* Moore tried to understand what caused the tragic murders at Columbine High School in Littleton, Colorado. His conclusion was that we, as Americans, live in a culture of fear. This fear permeates our culture and directly affects how we view the world and operate our businesses. Many companies with which Radar works suggest that fear exists on many levels, whether from competition, different ways of thinking, or the unknown. Persistent among many companies is a real fear of change. So where did all of this fear come from?

Unfortunately, we're suckers for the exaggerations of reality that exist in popular media, whether in the tabloids, newspapers, or on television and radio. While the individual topics of imminent natural disasters, scary viruses, or road rage may seem absurd or foreign to many of us, we also let our imaginations feed on them.[8]

The United States is actually safer than ever, but a persistent emphasis on safety can create a double-edged sword for brands and consumers. First, people are driven to purchase more safety-oriented products. Remember all the fear surrounding Y2K? An awful lot of money was spent on security. Likewise, with the ongoing threat of terrorism playing such a prominent role in our cultural consciousness today, a lot of money continues to be spent on safety. The downside is that these fears can just as quickly drive customers *away* from your products and services, decimating industries in the process. Think about the airline industry. While, statistically, flying is still one of the safest ways to travel, the veil of terrorism has significantly cut the industry's customer base.

While companies can benefit from the emphasis on safety in today's culture, they can just as easily be caught by surprise following a negative news report that plays on their customers' fears. There are numerous examples of automobile companies being caught off guard when a number of customers have a bad experience with a specific model. Even though an issue can be small, say a problem with a sticky latch on a door, it can easily explode into an uncontrollable wildfire of bad publicity, affecting the long-term health of the product.

Just as failure should be an inherent part of any company's strategy, fear must also be recognized—but not given too much power. I'm not suggesting that we ignore our own concerns or those of our customers; these are valid, human feelings and play into many of our decisions. What I am saying is that fear can also be used to motivate change and open us up to different opportunities, if we're willing to get past it and really look around. Companies must not let fear override their judgment or tie their hands; likewise, it is risky to build too much on anyone else's fears—especially those of your customers.

THE ROLE OF CHANCE

Just as science has already done, the business world is starting to realize that chance must be accounted for in the planning process. In science, the ability to incorporate chance has profoundly altered our worldview. One of the most profound realizations was that the observer cannot be objective—that just the act of observation changes an experiment. To incorporate this finding, a much more complicated model that treats the observer as a subjective part of any experiment or outcome has been developed. Likewise, companies must be aware of the role of chance in their dealings with customers and recognize that they are inextricably tied to their customers and to the world in which they all co-exist. For many companies, accepting the random nature, or chaos, of their world is incredibly challenging.

The meteorologist Edward Lorenz developed a better understanding of chaos for the average person in 1961.[9] At the time, he was working on the problem of weather prediction. He had a computer running a set of 12 equations to model the weather. This computer program did not predict weather but, instead, was designed to theoretically predict what the weather might be. While trying to repeat an experiment, Lorenz started in the middle of the computer program sequence instead of the beginning, to save time.

Instead of getting a sequence very close to the original, the model predicted radically different outcomes. He found that, by changing initial conditions only slightly, he could drastically change the long-term behavior of a model. Lorenz called this outcome the butterfly effect. Ian Stewart described the ramifications in his book, *Does God Play Dice:* "The flapping of a single butterfly's wings today produces a tiny change in the state of the atmosphere. Over a period of time, what the atmosphere actually does diverges from what it would have done. So, in a month's time, a tornado that would have devastated the Indonesian coast doesn't happen. Or maybe one that wasn't going to happen does." While there are always factors in the world that can cause an economic "tornado," some economists have begun to use chaos theory to understand complex, nonlinear, and dynamic systems such as the stock market. Companies can incorporate this kind of thinking to understand better their internal dynamics as well as the external, customer environment in which their brands live. While many factors can be planned, carefully strategized, and explained, companies can also learn and benefit from the slightest flutters in the marketplace. To do so, they must be willing to get out there, observe, and learn from the bottom up.

LEARNING FROM BEHAVIORAL ECONOMICS

In much the same way that chaos theory has given us a new perspective, behavioral economics has led to the evolution of traditional economics. By rejecting a basic premise—that man is a rational economic being—behavioral economics has brought about a new world view—that human emotions and irrationality have a large effect on economic activities. Businesses can learn from this new academic movement and inject the reality of emotion and irrationality of their customers into their business models. Let's take a look. Behavioral economists are generalists, pulling experimental methodologies from a number of fields. The study is defined, not on the basis of the research methods that are employed, but by the application of psychological insights to traditional economics. It has gone outside of economics to find academic inspiration from other fields, including psychology and neuroscience. Behavioral economics' goal is to increase the realistic psychological foundations of economics.

The economic model that the analysis of our society is based on is beginning to shift, and a much more organic and complicated model is being developed. For example, traditional microeconomics says that consumers look first and foremost at the price/benefit of any purchase. This might be true in some cases (remember our Wal-Mart shoppers?), but in reality, consumers don't consistently think this way in every purchasing decision.

Think about how you approach buying a car. Is the price benefit of a particular car the first thing—or the *only* thing—you think about? If you're at all like me, you probably think about what cars you like, how you might feel driving a potential car, how your family might like it, or what your specific needs are at the moment. If it were only about price, wouldn't we all be driving the cheapest option available?

The reality is that we live in a much less linear world than most economists would like to believe. We are human beings full of urges and exhibiting strange behaviors that have more to do with status and our historical perceptions than rational decision making. In a strictly rational, price/benefit world, why would anyone eat something that they know is bad for them? Such a decision has nothing to do with personal benefit and everything to do with personal taste.

The best example of how behavioral economics is changing the economic conversation is loss-aversion. Loss-aversion can be defined as the difference between the strong aversion to losses and the weaker desire for gains of equal size. Loss-aversion is more realistic than the economic utility smooth curve. Formerly the standard model, the smooth curve stated that the aversion to losses *equals* the desire for gains. Behavioral economics is doing a better job at illustrating the reality of our world.

Some of the work in this field that can directly help companies rethink their relationship with their customers includes hindsight bias, framing effects, and context effects.

Hindsight bias (or its slang term, "buyer's remorse") involves the very human process of second-guessing. Have you ever bought something and been very excited about it, only to find that much of your excitement came more from the purchasing process than the product itself? Coming back to the car example: I really wanted an Audi S4, because I always thought it would be fun to drive. A couple of months after finally buying it, I realized that I've always ridden my bicycle to work. The car just sat in front of my house, and I wondered, "Did I really need to spend that much money on a car that's parked most of the time?" Certainly, second-guessing is a part of many of our experiences. Did I prepare well enough for the test? Did I make a good impression at the meeting? And so on.

Framing effects illuminates the concept that the way a preference is framed can change the response dramatically. One example is the difference between these two statements:

1. We just bid on a $10 million contract and won it.
2. We bid on a $30 million contract and won $10 million of it.

Although the outcome of the two statements is identical, most people react more favorably to the first.

Context effects refers to the fact that a person's choice depends on what other specific options are offered. For example, if you got a phone call and the person on the phone said, "Congratulations, you've just won a new car. You can choose between a Ford Focus and a Volkswagen Jetta," you would feel very differently than if the caller said, "Congratulations, you've just won a new car. You can choose between a Ford Focus, a Volkswagen Jetta, and a Porsche 911." The context effect is one of the reasons that a primary tool for marketing research—the focus group—doesn't work very well. When you stuff people into a tiny conference room with a one-way mirror and ask them questions about how they cook a meal, for instance, it's very hard for them to explain it in detail. The experience is completely out of context. It's much easier for everyone if you ask the questions in the context of their own kitchen, while they're actually preparing that meal—the answers will be very different.[10]

Behavioral economics provides some relevant tools to help you rethink the relationship with your customers, the context of their lives, and the marketplace in general. Hindsight bias, framing effects, and context effects can all be used to deepen the dialogue you have with your customers; these tools will help you better understand the way they think and second-guess their decisions, the way a response can change as a question is reframed, and the way context affects choices between options.

WHAT THIS MEANS TO YOU

Most businesses continue to operate under the belief that the marketplace is controllable in the top-down fashion that executives learned in business school. One of the most common methods used in business today that reflects this top-down process is traditional branding. Many business people believe that a good top-down brand strategy is, hands down, one of the most important factors in making a business successful.

But the events of the past couple of years have come to challenge the notion of control in significant ways. We've all heard the media stories about some of the most established companies in the world fighting for their very survival. Dramatic shifts have occurred in the business environment at a grass-roots level, including the antiglobalization movement, unstable macroeconomic conditions, disruptive technologies, the rising power of retailers, the culture of fear, and the general uncertainty of our dynamic world. Now businesses must prepare to survive—and even thrive—in a new, bottom-up economy.

To participate successfully in this bottom-up economy, executives must accept a higher degree of risk and be willing to make mistakes when exploring new opportunities. Companies must view failure as a learning opportunity, actively integrating and accepting it as part of their culture.

Think about all of the external forces discussed in this chapter: global cultural shifts, radical changes in the macroeconomic environment, disruptive technologies, the power of retailers and private labels, the culture of fear, and the role of chance. Are there still others that specifically affect your company? Can you see the subtle signs of changes on the horizon that haven't been formulated into a formal strategy? Do you know intuitively that your company will be affected by some of these, but you can't quite put those feelings (or fears) into words?

Consider what *has* worked in your company lately. Has a successful new product or brand worked because of a well-thought-through plan or more by chance? Alternatively, has a product failed because everyone was so focused on their own work that they never took the time to think about how external forces might affect the company's future? Think about what can happen if your company gets past the distractions and fears it encounters every day and concentrates on gaining a more intimate understanding of your customers' needs. Can you help drive the culture of your company to be open to listening more actively to the massive changes happening around it?

2

THE ADVENTURES OF BRANDING

*I notice increasing reluctance on the part of marketing
executives to use judgment; they are coming to rely too
much on research, and they use it as a drunkard uses
a lamppost–for support, rather than for illumination.*
DAVID OGILVY[1]

Do you remember the story I told in the Preface about going to a
party and listening to an attractive woman holding court over the
crowd? She was interesting but only told stories about herself. While the
stories were fascinating, she never engaged anyone around her in a dialogue. In an ideal conversation, both parties are actively engaged and
have the opportunity to speak their minds.

Branding, on the other hand, has been appropriated as a distorted
form of communication, in which the company always assumes the position of power and is not required either to listen or respond to feedback. People are expected to sit quietly and listen; many react to this by
tuning out much of what is said. People are developing a "brand immune system": they will only pay attention to your brand or your product when they actually need or want your product or service—not before,
and usually not after. Most companies have failed to stay engaged in the

ever-evolving lives of their customers, making it impossible for them to notice the subtleties of the two-way conversation (if they're allowing it in the first place). When they stopped paying attention, customers also disconnected from the relationship. But maintaining this relationship can be both profitable and potentially more defensible in today's competitive marketplace.

This dysfunctional dynamic between companies and their customers often leads to companies that spend much of their time, energy, and money using top-down tools to promote their existing brands or products aggressively, rather than finding out what is relevant to their customers from the bottom up. Likewise, many companies outsource their most important relationship—the one with their customers—giving outsiders full control to attempt to understand their customers by using traditional top-down tools in often static and tightly controlled conversations.

One of the tools that has supported branding is market research. Much traditional market research is based upon the belief that, through the effort of gathering vast amounts of consumer data, a marketer can automatically gain a deep understanding of who people are. While massive data files, sorted with powerful computers, can yield interesting information on where and when people shop, it fails to reveal why they behave the way they do. Part of the problem is the assumption that more is better and that statistical verifiability is what matters. While a large number of responses can be interesting, many studies have shown that a couple of dozen customers can yield the same answers as several hundred. The biggest issue with becoming too reliant on quantitative tools is that people answer only the question that is asked. What happens when the question is wrong?

Another top-down tool that dominates the conversation between companies and their customers is the focus group. While companies spend over $1 billion on focus groups, some basic flaws plague this methodology. First, they are conducted in facilities that strip away the context of the customer's life. How can anyone talk about the experience of driving a car without sitting in a car seat and talking about it in the context of the activity? Other issues, such as groupthink and bullying among participants, only compound the problems with focus groups. How do you take people out of the context of their lives and spend two hours in a strange environment trying to cover ten topics with eight people? This gives each participant only a couple of minutes to react. How can you make significant strategic decisions after only getting to know a person for a couple of minutes? Can you really use this information to design a product or marketing campaign that expresses a deep understanding of your customers' needs, creating a space that allows them to co-create?

When companies concentrate primarily on increasing their sales by using static, top-down techniques, with only a secondary aim of developing deeper relationships with their customers, no agency or consultant can benefit them in the long term. To enact real, bottom-up change in the marketplace, companies must incorporate their use of consultants and agencies, as partners, to help shape their brands and products based on their customers' wants and needs—they must intimately know their customers at the front end of the process, not only as an afterthought. This ongoing engagement allows the essential space for co-creation.

The bottom line is that an intimate relationship with your customers has to begin *before* you offer them a product, brand, or service. Their insights, needs, and desires should be driving production from the bottom up at the front end.

THE HISTORY OF BRANDING

Branding today is a combination of ideas, products, and the advertising and marketing efforts of companies to put those ideas or products in the public spotlight. This is not too far removed from branding's roots, although the motivations and methods have changed considerably. Branding was initially used as a way for ranchers to identify their cattle; the distinct symbol of the ranch, burned into a calf's hide, made it immediately obvious that the calf belonged to someone. There was no variation in the method of identifying cattle; all ranchers used the branding technique—the only difference was in the actual symbol representing each ranch.

This "magic formula" of branding is obviously attractive to companies—an identifiable and well-positioned brand ultimately equals money in the bank. Unfortunately, this equation leads many companies to seek out brands or branding that will directly result in dollar signs. This emphasis on results has dramatically influenced the branding environment, where many brands are in direct and aggressive competition to get people's attention. Given the speed of information technology today, any unique attempt that companies make to attract this attention is quickly copied, resulting in its becoming just another ubiquitous branding technique. That is not to say there aren't examples of great branding strategies that allow the space for co-creation—think about the "Got Milk?" campaign. Branding can still be an important tool in building trust and deepening the conversation with any company's customers; it just needs to evolve along with a rapidly changing world. But this process has become much more difficult.

Originally, brands were used to differentiate products from the generic offerings available. For instance, Quaker Oats stood out distinctly from the bulk oats at the general store. Brands also conveyed a guarantee of quality and a sense of security regarding the source of the product: the company behind them. In these early days, advertising served primarily to increase public awareness that a new brand existed. It wasn't until the mid-1920s that Claude Hopkins proposed, in his book *Scientific Advertising,* that advertising should be systematized. He viewed advertising as an extension of the sales pitch with his philosophy: "The more you tell, the more you sell."[2]

As branding evolved, its basic goal remained the same: to establish a name for any given product that conveyed its legitimacy and stability. As brands in every category became more prevalent, it also became important to educate people about a product's value and use. To do so, advertising was incorporated as a form of entertainment—treating people as an audience while relating the merits of using a particular product or brand.

In the 1940s and 50s, the famous adman Leo Burnett took the use of entertainment in advertising to new levels; he introduced the use of lovable characters to represent products. During this period, Burnett launched the advertising "careers" of the Jolly Green Giant, Tony the Tiger, Charlie the Tuna, Morris the Cat, and the Marlboro Man—many of whom remain cultural icons to this day. Burnett challenged himself to find attractive brand images for "boring" products, such as peas or tuna. Later, Burnett extended the iconic use of characters to specific places (e.g., the Chevy Tahoe) and even situations (e.g., "Kodak moments"). While Burnett used strong characters and images to draw people to the products he advertised, he felt that the products' attributes, or what he called the products' "inherent drama," played an important part in successful advertising.

In the late 1950s, led in particular by another legendary adman, David Ogilvy, branding began to supersede the products themselves. Three major societal trends acted as the foundation for the success of Ogilvy's message. First, the United States experienced the greatest gross national product (GNP) per capita increases in the country's history, which created significant disposable income gains for the average American. Second, the development of television created a new medium for persuasive communication. Third, with more disposable income, Americans abandoned the cities for the suburbs. As suburbs spread out to surround cities, the automobile became a much more important tool for people's everyday interactions. Instead of being confined to one neighborhood defined by a reasonable walking distance, within which all of the needs of daily life could be satisfied, people began to live in one city and work in another. One consequence was the redefinition of neighborhoods, where neighbors were strangers. Instead of relying on a specific location to define what "the good life" meant, brands—through the new medium of television—helped to serve as indicators of success. Many companies celebrated the newfound economic freedom of their customers by helping them find brands—their own, of course—that could project this image of success.

In his quest, Ogilvy championed the idea of advertising as entertainment. He also developed several techniques to specifically promote the brand image—not the product itself—in television advertising. His ideas, such as "open with fire" (starting the ad with excitement) and "supers" (superimposing text over the ad to reinforce the brand message) are still cornerstones of today's advertising. In his book *Ogilvy on Advertising*, Ogilvy said: "Have they [consumers] tried all three [most popular whiskeys on the market] and compared the taste? Don't make me laugh. The reality is that these three brands have different images, which appeal to different people. It isn't the whiskey they choose; it's the image. The brand image is 90 percent of what the distiller has to sell."[3]

During the same era, Raymond Rubicam began to hire pollsters, such as Dr. George Gallup from Northwestern University, to conduct market research and try to understand what could be learned from people. Using polls, surveys, and focus groups, Rubicam set out to understand and differentiate various segments of users of a product. Hence, demographic research was born, allowing marketers to view people as statistical data, rather than emotional, largely unpredictable beings.

Following these early forays into market research, companies were tempted to rely on intelligence and analysis that reduced their customers to specific and manageable numbers, instead of a vague, often elusive group of people. Statistical analysis offered a means of "classifying, organizing, and labeling" people, which appealed to companies looking for quick, black-and-white information. Marketers would then reconstruct these "consumers" in the convenience of their office, look at their historical buying habits, and attempt to predict what they *might* want to buy.

But can you really scientifically deconstruct a person, reducing them to a few data points, and then reconstruct them—completely out of context? This thought process influenced product differences that were only quantitative and mechanical. This type of homogenous technique limited the interpretation of the customer's voice, erased idiosyncrasies from the marketers' observations of the culture, and ultimately marginalized risk taking by companies.

Because they were considered components of a legitimate science and were supported by academic research and education, market research and branding became significant strategic tools used pervasively within companies. As branding became more scientific and the communication of superior practices became widespread—through peer-to-peer interactions, the movement of managers between firms, and the use of consultants—a common branding philosophy was developed.

The concept of brands acting as cultural creators—doing more than just participating in or representing the culture but actually helping to create it—began to emerge in the 1960s. Bill Bernbach from DDB proposed the idea that products should be culturally authentic. To achieve this goal, brands had first to become disengaged from a company's economic agenda. DDB's solution was to give products an ironic brand persona; their campaign for Volkswagen's Beetle is a great example. Instead of speaking to people in the paternal, condescending voice that much of the era's advertising used, DDB created the voice of an honest friend by poking fun at the Beetle in classic ads such as "Think Small."

Inspired by DDB's example, other agencies, such as Chiat Day and Wieden-Kennedy, further developed the concept of the ironic brand persona for such clients as Nike, Eveready Batteries, and Levi's.

In the 1980s, in an attempt to increase the authenticity of the brands they worked with, agencies also started to explore the connection with what they termed "cultural epicenters." These epicenters of the marketplace included arts and fashion communities, ethnic subcultures, and creative and sports communities. The philosophy became one of identifying and developing a deep relationship with an epicenter to better position a brand as a cultural producer. A good example is Mountain Dew's early sponsorship of the X-Games produced by ESPN in the early 1990s. This relationship gave Mountain Dew credibility with the rapidly growing youth market and gave the brand an authenticity that still defines the product today.

To understand these epicenters, agencies established specialized entities that offered authenticity specific to the cultures with which they sought to connect. Such an example is DDB's collaboration with filmmaker Spike Lee that formed Spike/DDB. Agencies worked hard to become a part of the conversation in these epicenters. Done successfully, becoming a part of these communities gave some brands the ability to become tastemakers.

The power of the streets and the credibility gained from capturing it have changed the way brands are communicated. Brands now try to emulate the *personalities* of those found in certain cultural epicenters. As brands strive for this authenticity, a new "real" style of advertising has developed, as illustrated in candid spots in the ad campaigns of companies such as McDonald's and John Hancock. Similarly, in a recent campaign for Red Code, Mountain Dew's new subbrand, basketball stars Tracy McGrady and Chris Webber join an actual pickup game on the streets of New York City. The ad features the reaction and excitement of the amateur players and spectators as they realize they are playing with McGrady and Webber. The tagline, "Code Red. As real as the streets," even tips its hat to the effort to gain—and the value of—street credibility.

In their efforts to be seen as credible and authentic, companies engage in grassroots, viral, tribal, and buzz techniques. These methods range from the more traditional (grass roots) to the sensational (buzz), and are seen as slightly desperate attempts to gain people's attention. As an example, a company employing grassroots techniques might "seed" its products to tastemakers in cultural epicenters, hoping to gain the favor of its influential members. This method makes a lot of sense for culturally authentic brands, like Burton snowboards, which have a direct connection with their customers "on the street." But when larger, nonendemic brands begin to flood epicenters, community members tend to recognize the companies' motivations and mock their efforts. Instead of the technique working in their favor and suggesting authenticity, these nonendemic brands gain the reputation of cultural gadflies as they try to co-opt authenticity without paying their dues.

The speed of today's technology has made any successful branding technique so quickly emulated, that its novelty and success are marginalized through the flood of similar ideas. Consider the realm of reality television. In its first year, the popular show *The Bachelor* pulled in over 40 million viewers for its finale. One year later, the show averaged less than 6 million viewers for the first three episodes. Reality TV was a brilliant idea; the first few shows successfully captured the imaginations (and viewing habits) of a wide variety of people. But in one short year, the airways became clogged with variations on the same reality themes, with few points of differentiation. It's great to be one of the first to capture a market, but it's risky to rely on staying at the cutting edge as a successful strategy. Too often, the cutting edge becomes the bleeding edge.

THE CART BEFORE THE HORSE

Today, the concept of branding has become a driving force as a business strategy and an industry of its own. Thousands of branding books are available through Amazon.com, and hundreds of marketing and advertising companies sell their "unique" branding services. These branding experts instruct companies to extend their brand identities to every corner of the company. Branding experts in Oregon have suggested that the best way for Oregon to become a better state is for it to become Oregon,® the brand.[4] Likewise, Mongolia (that's right, the country) has retained a London-based branding agency to develop Mongolia,® the brand.[5] Mongolia is certainly not the first country to develop their brand. Britain has done it; so have Australia, Poland, and Slovenia. A couple of years ago, the U.S. government even got into the action by hiring Charlotte Beers, an ad exec who worked on the Uncle Ben's brand, to promote "brand America" to the people in the Middle East. It seems that branding may have become too much of a good thing.

Branding reached its real zenith during the dot-com era, when many start-up companies raised money with the specific intent of branding themselves. In fact, according to Forrester Research as much as 90 percent of the money raised from some venture capitalists was spent in this endeavor. While trying to build a Web site into a distinctive brand is an honorable goal, building a business around satisfying the needs of real customers who are willing to pay for a real service or product obviously has more lasting value.

Branding has become an industry perpetuating its own dogma; look at the self-help book market. Some new books, such as *The Brand Called You*, encourage people to develop a "personal branding philosophy" as a way to gain greater happiness and material success. Author Peter Montoya writes, "Personal branding lets you control how other people perceive you . . . You're telling them what you stand for—but in a way that's so organic and unobtrusive that they think they've developed that perception all by themselves . . . When done right, it's irresistible."[6] Okay, but whatever happened to just being yourself—a real person with genuine integrity?

The good concepts behind branding have simply gone too far, and people have become cynical about its mechanics. With branding's presence obvious in everything from products to personal lifestyles, people are growing tired of the smoke and mirrors. People—your customers—seek the reality of a company that is willing to act like a local merchant, a citizen of the community. What people want is true corporate transparency, in everything from marketing to manufacturing. This direct and honest approach can be, in itself, a unique branding method in today's environment.

As people grow more skeptical about common branding practices and the presence of branding in the marketplace becomes more pervasive, let's consider how some branding myths prevail, even as branding's weaknesses are coming to light.

Myth #1: Happiness Can Be Bought—and Sold

There is an assumption among both companies and people in America that the products we buy will make us happy. Companies—and brands—may be relying far too heavily on this assumption; the reality is that, after being exposed to as many as 3,000 branded messages a day, many people have developed a strong brand immune system.

Daniel Gilbert, a Harvard psychology professor, has spent the past decade trying to discover what really makes us, as humans, happy. He suggests that neither products—nor brands—are the answer. Gilbert's research indicates that both matter much less than we *think* they will; that it's basic human nature to overestimate how large a difference something will make. This concept of adaptation was developed by psychologists in the late 1950s to refer to how we acclimate to changing circumstances; as humans, we adapt quickly. Gilbert's team viewed happiness as a signal our brains use to motivate us to do certain things. In the same way that our eyes adapt to light, our brains are designed to find their "happiness set point." Our brains are not trying to be happy. Rather, they are simply trying to regulate us.[7]

Part of this internal adjustment is reflected in how quickly we adapt to a pleasurable event. As soon as we actually buy something, we immediately start to see it as ordinary. Often, in the days or weeks following a purchase, we lose our initial pleasure: when we buy that new car, it fails to provide the happiness we thought it would.

Myth # 2: Brands Are Empathetic

Agencies and marketing departments continually strive to make their brands appear empathetic, yet most corporate executives are so preoccupied with the bottom line and so removed from their customers' reality, that they have no real empathy.

Procter & Gamble once suggested that a competitor's laundry detergent destroyed fabric. When the accused company researched the issue, one of their most surprising findings was that not one of the company's executives, or their wives, even did their own laundry. They couldn't begin to understand the laundry experience. This disconnect happens inside many companies; while executives are busy working, their customers are living the daily experiences that should be influencing company decisions.

Some companies are taking steps in the right direction. Ford Motor Company recently purchased 12 empathy-belly pregnancy simulators from Birth Ways, Inc. The suit—originally designed as an educational tool to discourage teen pregnancy—gives Ford's designers the ability to feel what it's like to be pregnant. Each suit features the large breasts and bulging stomach of a pregnant woman, a six-pound sandbag under the suit simulates pressure on the pelvis and the bladder, and two seven-pound lead balls can be inserted into the suit to simulate the weight of a growing baby. In total, the suit weighs more than 30 pounds and gives designers a sense of how a pregnant woman really feels trying to drive one of their cars. Ford's designers also employ the use of a "third age suit" to help simulate the aging process. The third age suit helps to mimic symptoms of aging, such as blurred vision and arthritic joints. By using the empathy-belly suit and the third age suit, Ford is going beyond just *listening* to customers in their design process; such tools give their designers the ability to *be* their customers, if only for a few brief moments.[8] Only by actively understanding the context of its customers' lives can a company begin to take the journey toward deeper empathy.

Myth # 3: Labels Have Meaning

It's human nature to use words as a way to classify other people's actions or behaviors. Whether it's right or wrong, we all categorize people at times. Companies, and especially their marketing departments, do the same thing. A recent popular example of how words can be appropriated is the term *metrosexual*. Marketers now use this term to describe sensitive, image-conscious guys. "Their heightened sense of aesthetics is very, very pronounced," said Marian Salzman, chief strategy officer at Euro RSCG, to the *New York Times*. "They [metrosexuals] are the style makers. It doesn't mean your average Joe American is going to copy everything they do," she added. "But unless you study these guys, you don't know where Joe American is heading."[9]

It is somewhat ironic that gay writer Mark Simpson originally coined the term *metrosexual* to mock everything marketers stood for. In the mid-1990s, Simpson used the word to *satirize* the way that brands and consumer culture promoted the idea of a sensitive guy: one who shopped, used products for his personal appearance, and read magazines like *Men's Health*. Simpson felt that consumerism had taken its toll on traditional masculinity. From his point of view, men really didn't go to shopping malls, use personal-care products, or read self-help magazines. It was all a fantasy propagated by marketers.[10]

However, in 2001, British media latched onto the word *metrosexual*, and Britain's Channel Four produced a show about sensitive guys called *Metrosexuality*. Soon after, Britain found as their poster boy David Beckham, the English soccer star. Beckham has become a social icon by mixing his soccer stardom and marriage to singer "Posh" Spice with his habits of painting his fingernails, braiding his hair, and posing for gay magazines. As Americans became equally fascinated with Beckham, marketers gave new life to the term *metrosexual* in describing this new, sensitive man.

Companies should be hesitant to ascribe general classifications to their customers. While a label often does a fair job of describing its target population, individual characteristics are completely subject to interpretation. Relying on a simplistic descriptive tool to give life to someone as important as your customer, or potential customer, is dangerous. Get out of your office and spend time in the context of your customers' lives. A bottom-up strategy will give you a deeper understanding of how your customers live and help you avoid the need to develop or depend on generalized labels.

Myth # 4: Companies Control the Conversation

When sales are down, a popular solution for many companies today is an attempt to "rebrand." Following a misguided drive to turn Las Vegas into a family destination in the 1990s, the town is quickly shifting its gears back to the future. With the latest rebranding effort, Las Vegas has come full circle, back to the glory days when the Rat Pack glamorized the lifestyle of drinking and womanizing and the word *family* had a very different meaning. When was the Las Vegas brand *ever* about family entertainment?

Las Vegas first decided to market family-friendly entertainment following a few consecutive years of falling gambling revenues. The idea of attracting families was great in theory, until people actually started showing up with their kids. Casino owners came to a quick realization that this family market would never drive gambling revenue: Nobody maneuvering strollers and carrying diaper bags would be spending big money.

Now Las Vegas, with over 34 million tourists visiting each year, is in the process of rebranding itself again. "The new brand we're creating is one of freedom based on sensuality," said Oscar B. Goodman, the mayor of Las Vegas. The city's new slogan, "What Happens Here, Stays Here," reflects its new ad campaign. "The bottom line is that people can come here and go to the brink of whatever's legal, without having anyone look over their shoulder," the mayor said.[11] People who come to Vegas for its infamous attractions don't want to be dodging baby strollers on their way to the party.

The mistake that Las Vegas made was in switching its allegiance from a historically powerful, and very authentic, customer base in pursuit of immediate financial rewards. Pursuing the family market didn't necessarily make sense to the executives behind Las Vegas's rebranding decision; they just failed to trust their gut.

Myth # 5: The Vulnerability of Youth

As branding has become more challenging in today's crowded marketplace, marketers have turned their attention to kids as future consumers. Their messages are getting through to these young and malleable minds. Studies have shown that the average American two-year-old can recognize the McDonald's logo. As a father of two toddlers, I am constantly amazed at how my children connect with trademarked characters and products. My son Charlie walks around the house every evening yelling, "Pooh, Pooh, Pooh." Although my boys are not in the position to buy anything, heavily branded video programs, clothing, food, and books are sure to make a lasting impression.

Companies such as General Motors know this and have begun to advertise to "backseat consumers" (the 13- to 17-year-old demographic). They currently run ads in *Sports Illustrated for Kids* to advertise their minivans, hoping to influence these kids, who in turn will influence their parents.

While companies understand that they can help form future buying habits by cultivating relationships with kids, the downside is that with so much exposure, kids become numb to many of the messages. The group of kids marketers call Millennials (aged 13 to 21) deeply understands how companies advertise and try to influence their purchasing habits. They have become so immersed in the language of branding that, in many cases, they can flip the paradigm and parody the companies trying to sell to them. This deeper understanding and distrust of branding messages means that the marketer's job is that much more difficult, and the messages need to change.

In effect, a branding arms race is taking place. Companies that choose to reach out to a younger market need the knowledge and the tools to do so effectively. Conventional branding has lost much of its effectiveness—talking down to this market won't work; neither will aggressive or absurd messages. Kids are savvy and demand authenticity. They won't be fooled or impressed by anything less.

Myth # 6: The Myth of the "Consumer"

The word *consumption* first appeared in the 14th century and meant to waste, use up, devour, or destroy. Its opposites—*production* or *productive*—appeared in Middle French in 1612 and meant to be creative or generative, but the idea of consumption being the *opposite* of production did not appear until 1745.[12] To further confuse things, tuberculosis is historically known as the disease called consumption; at the beginning of the 20th century, "consumption" was still considered a disease. It was thought that people were sick if they thought about consuming goods. This hasn't stopped companies from typically looking at their customers as "consumers."

This classification is just as dangerous and potentially inaccurate as any stereotypical label. Do individuals, who just happen to buy products, want to be considered *primarily* as consumers? Do *you* spend 24 hours a day, 7 days a week, overtly consuming? Or are you a person with passions and relationships who has a life beyond that label?

Today, an increasingly diverse mixture of both cultural consumption and production threatens the corporate dominance of culture. New forms of resistance to a homogenized culture are beginning to appear. People are showing an interest not just in choosing the products and brands that are relevant to them but in helping to co-create those products. These "prosumers"—as Alvin Toffler called this emerging class in his 1980 book, *The Third Wave*—combine the roles of consumer and producer.[13] Toffler spoke of consumers of the future being interested in participating in the creation of their own products. He was right. Today, people are opting to gain local knowledge rather than simply succumb to the available market information. They choose to work creatively on everything they purchase to make it their own. They are also cultural DJs, sampling and mixing, cutting and pasting inspirations to develop and define their own new cultures.

CASE STUDY: THE FASHION INDUSTRY

The fashion industry is an interesting example of a business that has relied heavily on branding—how much more functionality can a $1,500 shirt have than a $15 shirt?—to gain revenue and profitability. So what has happened to the fashion industry, among the largest employers in New York City? Somehow, fashion got flipped upside down. In the past few years, it has become more about the money than about creativity and artistic expression. Many experts see parallels between the fashion industry and the fine art industry. In the 1980s, the art world became an industry—and was killed off.

From the 1980s to the late 1990s, fashion became a cultural icon produced by creative people on the streets of New York, Paris, and Milan. The industry became known as a hotbed of creative and branding ideas, with a following of actors, artists, and billionaires looking for ways to be unique. Designers became media darlings and shared the celebrity limelight with the stars who bought their clothes. Fashion used to be about exclusivity. It came to symbolize decadence, excitement, and a passion for clothes with a margin for error.

Today, with new communications technology, it is simple for a large retailer to see something interesting, take a digital picture of it, and produce a copy even before the original item hits the stores. Mainstream marketers have people figured out. They can now capture the subversive, the margins, and the fringes as well as any other specialty retailer can. Now fashion is mainstream: everyone has access.

Target and other retailers have flipped the paradigm by hiring designers, such as Isaac Mizrahi, to create collections that aren't following the trends but rather setting them. Now the hot item for fall is the Mizrahi blouse for $15—available at your local Target.[14]

In a world were everything quickly becomes the same, brands have an increasingly hard time competing for people's attention.

THE END OF BRANDING AS WE KNOW IT

People today expect the ability to co-create and lead innovation, forcing companies to devise creative solutions to be competitive in this new, bottom-up age. Such an environment creates opportunities for companies who are creative and intimately listen to the cultures with which they are involved—joining forces with other creatives including artists, journalists, filmmakers, and musicians to create new ways of expression and creation. The resulting products, which demonstrate a real understanding of their customers and the context of their customer's lives, will be successful. Instead of thinking globally and acting locally, the successful philosophy will be to think locally and act globally.

In the vast middle of the market, people will continue to treat brands as resources. These people do not have the time or the energy to be proactive in developing their own, relevant products. Instead, they will allow their peers to do most of the heavy lifting in creating new cultural materials—then adopt those products as their own. Brands that connect with people's imaginations, that inspire, provoke, and stimulate, helping them interpret the world that surrounds them, will be successful. Brands that can make the transition to provide honest, original, cultural materials, offering space for co-creation, will win. Proactive people will carefully weed out and broadcast those products, and companies, that they do not trust. Many companies have already discovered that being good corporate citizens can be good for their brands. In this new era, it's the creative citizens of a community—the people and the brands—that will help companies survive by co-creating from the bottom up.

WHAT THIS MEANS TO YOU

While branding has been an incredibly effective tool to communicate with people, it has evolved to the point that, often, the conversation between a company and its customers is a one-way monolog controlled by the company. Customers are given no choice but to listen to these one-sided conversations happening all around them. In response, people are developing brand immune systems. Have you noticed that people are becoming immune to your branding efforts? How do you stay engaged in the lives of your customers beyond your branding and advertising? Do you feel isolated from your customers? This relationship is too important in our dynamic world to be conducted from arms' length.

People want companies to act like a local merchant and a citizen of the community. They want transparency in everything the company does. Do you use the terms *community* and *transparency* in your internal language? Do you join your customers in co-creating and innovating? Products that express a company's real understanding of their customers and the context of their customers' lives will be successful. Instead of thinking globally and acting locally, the philosophy must be to think locally and act globally.

Think about your company's brands. Have those brands themselves been successful or the ideas behind them? Is your company's branding strategy best described as "one size fits all"? Or do you connect with your customers' imaginations in a way that inspires, provokes, and stimulates, helping them to interpret the world around them? Do you know who your leading customers are? Does your company currently produce honest, original, cultural brand materials for those customers?

3

POWER TO THE PEOPLE

You must be the change you wish to see in the world.
MAHATMA GANDHI[1]

The Internet promised that it would radically change the way companies operated: Amazon would destroy Barnes and Noble, and Enron's oil-trading business model would shutter Exxon. While technology has indeed had a dramatic effect on the way companies operate, the more radical change is the shift in people's behavior; suddenly they have infinite options immediately available to them. With the touch of a button, people can find vast amounts of information, products, and services. They can communicate, create, and conduct their own lives, much as the conductor of an orchestra uses the various sounds produced by the company's members to coordinate a completely new sound. Their newfound power gives people the interest and the ability to lead companies to produce what they want—to co-create their ideal products. By better understanding some of the roots of this power, you will develop the foundation for a new, deeper relationship with your customers.

What would happen if one of your customers were dissatisfied enough following an interaction with your company to make an "anti-advertising" movie that would reach over a million viewers and be previewed on CNN? That's exactly what happened to Apple and their iPod mp3 player.

After being told by an Apple Computer technical support person that replacing the dead battery in their 18-month-old iPod would cost the same as buying a brand new device, brothers Casey and Van Neistat decided to create a video as an expression of their feelings regarding Apple's replacement policy. In the video, the brothers take a handmade stencil and cruise through New York City, painting the words, "iPod's unreplaceable battery lasts only 18 months," over every iPod poster they can find. Ironically, the brothers announce at the end of their video that they used Apple's video editing software to create the movie.[2]

It only took a couple of weeks for the Neistat brother's Web site (http://www.ipodsdirtylittlesecret.com), containing the video, to receive as many as 50,000 hits a day. After three months, more than a million people had visited their site.

Fortunately, Apple is a savvy enough company to recognize the powerful impact the Neistat brothers' video was having on the marketplace, and within a couple of weeks, the company announced plans for a revised battery replacement program.

The power that people use to express their disappointment in products to a wide audience is not the kind of reactionary co-creation that any company willingly brings upon itself. This new freedom that people exercise in how they consume, produce, and react to products has profound effects on how they expect to be treated by brands and companies.

THE RISE OF PEOPLE POWER

People today have incredibly fragmented lifestyles; we all feel the pressures of living in a fast-paced, busy, and often chaotic world. While there are countless benefits to technology and most people appreciate having instant access to information, products, and services, the downside is that we aren't always able to step off the fast-moving treadmill; the world just keeps humming along whether we like it or not. To capture people's attention in this dynamic environment, companies need to take the time to view the world from their customers' point of view. The passive "consumer" of the past is disappearing; your customers are educated, well-informed, creative people who want a voice in the shaping of the products and services available to them. With so many companies trying to get their attention, people need to feel that companies are listening to what *they* have to say.

Three cultural factors are contributing to the rise of people's power. First, people today have greater freedom, which manifests itself in a growing culture of copying and sharing. Second, people are bombarded with too much information; in response, they seek out or create filtering mechanisms for sifting out what is relevant to them. This tendency has greatly increased the importance of reputation in the success or failure of a business, product, or service. Lastly, people are faced with too many choices at every turn, which leads them to be very protective of their time as well as of their financial and emotional resources. Today, quality of life is an important *daily* goal.

THE CULTURE OF COPYING AND SHARING

Most Americans don't need more stuff. There are already enough televisions in the United States to supply each home with two. A great many of us live in houses several times the size of our grandparents'. Most families have more than one car. We are now living the old perception of "the good life." We have greater freedom to personally decide which products, companies, and brands might best fulfill our needs; we can ask ourselves, for instance, what kind of car might best project our unique personality. The flipside is that, in this quest to become self-actualized, people regularly exercise the freedom to copy and take what they want from brands, constantly reinterpreting how brands fit in the context of their lives. In this environment, brand loyalty only happens if and when people truly connect with both a brand and the company behind it—and both stay relevant to their lives.

The Internet has been disruptive for many businesses due to its major impact on how people do things today. People have more power to easily compare products, make more subjective purchasing decisions, and exploit price variances; all these factors radically alter the traditional business environment. In addition, people are actively participating in a new culture of copying; there is a new ethic that, as long as you can get it, it doesn't really matter how. The Internet has become a metaphor for a new cut-and-paste morality. Some would argue that the Internet is only one factor contributing to the rise of copying. A much larger factor is the pervasive trend of copying by corporations.

People have become fully aware that companies often buy products and simply copy their brand name onto them. For many companies, production has come to be viewed as a liability rather than an asset. Naomi Klein, in her book *No Logo,* calls this a "race towards weightlessness." In today's culture, a product itself does not always hold value, but prominently displaying a company's logo on any product automatically produces a perception—and expectation—of certain brand attributes.

This internal focus on improving productivity and efficiency has spawned many companies that don't actually make anything at all. Enron was a classic example of an American company that accomplished the "weightlessness" that Klein mentions. With higher productivity has come higher profits and more financial rewards for corporate executives such as Martha Stewart, Dick Grasso, Bernie Ebbers, and Ken Lay. Such executives, even in today's consumer culture, epitomize the disconnection between some executives and their customers and companies that are better known for their greed and corporate malfeasance than for understanding their customers and running a good business.

Today's culture supports the mentality of DJs, file sharers, and product cloners, who are all doing what has become a cultural norm: reproducing things at a cheaper cost (or in less time) that were originally produced somewhere else. "Somehow everybody makes out," said a woman on the streets of New York after buying two copied Louis Vuitton handbags. "I don't see any poor rock stars. I don't see any poor designers." All of a sudden, buying fake is cool. Shopping for copies has become a trend in itself.

This culture of copying, or a cut-and-paste view of life, is affecting all levels of society. It engenders a "think globally, act selfishly" attitude and is a natural result of people having access to more information, more choices, and the technology to combine the two for personal benefit. It also speaks of the connection people are striving to make with one another in the face of a very disjointed and frenetic environment.

While the Internet has certainly made global business transactions much more efficient, it has simultaneously enabled this new culture of copying. People's ability to download something from the Internet, remix it, and immediately distribute it has directly contributed to their power.

Linux and open-source code is a wonderful example of this cooperative, creative ethos. In reaction to Microsoft's stranglehold on the software market, software developers have cooperatively developed open source software, such as Linux, giving everyone the ability to access and modify the source code, instead of hiding it as a corporate asset. This open-source philosophy is not only a challenge to Microsoft but can be seen as a challenge to many other industries as well. Lawrence Lessig, a professor at the Stanford Law School, has called open-source software an example of "creative commons," or a place where intellectual resources can be shared.[3] In effect, it is a way of creating a healthier democracy through the open sharing of knowledge.

The Internet has created the ability to share information on a global basis, and as importantly, it offers people a new forum within which to borrow, sample, and remix information quickly and easily.

Case Study: The Music Industry

The music industry is a sobering example of an industry caught in the crossfire of disruptive technology's radical changes. The industry's model has always been to find new musicians and make them into stars by controlling the distribution of the music. With the development of the Internet and file-sharing services such as the groundbreaking Napster and its followers Kazaa, Morpheus, and Grokster, record companies, trying desperately to control distribution, were thrown for a loop. In May 2003, more than 11 million Americans used Kazaa, the most popular file-sharing software, according to Nielsen/Netratings.

In September 2003, in a reaction to the popularity of various programs, the Recording Industry Association of America (RIAA) brought lawsuits against 261 users of file-sharing programs. Each defendant in the first round of suits (including a 12-year-old girl and a grandfather whose grandson used his computer) had more than 1,000 songs in accessible folders that allowed millions of strangers to copy them. While these lawsuits were initiated to give the music industry some short-term relief, people reacted by digging in and demanding access to what they really wanted—not just what record companies wanted to sell to them.

One of the main reasons given for initially taking such drastic measures was protecting the rights of the musicians. But many of these "protected" musicians found themselves in the middle, watching helplessly from the sidelines as their fans were taken to court. Many artists felt that the actions went too far and negatively affected their relationships with their fans.

One artist, Moby, had an especially hard time understanding or endorsing the record industry's aggressive tactics. On his Web site (http://www.Moby.com), he suggested that music companies might want to think about treating users of file-sharing services like fans instead of criminals:

> How can a 14-year-old who has an allowance of $5 a week feel bad about downloading music produced by multimillionaire musicians and greedy record companies? The record companies should approach that 14-year-old and say: "Hey, it's great that you love music. Instead of downloading music for free, why don't you try this very inexpensive service that will enable you

to listen to a lot of music and also have access to unreleased tracks and ticket discounts and free merchandise?"

The singer David Bowie envisions an even more radical paradigm shift. "I'm fully confident that copyrights, for instance, will no longer exist in ten years, and authorship and intellectual property is in for such a bashing," Bowie said in an interview last year. "The future of the music industry," he suggests, "is that songs are essentially advertisements, and artists will have to make a living by performing on tour."[4]

The idea of suing the record industry's fans was really the industry's last-ditch, desperate effort to react to disruptive technology. Many executives in the record industry agree that their problems go much deeper than file swapping. These problems include the consolidation of radio stations, which makes it harder to expose new bands to the public, and the lack of a popular music style, like teen pop and its packaged stars such as the Backstreet Boys, N'Sync, and Britney Spears. Other factors include the economy and the ongoing competition for people's time in a world full of video games and DVDs.

Ironically, while file sharing is seen as the embodiment of evil in the music business, many companies within the industry currently benefit from the services of Big Champagne, a company that uses its software to see what Internet users are sharing on peer-to-peer file-swapping services (like Kazaa) in greater detail. They have the ability to watch all file-sharing activity, segmented by artist and zip code. This is an extremely powerful tool for music companies. They can monitor what's being traded versus what's playing on the radio. If there is a discrepancy, they can use the information to convince radio stations to give their acts more play time. Big Champagne sells subscriptions to its service for between $7,500 and $40,000 per month. Not many record companies will admit to using Big Champagne's services, yet their client list reads like a "who's who" of the record industry, including Atlantic, Warner Bros., Interscope, DreamWorks, Electra, and Disney.[5]

Additionally, there is some overt hypocrisy in the music industry's actions. Josh Bernoff, the principle analyst covering media and entertainment for the research giant Forrester Research, got a call about some industry-specific research from a record industry executive whose company aggressively discouraged file sharing. After listening to the executive's questions, it was obvious that he had read the report. Bernoff asked him if he was a subscriber and, if not, how he had seen the report (Forrester sells it for $895). Apparently, the executive had gotten his copy from a colleague at one of the movie studios.

On a more positive note, some musicians have come away from the experience with a renewed interest in connecting directly with their fans. Pearl Jam has made an effort to reestablish this relationship, and it has paid off.

In 1995, Pearl Jam became frustrated with the high price of concert tickets and decided to put pressure on Ticketmaster to cut ticket prices. Since then, the band has become innovative and proactive in their relationship with their fans. Additions include producing live, band-produced bootleg CDs, lower ticket prices, and online ticketing for fan club members. Even though Pearl Jam has not produced a music video since 1993 or had a top-ten radio hit since 1999, their concerts are among the best-selling events in the industry. In September 2000, Pearl Jam released its first wave of bootleg, contra CDs produced by the band. The CDs were so well received that 5 of the 25 albums hit the billboard top 200 chart in their first week.

This powerful relationship with their fans has given them the ultimate freedom. The band is considering dropping Sony Epic, its record label of 12 years, and getting out of the corporate music world altogether. And promoters have a love/hate relationship with the band's policies, especially the policy that dictates that fan club members get the best seating at concerts. It must be a shock for some music industry executives to sit *behind* the fans at a Pearl Jam concert.

While some may feel that the music industry's experience is unique, no industry is immune. The founders of Kazaa, Nikolas Zennstrom and Janus Friis, and the same team of programmers who wrote the code for Kazaa, reunited in the fall of 2003 to create and launch Skype, a way for people to make free, high-quality phone calls over the Internet. Skype relies on technology called "voice-over Internet protocol" (VoIP). It routes calls through the Internet, turning computers into phones. VoIP is being used by a number of new, small phone companies and is becoming incredibly disruptive for traditional telecommunications companies, because these new companies can charge next to nothing for their service. Mr. Zennstrom has a big ambition with Skype: to make it *the* global telephone company.

What happens when someone finds a way to charge nothing for the products that you make? Today, it's happening in the music industry; tomorrow, the telecom industry. Will your industry be next? Will you be ready?

THE POWER OF REPUTATION

All too many irrelevant messages are floating around the cultural ether and getting in the way of listening. People are becoming much more sensitive to the amount of information available and much more discerning about where they will focus their attention. This happens for people at work as well; there is an abundance of information to absorb about markets, competitors, and customers. All of this secondhand data can perhaps be useful, but not if the time required to digest it precludes sitting down with customers and getting to know them. People within companies, just like their customers, must actively prioritize both their sources of information and the data itself. Having access to vast amounts of information might seem ideal, but the real value lies in the messages themselves. Don't allow yourself to become distracted by trying to listen to everyone and everything being said in the marketplace. Find the right voices, and commit yourself to really listening to them.

It's a big challenge for individuals and companies to filter the messages they receive on a daily basis. Nobody wants to overlook something important or give too much attention to something of little value. One tool that has played a vital role in human evolution, and that is gaining more power in our complicated world, is reputation. People are placing a great deal of importance on the reputations of the companies with which they choose to interact and are actively networking with others to share information. Given the immediacy of shared knowledge (remember Apple's experience?), companies are starting to realize that their long-term success will be based on a combination of intimately knowing their customers, doing a consistent job of satisfying these customers, and simultaneously upholding positive corporate reputations.

To understand the power behind reputation, it's important to look at it as more than just a persistent "image" people hold for each other or for companies. In the context of our evolving society and the demands placed on each of its members, reputation carries weight largely because it springs from the cooperative, word-of-mouth transfer of information between people. Remember how important your reputation was to you in high school? We all have at least some concern about how others view us; for any company, this is especially important. We know that customers are demanding more authenticity from companies and their products, that people want to be heard by companies, and that people value corporate commitment for the long term, not just for quick financial gains.

If companies fall short in any of these areas, people will talk about it. They'll share their opinions with as many people as they can reach—and, as we saw with Apple's iPod "mistake," the power of the people is abundantly clear. Two "small" voices reached the ears (and eyes, in this case) of over a million potential Apple customers. Apple's reputation—and some very quick acting on their part—saved them from serious trouble. The power of reputation comes from building a good one in the first place, then being able to defend it legitimately. When your customers expect more of your company, you'll be more likely to meet, or exceed, those expectations. Henry Ford, one of the greatest businessmen in the history of this country, claimed, "You can't build a reputation on what you are going to do." He knew that a good reputation is one of the greatest assets a company can have.

For a couple of decades, companies have had the ability to capture and analyze their customers' reputations through formal gossip networks or credit reports. It's easy for any company to view a person's credit rating and see what type of customer reputation they have. If you have a frequent shopper card at your local grocery store, the grocer is collecting information about what you buy as you save a few dollars on those purchases. People's individual buying habits are becoming widely tracked and just as commonly traded. This trend of gaining intimate knowledge of customer's behavior has only just begun.

Today's newly empowered customers—already active in gaining market knowledge—are also using their power to aggressively pursue and share information about specific companies. After decades of being the specimens under the microscope, today's shoppers have pulled off a role reversal. Your company is just as likely to be squirming on the slide under the watchful, critical eye of your customers. Can your reputation survive this close scrutiny?

As our world continues to be more complex, the power of reputation will grow even stronger. There are already many examples of reputation marketplaces playing an integral role in our lives. If you live in a U.S. city and enjoy shopping and eating, chances are you have read or own a copy of a *Zagat's Guide*. Tim and Nina Zagat have built their business by providing diners, shoppers, and theatergoers with a forum to express their opinions about restaurants, shops, and entertainment. The Zagat Survey's power is in the reputation of the grassroots methodology, which allows customers to write reviews and share information about their experiences. If you are a restaurant owner in New York City, you care immensely about your reputation in the Zagat Survey.

Today's electronic culture feeds on this grassroots buzz. As society becomes networked through the proliferation of new technologies, the process of reputation sharing is being greatly accelerated, while the cost is decreasing dramatically. A perfect example of how a reputation marketplace functions on the technology playing field is eBay. Often called the world's largest flea market, eBay is a fluid marketplace that allows transactions to happen with less friction between people—and more trust. Much of this trust may be attributed to its reputation system. Paul Resnick, an associate professor at the University of Michigan's School of

Information, describes the power of these systems: "Reputation systems seek to restore the shadow of the future to each transaction by creating an expectation that other people will look back on it. The connections of such people to each other may be significantly less than is the case with transactions on a town's Main Street, but their numbers are vast in comparison."[6]

Resnick has been a leader in the field of online reputation marketplaces for over a decade. In 1992, he and a few of his colleagues created a software program called GroupLens. The idea behind GroupLens was to give online bulletin board readers the ability to rate messages and make those ratings available to other readers. Today, Resnick runs a Web site devoted to academic research on the subject of online reputations, Reputations Research Network (http://databases.si.umich.edu/reputa tions/). This network was created ". . . for researchers who are studying how reputation systems should work in theory, how they actually work in practice, and how they could work better."

With its over 50 million members, eBay is an excellent example of a marketplace that has been greatly enhanced by the sharing of reputation. Resnick puts it this way:

> At eBay, for example, a stream of buyers interacts with the same seller. They may never buy an item from the seller again, but if they share their opinions about this seller on the Feedback Forum, a meaningful history of the seller will be constructed . . . Through the mediation of a reputation system, assuming buyers provide and rely upon feedback, isolated interactions take on attributes of a long-term relationship. In terms of building trust, a vast boost in the quantity of information compensates for significant reduction in its quality.[7]

Epinions.com is another example of a Web site that uses the power of reputation as a central business strategy. Contributors to Epinions are paid for their opinions about everything from movies to cars. It is a reputation marketplace. Visitors to Epinions.com rate contributors and opinions. The better the rating, the more you are paid for your reviews. "Epinions is one of the most active and varied ecosystems on the Web," *Wired* editor Mark Frauenfelder wrote. "It has evolved into a diverse community populated by cliques, clowns, parasites, symbiotes, self-appointed cops, cheaters, flamers, and feuders. It's swarming with people who were English or journalism majors but ended up stuck in other careers. And it has produced member-generated site refinements, such as the Web of Distrust."[8]

The power of these reputation markets increases as these forums continue to use more sophisticated self-regulation techniques, like rating the quality of reviewers' comments and keeping out blatant self-promotion or excessively negative comments.

The phenomenon of Web logging has also contributed in a major way to the online reputation marketplace. *Web logging* is a term used to represent the activity of writing a hypertext diary online. Millions of people keep Web logs, or "blogs" as they are affectionately known, to express their opinions. Bloggers can offer not only their own points of view but also links to other sources. Henry Jenkins, a Professor at MIT, sees the power of blogging as the power to reframe issues. Jenkins believes there are two kinds of media power. One comes through media concentration: a message gains its authority by being broadcast on network television. The second kind of media power comes through grassroots intermediaries: here, a message gains momentum only if it is deemed relevant to a loose network of people. "Broadcasting will place issues on the national agenda and define core values; bloggers will reframe those issues for different publics and ensure that everyone has a chance to be heard," says Jenkins.[9]

Companies are beginning to realize the power of these self-selected reputation markets and are both seeding products to user/reviewers and using their reviews in their marketing. For instance, on their company Web site, Laplink Software lists a review by "lucie30," the username of an individual user from an Epinions forum, right alongside reviews from traditional media.

What would you do if you found out that there was a grassroots protest against the highly anticipated launch of your new product? Intuit launched its Turbo Tax Deluxe in January 2003. Soon after the launch, the buzz throughout the Internet was decidedly negative, largely because of the software's antipiracy features, which made it difficult to install. Intuit had also decided to make each copy of its new version installable on only one computer.

A firestorm of negative comments flowed through reputation markets from Epinion.com to Amazon.com. Amazon alone carried 587 negative comments about the software. One customer wrote, "After using Turbo Tax for 13 years, I'm switching to Tax Cut."[10] Quite simply, the Internet has thrown open the doors to reputation marketplaces. Now customers can share and contribute to companies' reputations as easily as companies review their customers' credit ratings. This democratization of reputation marketplaces has significant implications for companies.

With these new online tools, people have begun to exercise their significant power. With this leveling of the playing field, companies must now dedicate their resources to really listening and responding to these reputation marketplaces.

By understanding the power of the reputation marketplace, Intuit's CEO, Stephen Bennett, was able to react in a positive, proactive way to a potentially damaging situation. Mr. Bennett e-mailed angry customers to reassure them that he would take care of the problems and that Intuit was not trying to do anything malicious.

The power of reputation has the potential to have a dramatic effect on traditional marketing, also. "The more consumers come to trust the opinions posted in online forums, the less effective traditional advertising will become in influencing consumer behavior," said Chris Dellarocas, a Professor at MIT. The fluid reputation marketplaces of the future will certainly challenge the power of branding.

In direct response to these reputation markets, Amazon has cut its traditional advertising budget and focused its energies in other areas, offering free shipping for orders over $25, for example. By listening to what their customers have to say and offering to give something back to them, Amazon is taking a step toward deeper trust and a more honest, intimate relationship.

Because reputation can play such an important role in the way people relate to brands and companies, it's important to think about how to make sure you stay engaged in managing your reputation in this bottom-up economy. Here are things to think about:

- *Research your reputation.* Think about what kind of reputation your company has. Is the internal view of your company consistent with the external view?
- *Understand your reputation.* Who really owns your products and brands: you or your customers? Is your company ready to acknowledge the illusion of control and start to listen to what people really have to say about you and your products?
- *Tap into the conversation.* There is a current conversation going on in the world about your company. It's hard to really listen to the conversations that are happening in the marketplace unless you get out of your office and seek them out.
- *Let go.* The idea that you can completely control your reputation is another illusion. Try to let go now and then and focus on the relationship with your customers in the context of the journey. Enjoy the day-to-day experience.
- *Participate in improving your reputation.* The best way to start participating is to ensure that the actions of your company are consistent with your philosophy. Do you do what you say you're going to do?

TOO MANY CHOICES, NOT ENOUGH TIME

Just as people are creating filters and using other tools to make sense of the many messages that bombard them every day, they're reacting in a similar fashion to a culture that offers far too many tangible offerings. In every category of business, there are more product choices than anyone could ever try, let alone purchase. No matter how much branding or advertising a company does, it's increasingly difficult to wade through the clutter. I was in Russia recently, and many of the people I met in my travels had visited the United States. Their general impression was that the number of choices here, whether at the supermarket or the shopping mall, was simply overwhelming. In some fascinating recent research, Dr. Sheena S. Iyengar, an assistant professor at Columbia's business school, and Dr. Mark R. Lepper, chairman of Stanford's psychology department, have demonstrated that providing *too many* options—particularly when the real distinctions between them are small (there are over three dozen different flavors of Crest toothpaste, for example)—can cause people to feel overwhelmed and overloaded and, as a result, less likely to pursue *any* of the options available.[11] People want variety, but they want companies to be reasonable at the same time. When the products available to them are relevant to their needs and their lifestyles, customers will feel that the companies behind those products have actually done their homework. Throwing out dozens of choices and assuming that people will find something they like doesn't foster feelings of intimacy between companies and their customers. People don't necessarily need more choices; they need choices that are personally relevant.

The reality is that, in response to this product overload, people are suggesting that more isn't always better, that perhaps quality—or at least relevance—is more important than quantity. The only possible exception to this way of thinking is in people's ongoing quest to find, somehow, more *time*.

Do you remember the articles in the 1960s and 1970s about the rise of leisure time we would experience by the year 2000 because of increased productivity following the development of technologies like the computer? Remember how many futurists accepted the notion of a four-day workweek as the norm for most of us at the turn of the century? What happened? With our infinite choices, from 500 television channels to 125,000 new books every year, among others, we've filled up our "extra" time pretty fast.

If there is one constant for all of us, it is our lack of time, whether real or perceived. I look at it this way. I'm 43. The average American male lives 72.3 years (according to the National Center For Health Statistics). That's 26,390 days, so I've got about 10,694 days left. If you're like me, you sleep 8 hours per day (if you're lucky)—that's 3,565 days, eat 2½ hours per day—1,114 days, spend half an hour per day in the bathroom (hot showers rule!)—223 days, work 8 hours per day (25 years, maybe, maybe not)—3,042 days; work out 1 hour per day (hopefully)—446 days, commute 1 hour per day (at least)—446 days; hang out with the family 2 hours per day—892 days, do things you don't really want to do (pay bills, listen to telemarketers, do yard work) 1 hour per day—446 days. That leaves 516 days, or about 1 hour per day, left for following your bliss. I don't know about you, but anyone hoping to get my attention these days better make it really mean something to me, especially if it infringes on that one sacred hour.

WHAT THIS MEANS TO YOU

People have more power today in our dynamic world. They act as both consumers and producers and work creatively on everything they purchase to make it their own. Have you experienced people sampling and mixing, cutting and pasting your products and marketing to make them their own? How does your company proactively respond to the cultural trends that have given people more power?

People have developed a brand immune system, as they are exposed to over 3,000 branded messages a day. How have the effects of this immunity challenged your branding efforts?

As the dynamic changes happening all around us continue to accelerate, your company must take steps toward building a deeper relationship with newly empowered customers. Do you understand the factors causing customers to approach your company differently and carry new expectations for that interaction? How is your company thinking about your customers' fragmented lifestyles? In a world where people are both consuming and producing, how do you fit in? Can you help your customers in their quest to become active participants in developing their own products and culture?

If your company is feeling disconnected or left behind as people react to having greater freedom, too much information, more choices, and less time, what steps can you take to begin to understand and participate in the changes taking place? One important step in becoming more proactive is paying attention to the developing reputation marketplace that surrounds all companies today.

4

GETTING BEYOND
THE BRAND

You see things as they are and ask, "Why?"
I dream things as they never were and ask, "Why not?"
GEORGE BERNARD SHAW[1]

In a world where people are demanding authenticity and originality more than ever, formulaic branding has lost much of its magic. As discussed in Chapter 2, many things have contributed to the declining effectiveness of the success of top-down branding techniques. Compounding the problems for companies, people's behavior is radically changing. Customers now want to act as both consumers and producers, working creatively on things they purchase to make them their own. People now have greater freedom, too much information, too many choices, and a lack of time and are more unwilling to buy products from companies that are not prepared to engage them in a dialogue, as described in Chapter 3.

This challenge to companies to bring the right customers directly into the planning process is compounded by changes in the environment in which brands exist. As discussed in Chapter 1, the antiglobalization movement, unstable macroeconomic conditions, and disruptive technologies will continue to be major issues, having the power to impart real damage on companies that remain disconnected from their customers and the communities in which they work. Additional factors, including the rising power of large retailers and the prevalence of fear, interject still more uncertainty into the branding process. This uncertainty is difficult to predict or prepare for. The only way to deal with it is to accept its presence and actively work to gain a deeper understanding of the environments in which brands work. Brands must continually strive to act like a local merchant, like a citizen of the community. In Latin, *cum* and *minis* mean "shared together." In a true community, participants share their personal experiences. If companies want to identify with and be relevant to their customers, they must first become trusted, committed community members. With this step, companies can begin the journey toward creating long-term, sustainable relationships.

Most of us have been trained to think that there is always a "right way" to do things, and we often try to impose that perspective on our customers and the communities in which we do business. Last year, there was a story cruising around the Internet about how out of touch American businesspeople can be with the environments they enter.

An American executive had just sold his business and was taking some time to think about his next business opportunity. He decided to head south and spend the season in a coastal Mexican village. One day, he was standing at the pier, thinking about his next business move, when a small boat with just one fisherman aboard docked at the pier. Inside the small boat were several large yellowfin tuna.

The American complimented the Mexican on the quality of his fish and asked how long it took to catch them.

The Mexican replied it was only a little while.

The American then asked why he didn't stay out longer and catch more fish.

The Mexican said he had enough to support his family's immediate needs.

The American asked, "But what do you do with the rest of your time?"

The fisherman said, "I sleep late, fish a little, play with my children, take a siesta with my wife, Maria, then stroll into the village each evening where I sip wine and play guitar with my amigos . . . I have a full and busy life, señor."

The American scoffed, "I am a Harvard MBA, I've just sold my company for millions, and I can help you. You should spend more time fishing and, with the proceeds, buy a bigger boat. With the proceeds from the bigger boat, you could buy several boats, until eventually you would have a fleet of fishing boats. Instead of selling your catch to a middleman, you would sell directly to the processor, eventually opening your own cannery. You would control the product, processing, and distribution. You would need to leave this small coastal fishing village and move to Mexico City, then Los Angeles, and eventually New York City, where you would run your expanding enterprise."

"But señor, how long will this all take?"

"Not long. Maybe 15 to 20 years."

"But what then, señor?"

The American laughed and said, "That's the best part. When the time is right, you announce an IPO, sell your company stock to the public, and become very rich. You would make millions."

"Millions, señor? Then what?"

"Then you would retire and move to a small coastal fishing village where you would sleep late, fish a little, play with your kids, take siesta with your wife, then stroll to the village in the evenings where you could sip wine and play guitar with your amigos."

This Mexican fisherman acts very much like most customers. They're living their own lives without staying up at night thinking about which laundry detergent brand will make them a better person or more popular with their friends. Yet, in the context of the executive's world, a customer is just that—a customer—rather than a person. Many brands today are seriously out of touch with their communities and customers. But these same companies act surprised when their customers get upset and suggest that they seem out of touch.

CHANGE AND LEARNING

In turbulent times, many companies act like deer caught in the headlights of an oncoming car. It is hard to get out of the habit of doing what the company has always been doing and shift gears to be proactive in the face of change. Like people, companies resist change with tenacity, yet a changing environment and changing customer needs require—or demand—that the corporate status quo must change. To engage their customers, companies must place their brand within a deeper context of their customers' lives.

Many times, companies get so wrapped up in finding that right, distinctive branding message that they lose touch with their communities. Hence, brands become defined by their own self-imposed boundaries from a lack of connectivity. They must broaden their view and understand that they are part of a larger community. A community is defined by its collective dialogue and, hence, has no boundaries. Instead, communities have horizons. A horizon is a place one never quite reaches. It is not a boundary or a goal. It is not defined as a final destination but more as a relative journey. Companies must recognize that, to deal with the uncertainty that the world presents, they must strive to jump into the community—like the Mexican fishing village—and enjoy the collective journey of being part of that community. By doing so, brands can develop more profitable, long-term, sustainable relationships built on mutual trust and understanding.

How can businesses accomplish this? Well, it starts with creativity. Creativity can be found in anyone who is prepared to enjoy the journey of interacting in a community. Most businesses are isolated from the central experiences of their customers and the context of their lives. They must be willing to get out of their offices and use their curiosity to rediscover the reality of the communities in which they live from the bottom up. Companies must take the time to wonder. Introducing creativity and wonder means that they must strive to live by more human values like honesty, friendship, and empathy. It means that companies must reframe and recontextualize their current world view. They must be willing to take the leap of faith, try and fail, and, most of all, use a bottom-up strategy to learn and become competitive in today's dynamic world.

DEVELOPING YOUR BOTTOM-UP STRATEGY

Many companies focus their strategic thinking around current market needs by getting into a conference room and divining the future (or attempting to). It's a very inside-out or top-down approach. In a reversal of this traditional process, exceptional companies use an outside-in approach, or bottom-up strategy, to focus their thinking on engaging in a dialogue with the other members of their community, allowing them to co-create innovations with their customers. This holistic, organic strategy allows companies to recontextualize and reframe their brand continually, making necessary adjustments as the community and customers evolve.

I heard an interesting story when I was in New York recently, talking with an account planner at a prestigious global advertising agency. He said that, throughout the advertising industry, clients are often nervous about relying solely on the intuition of the creative teams at the agencies they use. Thus, many of them direct their agencies to "be creative" and propose a few new concepts; then clients test these ideas on their "customers"—using focus groups. Because most clients strive for an efficient process, their agency's creative concepts are sent off to the same focus group facilities and moderators, using the same respondents from the same databases, as everyone else in the industry. It's no surprise that clients get nearly identical answers.

While companies recognize the value of intuition and creativity in their planning processes, most are unprepared to jump all the way into a radically new way of thinking. However, asking for a "second opinion" in a completely different context—like the focus group—does as much damage as not being creative at the front end of the process.

Most strategy based solely on traditional research methods is in trouble. As practiced today, most strategy works *against* creativity and the risk taking that is crucial to creating innovative products and services. Its typical pattern is linear.

Idea ➔ Strategy ➔ Action

This makes sense in highly logical, predictable situations. But a company's strategy needs to be contextual and open. It has to be human. Hence, a bottom-up strategy takes these factors into consideration. In this way of strategizing, the pattern needs to be as shown in Figure 4.1.

And it's a perpetual cycle.

So what is a bottom-up strategy, really? In many ways, the concept mirrors the computer software industry's idea of open-source development, which is usually linked to the development of the Linux operating system. Linus Torvalds wrote the original kernels of Linux in 1991. Twelve years later, Linux has a user base of more than 18 million people around the globe. Linux has proven to be robust, capable of running the world's most powerful supercomputers, while also humming along inside TV cable boxes. Torvalds wanted help developing his operating system, so he came up with a radical solution: He'd make the software free. Linux's licensing agreement gives people the ability to make money selling Linux-based products, as long as they share the source code on any additional features they develop.

The idea of creating just the initial seed of the software, then asking for help to develop it into a robust program, has solicited the participa-

FIGURE 4.1 *A Bottom-Up Strategy*

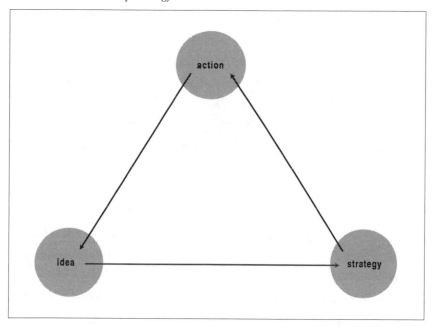

tion of thousands of contributors. These volunteers create software that is comparable to the work produced by the legions of salaried software engineers at Microsoft, Sun Microsystems, and other software giants.

Torvalds's open source philosophy has created an environment where users actually help create the product. It has made Linux's customers fearlessly loyal and has spawned many successful businesses, including Red Hat and VA Software. Linux is a meritocracy, where the merits of the software are judged and evolved by the participants in the Linux community. Torvalds has also appointed "maintainers," volunteers that he has selected based on their participation, to help run different sections of the program.[2]

A bottom-up strategy takes the open-source philosophy a step further. First, it's about loosening the control over the strategic process and focusing on guiding it instead of owning it. It's about inviting the right customers, suppliers, and employees to participate in an open, informed process based on solid guiding principles. To do this well, companies must focus their strategic energies on building consensus and communities. The strategy has to be human. The focus has to be on the quality of the input into the strategy and the communications of those ideas to the community. Companies must focus on being evolutionary.

A great example of focusing on a bottom-up strategy that resulted in disruptive innovation is Dutch Boy Paints and their revolutionary new can. Driving innovation that anticipates the customers' needs means thinking outside the box (or in this case, the paint can). While many marketing executives complain that designing something truly new and original is difficult in today's world, especially in traditional categories, it obviously can be done.

Instead of focusing on finding the next Ralph Lauren or Martha Stewart to cobrand their paint, Dutch Boy Paint, a unit of Sherwin-Williams Co., went back to the drawing board and asked a simple question: "How do people really use paint?" Their investigation led to the reinvention of the paint can. The company rethought and redesigned the simple paint can in a spectacularly creative way. The team worked on the design of the new can for two years, with the goal of reinventing the customer's painting experience and changing an everyday object, the paint can, into something of much more value and usability. The result was Dutch Boy's transformation of the traditional metal paint can into a sleek, square, plastic container with a unique spout, called the Twist & Pour. The new container is easier to open and close, reseals more tightly, allows paint to pour more evenly, is easier to carry, and produces fewer spills. It is also ergonomic and more aesthetically pleasing. It is molded of high-density polyethylene and features an easy-to-hold handle, twist-off top, and pour spout.[3]

By looking beyond the traditional paint market, developing insights and inspiration from deep conversations with the key voices of their customers, and using their intuition, Dutch Boy Paint was able to develop a breakthrough innovation that is destined to be disruptive in the paint industry. Thanks to this innovation, Dutch Boy Paint has tripled the number of retail outlets that sell its products. In addition, *Popular Science* recognized the Twist & Pour paint container as one of the year's best products in 2003.

Disruptive innovation, fueled by bottom-up learning, means companies must participate in an open way within their community. This approach requires true corporate transparency, in everything from marketing to manufacturing, and a more long-term, sustainable outlook on the community in which they participate.

Companies that can make the transition to providing honest, original, culturally relevant materials and products will win. People will carefully weed out and broadcast to their peers those companies and brands that they do not trust. Many companies have discovered that being deeply connected to their community is good for their brands. In this new era, brands will have to become good, *creative* citizens of the community to survive.

In the context of the rapidly changing business environment, it is time to question what we already know and how we attempt to learn what we don't. Are we using tools that provide us with meaningful and useful insights that can drive corporate strategy from the context of our customers, bottom up through the organization? Can data be transformed, from the bottom up instead of top down, into relevant innovation in branding and product development? The only solution is to develop new ways of understanding and finding meaning in the dynamic flux.

L ≥ C

The principle that learning has to be greater than or equal to change is at the core of a bottom-up strategy. The one constant in these turbulent times is that change is happening faster than ever; thus, learning has to happen even more quickly. Part of the learning process requires knowing what to do with the intelligence you acquire; this is the step that facilitates real change. This idea may seem quite simple, yet it may challenge many people who have traditionally been involved in product development. Let me tell you a story that illustrates this.

Last year I was invited to kick off the annual innovation conference for a *Fortune* 500 company. I was giving a talk about the power of storytelling with Barbara Perry, a great friend and esteemed cultural anthropologist. When the person introducing us launched into a discussion of Type 1 and Type 2 statistical errors—pure numbers stuff—it set off a nervousness that only escalated. I felt that we were in real trouble. Just as our introducer was finishing his remarks, I looked over at Barbara with fear in my eyes. I was surprised to see she had a mischievous smile on her face.

Once we were introduced, Barbara walked over to the whiteboard and said enthusiastically, "I have a formula, too!" She wrote $L \geq C$. She went on to explain that this meant Learning has to be greater than or equal to Change. During the course of the presentation, we demonstrated how storytelling was an essential part of and an invaluable tool in the process of learning. To my amazement, the talk went extremely well. Everyone agreed that, to solve complex problems, learning has to be greater than change.

More than that, the formula was an ingenious way to introduce a new idea, the power of storytelling, in the context of the engineers' world. In fact, many of the engineers contributed stories of their own. Far from being uninterested and remote, they were emotional when they told their stories about their own automobile experiences.

While learning has always needed to be greater than change for a company to grow, the rate of this change has accelerated from the old business environment, where change occurred gradually, during a decade or over the course of someone's career. Today, change seems to happen overnight. One day, you are ahead of the pack, and the very next day, you are struggling to keep up. This means that the rate of learning has to be greater for any company to survive. So what do you do? With more information available, people have to acknowledge that what they perceive as the whole picture is only a small slice of reality. Any company's world can be segmented into three areas: what we know, what we *know* we don't know, and what we *don't* know we don't know (see Figure 4.2).

One of the problems that we all face in today's more dynamic world is that the area of *what we don't know we don't know* cannot be blissfully ignored, due to its disruptive potential. Companies need to recognize

FIGURE 4.2 *The Whole Picture*

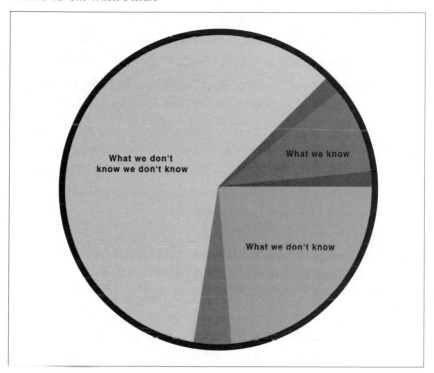

this segment of their world and try to reduce it, using inspiration from the bottom up.

Businesses often approach strategic planning as a very top-down, rigid process; even the language they use is far too structured and solemn. Planning, in its nature, requires an acceptance of the unknown and receptiveness to new ideas. Unfortunately, many companies' reaction to an influx of new information is to fall into the paralysis-by-analysis syndrome. Other companies react by panicking and making important decisions *too* quickly.

The ideal solution, but one that doesn't come easily to most companies, is to rely more heavily on intuition. This is a huge paradigm shift for most businesses. People need bottom-up tools that give them the confidence to rely on their intuition when exploring the world. Businesses need fast, "real," and connected ways of making meaning of their quickly changing realities. The goal of the second section of the book is to help you build your own set of bottom-up tools, giving you the ability to develop relevant innovation faster. Inspiration developed from a bottom-up strategy can give a company the confidence needed to drive real innovation.

Bottom-up learning demands that companies be prepared to make serious mistakes when exploring their communities with their customers. It means that people inside companies need to be unintimidated, spontaneous, unconditioned, and expressive in these explorations. They need to be allowed the space to learn through stories from their communities. Companies need to revel in these stories and be creative in their interactions with other community members.

THE SEARCH FOR MEANING (OR, WHY MORE AND MORE DATA IS NOT ENOUGH)

The information age has leveled the playing field; everyone now has access to the same data. So how do you transform that data into relevant innovation? In such a competitive environment, what can you do to stay ahead of the competition?

Once we've identified what we do (and do not) know, another crucial step has to happen. Companies must actively develop these bottom-up tools to understand and transform information into action. To find meaning in what they learn about their customers, they must identify what keeps the community balanced: its center of gravity. By deeply understanding this center of gravity (discussed in detail in Chapters 6 and 10), any company can move more quickly in driving *relevant* innovation for their customers, without spending time or energy going in the wrong direction.

Information really exists along a continuum, with one step leading to the next.

The continuum typically looks something like this:

Data ➜ Information ➜ Knowledge ➜ Insight

FIGURE 4.3 *The Full Information Continuum*

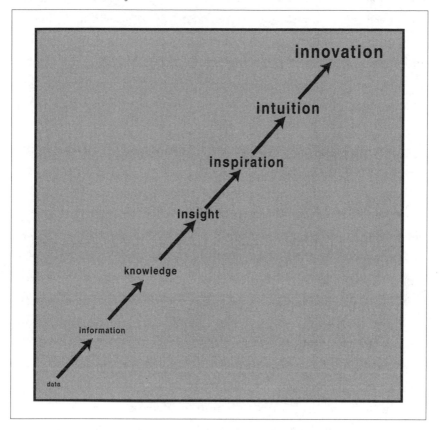

The problem with the information model above is that three important steps are usually left out. The goal is to drive innovation. With that in mind, three steps should be added to the continuum, making it look more like Figure 4.3.

As Einstein said: "Any fool can know, the point is to understand."[4] So many times, the act of knowing is based on a quick observation—I know Joe—versus a deeper connection I understand Mary. But new information can be challenging, both to an individual and to an organization. Companies need to be fearless about finding ways of learning and knowing that allow for deeper understanding of meaning, of context, and of the shared experiences of everyone involved in their businesses. The key is to listen to the stories that customers and noncustomers alike are telling about their lives, their cultures, and how they really feel about the company and its products. It is crucial to understand, on an intuitive level, what the community needs and wants.

Pursuing a bottom-up strategy means seeking enough inspiration and input to find the magic to drive innovation. It's hard work. It means breaking out of categories, words, and definitions. It means focusing on developing a renewed sense of wonder. It means really getting to know your customers, and suppliers, as people.

Here are five steps to follow in the pursuit of developing bottom-up strategic thinking.

Step one: Stop counting. So much of modern marketing strategy takes the ivory tower, arm's length, quantifiable approach to strategy. Strategy can't be sanitized and kept distant from what's actually happening in the market. Being so reliant on quantitative models misses the point. As Friedrich Nietzsche said, "There are no facts, only interpretations."[5] Many companies spend a great deal of time counting everything but seeing the significance of nothing.

When you count things, you first have to define them in measurable ways, letting the system manipulate the figures by narrowing the definition. The reality is that the more you count, the less you understand. I often find that, when asked by a client to solve a particular problem, the solution becomes clear after spending time in the field listening to people who use the product. I *might* get the same result by looking at internal reports and spreadsheets, but it would take a lot longer. I would also miss the opportunity to discover the unexpected, become exposed to new ideas, or learn how the customers' expectations of the product could lead to real innovation.

Meaning is best constructed as a story. As Joan Didion says, "We tell each other stories in order to live."[6] Even numbers have to be integrated into a story to be made meaningful. Hence, it makes sense that to understand our customers, we have to seek out the stories they tell. It still comes down to using common sense and intuition. Strategy has to be based on leadership, enthusiasm, or personal engagement. There's no way around it.

Step two: Don't begrudge complexity. In its essence, truth is complex. You can't reduce the complexities and idiosyncrasies of the world to black-and-white numbers and hope to gain any real understanding. I see this happening all the time in the sales department of many companies. Naturally, the focus of salespeople is to hit their goals consistently. In many instances, I've seen salespeople count orders that aren't really tied down or withhold excess orders until the next month, just to meet these rigid, predetermined goals. Instead of focusing on the needs of the customers, or even on the reality of what's sold and what isn't, the salespeople focus on the numbers that *supposedly* represent reality. Numbers can be manipulated; real people with complex wants and needs cannot.

The real problem is that quantitative tools for building strategy can't capture the complexity of human life. They provide a wonderful rearview mirror view of the world, but it's hard to drive a strategy into the future by looking backwards. Think about the stock market. We've become so enamored with the ups and downs of the markets that we tend to forget the complex reality of what they represent. The best market analysts are not those who can merely recite the percentages of growth or decline but the ones who can use their intuition to interpret correctly the reasons behind these movements.

Even the way most companies view their own structure—as a pyramid—suggests a static, top-down entity. Companies must recognize the complex world in which we live and begin to see their involvement in it in a new way. Instead of looking at the corporate structure as a pyramid, consider seeing it as a tree: a living, growing tree whose roots are planted deeply in the reality of its environment, with the sturdy support structure of a thick trunk, an efficient delivery system from the nutrients of the ground to the tips of the leaves and back again, and the ability to populate the ground (or market) with its seeds (its products). The only way to welcome the role of complexity in your strategy is to rely on more organic strategic methods.

Step three: Belong to your community. So many companies have isolated themselves from the communities in which they participate. It's easy to see what happens; it happened at Radar. I started Radar in my garage. While the garage was crowded, noisy, and full of interruptions from neighborhood kids, it sure was fun. It also functioned pretty well. We were all generalists. There was no need for meetings. Everyone always knew what was going on. Now that we are in an office on two separate floors, much more effort must be made to communicate; hence, there's less time for us to be out in the community with our customers. It is also much more difficult to keep the internal community of Radar as close as it was when we started. It's not a bad thing. But it takes a lot more effort and management than it used to, and that all can get in the way of spending quality time with the right customers.

While growth certainly demands more organization, it also means that you have to make a greater effort to be a part of all of your communities. Many of our clients are big, complex business organizations, and their executives often tell us that they're too busy to go out and spend time with their customers. Doing all their internal tasks precludes the time or the energy it takes to get outside the confines of their offices.

In this dynamic environment, the companies that will be successful will know their customers as they know their friends. They will be creatively engaged in their communities. To be a part of these communities, companies must develop new ways to communicate. It is a prerequisite for social and emotional connections. They must form community network strategies to give them the ability to understand and react to changes occurring in every corner of their community.

Step four: Always ask why. I was talking to a client recently about his company's access to customer information. He said that the company has spent the past decade developing enormous databases of information about their customers: they know precisely what is purchased, when, and where. But even with all of this information, the client's company was dismayed to realize they still didn't understand *why* their customers behave the way they do. All of the quantifiable data in the world won't help you understand a person's underlying reasons. It will not give you the cause, only the effect. Not only does the very act of asking yourself *why* force you to make leaps of faith and use your intuition, it also makes you more human, giving you the ability to connect to your customers on a deeper emotional level.

Step five: Develop narrative thinking. In this disruptive age, the power of stories is becoming recognized as an important tool. It's a move from cold hard facts to warm and fluid narratives. People crave a human connection with the companies whose products they buy. A cornerstone of good branding is good storytelling—but it's a two-way street. Companies must learn to go beyond telling their *own* stories to listening to and understanding their customers' stories. By being more human and relying on storytelling and narrative strategic thinking, companies have the opportunity to be more relevant to other members of their community.

Marketing strategy must be framed as a fluid, organic narrative instead of a static, immovable framework. It's the tree versus the pyramid. Telling and listening to human stories not only provides a context to people's lives, but also engages the imagination and interjects magic.

Founders of exceptional companies are seldom focused on their "brand" when they start their business. Instead, they focus on stories that eventually change the world, by using bottom-up strategies to see beyond the horizon. The reality is that, in the start-up phase, you inherently rely on your customers, suppliers, and employees to help develop your strategy. Established companies often forget this and try to distance themselves from their turbulent, risky beginnings. But companies would do well to rediscover their roots and revisit their own creative history.

Case Study: Williams-Sonoma

Every great company has an equally great story about its founder, who used intuition and intimate knowledge of their customers to, many times unknowingly, create disruptive changes in their industries. Think about Steve Jobs, Phil Knight, Charles Schwab, Bill Gates, and Sam Walton. All of these men saw the world differently than their competitors and created a whole industry by following their gut. Another great example is Chuck Williams, founder of Williams-Sonoma.

When Chuck Williams opened Williams-Sonoma for business in the fall of 1956, he ushered in a new era in America and became the founding father of the "foodie" movement. The idea for a gourmet specialty food shop was influenced by many of Williams's early life experiences. When he was a teenager during the Depression, he found a job at a date ranch in California, picking fruit for pennies. Soon, he began helping in their roadside shop. He enjoyed working with discriminating customers, a skill that would later come in handy at Williams-Sonoma. During World War II, Williams worked for Lockheed Aircraft as part of a traveling maintenance crew, stationed in East Africa and India. He enjoyed traveling to small towns and villages to sample the local foods.

These experiences set the stage for having broad horizons, but it was his trip to Europe in 1953 that gave him the idea for Williams-Sonoma. On the trip, he became enamored of France and French cooking. He noticed all of the interesting cooking equipment that was available to the French home cook—none of which was available in the States. So he started a business selling the cooking equipment that he found in France. Williams and his friends enjoyed French cooking and threw parties to enjoy the experience of cooking together. When Williams opened the doors of Williams-Sonoma in Sonoma, California, he focused on displaying his cookware as art. He would display each pan in the best possible way by putting it on a shelf in size order, with all the handles facing the same way. If somebody wanted to buy something, they had to ask Williams to get it for them, giving Williams the ability to start a conversation about French cooking.

Two years later, in 1958, Williams opened his shop in San Francisco. The idea of French cooking began to take hold with Julia Child's first television show specifically on French cooking. Gourmet cooking became a movement. To help spread the word, Williams published his first catalog in 1971. Every year in January, Williams would travel to France to keep the stores and catalog stocked with interesting new items.

Like many entrepreneurs, Williams saw himself as his own customer and filled the store with what he wanted in his own kitchen. He would find things foreign to American palates, such as balsamic vinegar, and introduce them to his American audience. In those days, if you wanted to know what was happening at the cutting edge of food, all you had to do was go to Williams-Sonoma. After 17 years of operating in San Francisco, Williams opened stores in Beverly Hills, Palo Alto, and Costa Mesa. Meanwhile, the catalog had grown quickly, and by 1977 it had to open a small distribution center.

In the late 1970s, Williams and his investors sold the company to Howard Lester on the condition that Williams would still be involved.

In 1983, Williams-Sonoma went public and really started to expand. The company bought the Gardener's Eden catalog, then Pottery Barn. By 1986, Williams-Sonoma had its first $100 million year in revenue. In 1991, the company published its first cookbooks in the Williams-Sonoma Kitchen Library Series. Over 17 million Williams-Sonoma books have been sold.

Today Chuck Williams's gourmet specialty food shop has transformed into a retailing giant with 478 stores and $2.3 billion in revenue. By seeing beyond the horizon, engaging his customers in a dialogue, and using his own intuition, Williams created a permanent home for gourmet cooking and forever changed the way we think about food.[7]

THE ROAD MAP AHEAD

A bottom-up strategy provides companies with the flexibility to be extraordinary. They become more prominent participants in their own communities and have deeper relationships with other community members. The second part of this book is a map of how to become more actively engaged in your community. It's about taking a journey to create this deeper dialogue in the context of your current and future customers' lives. The goal is to provide you with real tools that have worked well in driving inspiration and innovation deep inside companies. Embracing a bottom-up strategy means becoming more sensitive to the subtleties of the environments in which we all live. This is easily accomplished and can be done in seven steps.

Step one: Focus on key voices. It's easy to get stuck in thinking that your customers see the same power of your brand that you see. You've got to get out and have the right conversation about your brand, with the right customers, in the real context of their lives. Every company has a small set of customers that have a disproportionately large amount of power in the market conversation. You need to know who these customers are and ask them the *right* questions, which sometimes means the hardest ones.

Step two: Get the story. The key in getting the stories from the street is to get deep enough into the lives of the people you want to reach so that you can understand the underlying assumptions of their lives. Only at this level can the useful context and meaning behind outward actions and behaviors be fully understood. It is the primary source for new ideas and product innovation. And the only way to get to this level is by investing a lot of time and energy engaging in real, two-way conversations.

Step three: Listen. At the core of any relationship, a level of trust is required. People feel most comfortable with those who take the time to listen to them *in the context of their lives*. This makes them feel important, respected, and empowered.

Step four: Find inspiration. It's important to look in places in the market that are beyond your periphery but can bring unexpected insights and inspiration. It takes getting out in the marketplace, listening at the fringes, and understanding the power of networks in the community.

Step five: Hone your intuition. When you really get to know your customers with the key voices, you can greatly enhance your ability to beat your competition to market with breakthrough innovations by using your intuition. Utilizing a bottom-up strategy gives you the confidence to trust your gut.

Step six: Find the center of gravity. All of the great inspiration that you gain from your customers isn't worth anything, unless you can make meaning of that inspiration in the context of your company. At the core of finding the center of gravity is dialogue. This means that you have to maintain an ongoing dialogue among your internal team in regard to what you have learned from the conversations with your customers.

Step seven: Tell the story. Products today have become less important than the stories they convey and the way their audience or customers interpret them. Companies also need to have stories to tell internally—true stories that inspire action. They must themselves embody those stories with congruency and authenticity.

WHAT THIS MEANS TO YOU

In the past, companies used top-down tools to interact with their customers because that seemed most efficient. Who has time to answer all the e-mails and attend all the meetings and still be able to interact directly with customers in this dynamic world? The reality is, however, that the top-down tools are no longer sufficient in a highly dynamic business environment. Companies can use these top-down tools to find out the *whats* and the *wheres* of customer behavior, but they do not provide the learning opportunities that reveal the reasons *why*. Understanding these reasons is essential for staying deeply connected to the right customers and staying ahead of the competition.

To respond to dynamic changes, you must know your customer more intimately. This means finding new ways to get through the many layers of insulation and develop a deeper connection with the right customers from the bottom up.

Today, people are demanding to be more involved with the companies from whom they buy goods and services. Customers are demanding that companies employ a bottom-up strategy not only of listening to them but also giving them the ability to co-create the products they buy. Co-creation can mean many things to many different customers. For some people, co-creation might mean more personalized or customized products. For others, it means that a customer service representative took their concerns seriously and the company is willing to learn from them.

Think about how your company learns. Does it get stuck in the paralysis-by-analysis syndrome? Or does it panic and react *too* quickly to change? Also, think about your strategic decision-making process. Do you use a top-down or a bottom-up strategy? Does the information that your company uses result in insights but go no further, or does your firm make a genuine effort to drive innovation through intuition and inspiration? Are there cases in which products or branding messages have been truly innovative, offering your customers the space to co-create?

SEVEN STEPS TO GET BEYOND THE BRAND

5

STEP ONE
Focus on Key Voices

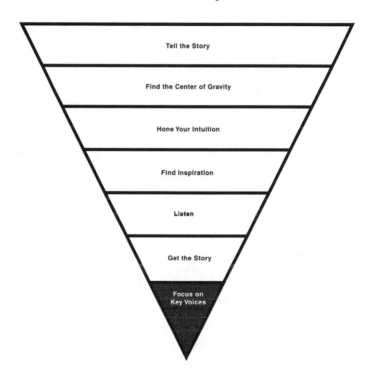

The ideal condition
Would be, I admit, that men should be right by instinct;
But since we are all likely to go astray,
The reasonable thing is to learn from those who can teach.
SOPHOCLES, IN ANTIGONE[1]

We know that both individuals and companies have more to do, listen to, and respond to than they have time. Successful companies understand the importance of identifying and listening to the *key voices* in their industries. The people with the key voices have been called many things over the past couple of years in popular books and magazines: connectors, salesmen, mavens, deviants, and influencers. But one question remains: How do you *find* these key voices? This process is much more than a business strategy; it is a matter of survival.

Case Study: Patagonia

Even though Patagonia—the company he founded and owns—is now 25 years old, Yvon Chouinard still understands the importance of listening to the key voices of his most important customers. Patagonia has become the philosophical leader of the outdoor industry and has a far-reaching influence on society because of its environmental and social practices. But how did this start? When Patagonia began, it was staffed by a group of climbers and surfers who wanted to focus all of their energies on climbing in the summer and surfing in the winter. The foundation upon which Patagonia was built was that passion for climbing and surfing.

In the beginning, Patagonia's customers were Chouinard's friends, so they were easy to listen to. As the company has grown into an outdoor industry leader, it has focused on listening to the key voices of those participating in climbing and surfing but has grown to include paddlers, mountain bikers, backcountry skiers, sailors, snowboarders, and fly fishermen. Each sport has its intricacies, its nuances of skills and expertise, which Patagonia understands. Chouinard believes that "Patagonia's success lies in the close connection to specific sports and the innovation that comes from constant participation." He and his staff are constantly out there, doing the sports themselves and listening to the key voices of other participants.[2]

Through this deep connection, Patagonia has provided an example for other companies. For instance, a Patagonia catalog is more than a collection of available products. It embodies the experience—through breathtaking photography and award-winning writing—of being out there using those products. The catalogs have also encouraged customers to get more actively involved in environmental causes.

Chouinard is concerned about the future of the world. He has used his connection with Patagonia's key customers to start a revolution in sustainable farming by only using organic cotton in his clothing. Patagonia has also reduced the amount of packaging around their products. Patagonia has focused its energies on making everything it does as sustainable as possible, from the quality of the clothes they make to the environmentally sensitive buildings they design. They have also spurred the idea of environmental auditing, by looking at the full cost of doing business, including what it would cost to replace the raw materials used in their products. These proactive business practices have done much to strengthen the commitment of the key voices of Patagonia's customers. Today, through the pages of their catalogs, at their retail locations, and on their Web site, many of their customers look to Patagonia to help them understand the impacts we humans have on the planet and what they can do about it. Such a deep connection is enviable. It is possible for most businesses to move in such a direction, but it requires listening to the key voices of your market.

So, who has the key voices in your market? How do you identify them?

TO WHOM DO YOU LISTEN?

In most industries, the early adopters or trend translators have the key voices. Why? Think about an innovation in your industry. Has there been an innovation that started out small, then really took off? Think about Kodak. They *owned* photography. All of a sudden, digital photography went from something for technophiles into the mainstream. This dramatic shift has left traditional photography companies, including Kodak, FujiFilm, and Polaroid, scrambling to keep up. Like most revolutionary new products, digital cameras were expensive and slow when they were introduced. After manufacturers fixed those problems, digital camera sales have seen dramatic increases, now outselling traditional film cameras. Aggressive advertising by camera manufacturers did not bring about the shift from traditional to digital photography. Instead, it happened due to the adoption of the technology by translators, who acted as evangelists to their family and friends. Digital photography's growth is now directly tied to its ease of use and quality of images. For a long time, film-based photographic companies believed that digital photography would be much slower to catch on because of the technical quality difference between film (approximately 18 megapixels) and digital (3 to 5 megapixels) images. The reality is that, for the average family snapshot, three megapixels is perfectly adequate. Another reason why digital photography has spread so fast is that it has been so easy for opinion leaders to communicate.

As with digital photography, in many markets, the real sales don't come until after the trend translators have been convinced of the need for the product. If they accept a product, and the market is big enough, the product will spread like wildfire with little help from any formal branding. Trend translators help create an environment of acceptance and safety where more people can feel comfortable getting involved.

When I owned *Women's Sports & Fitness,* one of the things that we noticed in some conversations with our readers was that they often found themselves being asked about products by their peers. On average, each of our readers was asked for help buying a product by 12 of their peers per year. This finding became core to our advertising sales strategy. At the time, our competitors had circulations of five or six times that of *Women's Sports & Fitness.* We grew our advertising substantially by helping our advertisers recognize that our readers were more important to reach than our competitors' readers, because they influenced so many others. The reality was that our competitors' readers were seeking out *our* readers to help them make purchasing decisions. These readers, who were not as passionate about sports, were listening to their more experienced peers. Our advertisers found that it was more important—and a lot cheaper—to engage in a dialogue with the readers of *Women's Sports & Fitness* than to advertise with our competitors. It seems so logical to skip the translators and focus on the middle of the diffusion curve, where the biggest number of customers resides, but a successful dialogue doesn't happen that way.

The reality is that, if you don't connect with the trend translators, the rest of the market won't take you seriously. They will look first to their respected peers to validate your product. Why is this? Well, most people further to the right of the translators on the diffusion curve simply don't think about your product and the problems it solves very often. They have bigger things to think about. They probably won't even take the time to listen to you. However, they will listen to their peers. Recently, my wife and I adopted our sons from Russia. Waking up one morning with two eight-month-old boys was an overwhelming experience. Neither Bridget nor I had the luxury of taking the time to read parenting magazines and seek out information. It was much easier—and faster—to ask trusted friends and family members for advice.

So, what is a trend translator? In the past couple of years, several books have described the importance of this group. Each book, from *The Tipping Point, The Influentials,* and *Crossing the Chasm* to *The Deviants' Advantage,* has its own spin on what to call these early adopters. All of these books are based on the groundbreaking research of Everett Rodgers. In 1962, Rodgers wrote *Diffusion of Innovation.*[3] In it, he outlined how different segments of a population accepted an innovation in what he described as a Diffusion Curve (see Figure 5.1).

Rodgers observed that every population of potential users breaks into five categories: trendsetters (innovators), trend translators (early

FIGURE 5.1 *Diffusion Curve*

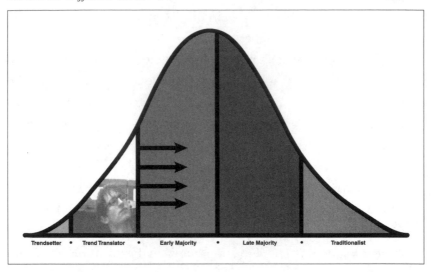

adopters), early majority, late majority, and traditionalists. Each group differs in its value orientations. The categories are described as follows:

1. *Trendsetters (innovators).* 2.5 percent of the population. Innovators are venturesome; they're always willing to try new ideas.
2. *Trend translators (early adopters).* 13.5 percent of the population. Early adopters are guided by respect; they are opinion leaders in their community and adopt new ideas early but carefully.
3. *Early majority.* 34 percent of the population. Early majority members are deliberate; they do adopt new ideas before the average person, although they are rarely leaders.
4. *Late majority.* 34 percent of the population. Late majority members are skeptical; they adopt an innovation only after the majority of other people have tried it.
5. *Traditionalists.* 16 percent of the population. Traditionalists are tradition-bound; they're suspicious of change, mix with other tradition-bound people, and adopt innovations only after they become major, recognizable trends.

So, who are the trend translators? They aren't the first to jump on a trend, but they are inquisitive about ways to improve what they do. They are usually good communicators, and others in the market tend to solicit advice from them. Translators achieve the capability of sharing a common language within a large group of peers—remember our *Women's Sports & Fitness* readers? A result of this confidence is the ability to become a leader and a seer, one who is able to initiate a conversation about a subject they are passionate about, an idea or innovation they find of interest and value.

As translators, they are opinion leaders and are always a little slower actually to decide about the acceptance of an idea or product than trendsetters, because they want to make a decision that is good—*good* meaning right, efficient, etc. The diligence expressed by these individuals in their decision-making process is an important part of their psychological makeup. It is important to them that their peers see them as trustworthy and thoughtful, yet also progressive and forward thinking.

Despite the attention that the popular books mentioned above have brought to Rodgers's ideas, many companies have shied away from engaging translators in a conversation due to their relatively small numbers. Springing from the general corporate belief in the illusion of control, the idea of statistically verifiable sample sizes is seen as a cornerstone of any conversation with customers. The anthropologist Dr. A. K. Romney, however, has helped to overturn that assumption. Romney built a mathematical model, the Cultural Consensus Theory, which supports the notion that, chosen well, small sample sizes of opinion leaders—as few as eight people—can be scientifically valid for conveying what the rest of the community thinks.[4] Typically these opinion leaders in the social network can see further ahead, helping you become more predictive in your strategic thinking.

These trend translators generally tend to be young, progressive, and artistic. They are expressive and thoughtful. When I mention the word *young,* I do not mean young in terms of age but in terms of acceptance of change. Trend translators are always looking for ways to improve themselves or their experiences. They also seem to focus more on enhancing their experience than on being the first to accomplish something; the journey is as valuable as the final destination.

In some senses, magazines can be trend translators. They are trying to share an experience with their readers. However, a printed medium lacks interactivity. The Internet and Web logs have recently succeeded in making the printed word more interactive. This interaction means that trends can flow through the Internet at a much higher speed.

Why Trend Translators?

In today's brutally competitive business environment, it is essential to find a group of passionate customers who are willing to spread the word about your product or service. Without a deep connection with a core group of customers, it is virtually impossible to compete. Think about how this works among you and your peers. Do you have a few friends that seem always to be ahead of the curve?

I have seen it happen personally. I've owned a house in a small town in Mexico for six years now. It's a small, beautiful little town on a beach with a great surf break. When we bought our house, there were only a handful of "gringos" who owned property. These trend translators were surfers who, over time, let friends use their houses. Some of these guests went on to buy their own property. Recently, our little town garnered a full-page article in the *New York Times*.[5] The telephone at the real estate office in town started ringing off the hook. For better or worse, in the past couple of years, the town has become "gringoized." Property values have tripled, and a development frenzy is happening. When we first arrived in town six years ago, you could tell that it was going to get very popular—there already was a tangible "buzz."

The key is to know and differentiate your customers. Focus on finding the translators. Even if you want to get to know your loyal customers better, it's important to seek out the *right* loyal customers. Which loyal customers influence others? Not only does focusing on key voices save you money, it helps you understand where the rest of the market will be and gives you an opportunity to prepare for changes.

Case Study: Trucker Hats

The meteoric success of Von Dutch is a good case study of how diffusion works. Von Dutch was the street name of Kenneth Howard, the legendary 1950s car customizer. The nickname was based on Howard's reputation of being "as crazy as a Dutchman." Howard is best remembered for his iconic symbol of a flying eyeball; he is also known as the first person to paint flames across the nose of a car. Mr. Howard's heirs sold the Von Dutch trademark in 1996.

Today, Von Dutch still represents 1950s hot rod chic. In 1999, the business started selling the Von Dutch logo on T-shirts and hats for car enthusiasts. In so doing, they relaunched the trucker hat and rode a wave to success. In 2001, the company had revenues of $1 million. Two years later, the company's revenues topped $25 million.

How did this happen? Von Dutch focused on a dialogue with a few trendsetting New York and Los Angeles shops in the late fall of 2002. The denim hats quickly became a hot item. Suddenly, stars such as Ashton Kutcher, Britney Spears, and Carmen Electra became translators, appearing in the media wearing them. But it wasn't until pop singer Justin Timberlake sported a Von Dutch hat to the Grammy Awards parties in February of 2003 that things really gained momentum.

By the time Timberlake showed up on magazine covers, most "fashionistas" were declaring that the trend was over. Yet at malls all over America, the hats were flying off the shelves. In today's connected world, around the time that trendsetters are declaring a trend as dead, it reaches the general population. By the end of 2003, retailers from Paris to Tokyo were carrying the trucker hats.[6]

While you may have seen the Von Dutch hats and heard the company's success story, you might say, "I don't work for a fashion company," or, "We don't sell trendy stuff." But would any company turn down increasing their growth in sales by a factor of 25 in two years? Start small, understand who to listen to—in Von Dutch's case, the key voices were small retailers in New York and Los Angeles—and understand what they need. While the Von Dutch story illustrates an example of being in the right place at the right time, it is also possible to work proactively at developing relationships with your key voices. This will not only inform your outside-in strategy in a profound way but also keep your company ahead in a dynamic, competitive environment.

THE DOWNSIDE OF FOCUS GROUPS

Many companies use focus groups as one method of listening to the key voices in their markets. While this seems appealing—and effective—on the surface, the reality is that you've got to get out and really have a conversation about your brand in the context of your customers' lives—not in a pseudoscientific setting.

In the United States, over a billion dollars are spent on focus groups every year. Focus groups are the current paradigm for most companies seeking customer input on new product development and marketing ideas. Yet 80 percent of new products or services fail within six months, even when customer opinions were actively solicited. Likewise, most new television shows fail even after being screened by focus groups. Many people within the advertising and marketing industry question the value of the traditional focus group, yet focus groups remain the standard research method, accentuating a huge gap between what customers say (in the focus group setting) and their actual behavior in the marketplace.[7]

I've sat in an awful lot of focus group facilities watching people who are supposed to be customers, when it is obvious they are not. Before I started Radar, I sat in on a focus group involving a new inline skate for recreational skaters. One of the primary screening criteria for participants was that they skated on a regular basis; it seemed highly unlikely the criteria had been met, when one participant had to ask the moderator to identify the skate sitting on the table.

The reality is that, for many reasons, most focus group participants tend to misrepresent themselves or even lie outright. First, it's only human that when someone asks a question, especially in a place that is out of context, we all tend to guess at the "right" answer. Product development and marketing shouldn't try to solicit one "right" answer from people. Companies need to hear what people really think about an idea, in the context of their lives. Isn't it much easier to be honest about any experience when you're actually involved in it, rather than sitting in front of a one-way mirror?

Another reason is that some element of groupthink always comes into play, no matter how hard a moderator tries to stop it: There will always be leaders and followers in every group. One famous story about focus groups has reached myth status.

An electronics company was conducting focus groups to understand customer preferences about a new portable boom box. Among other questions, participants were asked to pick between two colors: yellow and black. Everyone in the group talked about how cool the yellow was and that they would definitely purchase that color. As they left the session, each participant was instructed to stop by a room, one at a time. As part of their compensation for attending the focus group, they were being offered a boom box and could choose between the black and yellow boom boxes. *Everyone* picked a black boom box to take home—the exact opposite of what they had said in the focus group.

Lastly, many focus group participants simply don't know what they want. New ideas are hard to articulate. That's because most of the thoughts and feelings that influence people's behavior are unconscious. There is no way to tap into a participant's unconscious thinking in the span of an hour, in an out-of-context room, with a bunch of unfamiliar people hanging on their every word.

Another significant issue is that many of the people sitting on the *other* side of the one-way mirror aren't always fully engaged. I recently got an e-mail from a focus group facility owner. He emphasized the implementation of an exciting new innovation for the industry . . . exercise equipment in the client room. The idea was that, while the researchers conducted the focus group, their clients could be catching up on their treadmill workouts.

I've observed several focus groups where the nature of being behind the one-way mirror has only accentuated the problem of hearing what you think you want to hear, rather than what the focus groups participants are really saying.

Focus groups, however, are highly efficient, which is one compelling reason for their widespread use. Companies simply hire a focus group company that can quickly recruit people off of their standard database and run several groups an evening in their facilities. People have many motivations to participate in focus groups, even about an undisclosed subject. Some participate because they need the cash; others come for the refreshments or simply for the opportunity to interact with other humans. But what are the chances that they are going to represent the key voices you're looking for to give you honest, direct feedback and push your innovation forward?

Finding and listening to the key voices of your customers takes a lot of work. You can't outsource every element of the process and expect to learn something that will inspire real innovation. You've got to get out from behind your desk—or in this case, the one-way mirror—and find ways to locate and really listen to those key voices.

FINDING THE KEY VOICES

One of the things we've realized at Radar is that the current paradigm of recruiting from an established list is antiquated, not to mention unreliable. Where is the value in talking with professional focus group respondents? Here are ten steps to ensure that you're finding, and keeping, your key voices.

1. *Identify cultural cornerstones.* It's always easier to find the right people in the right places. Would you expect to find a fashion diva at a football game? Context is everything. Who really are your brand's key voices? Where do they hang out? What do they do? Are they online, in the mall, or hanging out with friends at someone's home? Get out of your office and spend time in your key customers' environments. By understanding the cultural cornerstones and understanding the context of people's lives, you can go a long way toward finding and understanding them.

2. *Identify the key voices.* Once you understand your key customers' environments on a firsthand basis, start to look around and listen. Who is talking? What are they saying? We always ask people who influences *them* in their thoughts about a certain subject or product. By always asking people this question, you can quickly understand who the opinion leaders are.

3. *Make them a part of the team.* If you want people to be honest with you, you have to be honest with them. One of the big problems with focus groups is that they are rarely honest—they exist apart from reality. How would you feel, and act, if someone was behind a one-way mirror in your office, watching your every move? To get people to open up, you've got to get into their environment, be human, and do more than just let them talk. Let them lead.

4. *Create a community space.* When I was publishing special interest magazines, I realized that to be successful, it was my job to set a community table and invite all of the members of the community to it. At the time, this included employees, advertisers, readers, writers, and photographers. I figured that if I could make one of our magazines into a community space, where everyone in the community would come to find out what was

going on and actively participate in an ongoing dialogue, I'd be successful.

A special interest magazine doesn't attract everyone in the market. It only attracts trendsetters and translators. For instance, when I published *Inline Magazine,* the biggest magazine in the inline skating market, our circulation was 40,000. That was a drop in the bucket compared to the 30 million active inline skaters at the time. Yet, creating a community space for this relatively small number of participants had a very large influence on the rest of the market. The community space not only provided a place for the company to connect with the key voices, but it also became a place for key voices to connect with each other.

5. *Create a dialogue with each trend translator.* If you really want to understand the subtleties of the marketplace, it is essential for each person you engage in a dialogue to feel that they are important and honored as an individual. Today, having an individual conversation with each and every translator is much easier with the power of the Internet. Include them in every corner of your business.

6. *Consistently bring in new blood.* Too many companies rely on the same key voices over and over to help them develop their strategic thinking. For instance, it's important for consultants to understand your business, but the reality is that any market is just too complicated to rely on a single perspective to understand it. Likewise, when developing a dialogue with translators, it is essential to refresh their numbers for every investigation. That's not to say that a few key voices shouldn't stay involved. But it is important to reinterview the translators in your dialogue for every project. This keeps viewpoints fresh.

7. *Compensate them well.* When I published magazines in the sporting goods industry, the common belief was that you could go out and talk to some translators and pay them by giving them a free pair of shoes—or better yet, socks. There was a feeling that

people should be honored just to be involved with giving these companies their opinions about product designs. But the bottom line is that everyone is busy and everyone's time is valuable. Cash is still the best incentive, and I'm not talking about five bucks. For Radar's cultural encounters, spending time with reporters in their world, the average compensation is $100 per hour. That might seem like a lot to pay a soccer mom or a high school kid, but our clients are trying to make decisions worth millions; they need to hear the real story, and that costs money.

8. *Respect their opinions and their time.* I've been in the field with way too many companies that consider their customers an inconvenience. It's always amazing to watch as a company has a conversation with its customers but doesn't respect their time or opinions. How many times have you heard someone say that their customers don't know what they want or dismiss an idea as one that has already been tried? The superior attitude comes through loud and clear when you're listening to someone. Just remember, there is always something to learn.

9. *Don't burn them out.* It's easy to establish a dialogue with a key customer and then begin to rely heavily on that one perspective. That person becomes your "go-to guy." It's great to have a few of these relationships in your quiver, but it's important to remember that, while you might spend 80 percent of your life thinking about your work, chances are that your customer probably doesn't. Connect with them often, but give them a break every once in a while.

10. *Keep listening.* None of us can be reminded too many times to slow down and listen. Even if you do nothing but listen, you can get halfway to your goal.

Case Study: Pabst Blue Ribbon

Pabst Blue Ribbon beer has been resurrected by finding and listening to a new group of key voices in the beer market. After a sales decline of more than 90 percent in the past 30 years and no real advertising in the past 20, a new buzz suddenly rose up around the beer. The buzz wasn't coming from the 45- to 60-year-old demographic that has traditionally been Pabst's customers, however. It was coming from younger, hipper consumers—most notably, bike messengers in Portland, Oregon. According to trend experts, Pabst was actually a part of a larger "retro-chic" movement. Recently, many other companies have gotten a tremendous boost in sales by reissuing products from the 1970s and 1980s.

Faced with their initial situation, many marketing professionals would have taken this odd little sales increase as a cue to step up the advertising in youth markets. Pabst took a more patient route and dispatched a young executive, Neal Stewart, to Portland to find out what was going on. Instead of surgically dissecting the marketplace through typical marketing tools such as focus groups, Neal decided to try a novel concept—simply hanging out in a couple of bars and listening to people. Soon Neal started to get a sense of why Pabst was hot: its very *lack* of a brand image. This had allowed the bike messengers in Portland to develop their own image of the beer. In other words, it had become *their* beer.

With this new appreciation of what was happening out in the real world, Stewart related their success in the context of Naomi Klein's book, *No Logo*. The book focuses on the backlash against the over-branding of the world. "It really articulated the feelings, the coming feelings, of the consumer out there," Stewart says of the book. "Eventually people are gonna get sick of all this stuff [marketing] and say enough is enough."[8]

Pabst's strategy is a reaction to this world and is based on looking and acting like the underdog. "Pabst is seen as a symbol and fellow dissenter," says Alex Wipperfurth, of Plan B, a Bay Area marketing agency.

Their goal is not to be invasive but become a resource for people to build and tell their own stories about Pabst. Stewart uses terms like *organic,* saying, "The customer must lead the brand."

To do this, Stewart has focused Pabst's marketing on pull rather than push strategies, reacting to grassroots sponsorship opportunities that have been brought to the company by their customers and nurturing organic, microrelationships in the field. These have included sponsoring skateboard movie screenings, art gallery openings, and readings for independent publishers. The goal is to help these small communities expand their own networks, while serving as a partially visible bonding agent.

By understanding their reputation, letting go of the control of their brand, and being a part of a community, Pabst has turned the marketing paradigm upside down. Truly, it has gone bottom up. For many companies, of course, this is a scary idea. But if the goal is to be more intimate with their customers, companies must realize that the idea that they actually control their own brand's image is built on false assumptions to begin with. By living in the community with its customers, having real conversations with them, and reacting to their needs in an organic way, Pabst has increased sales dramatically and reinvigorated the company through the simple, if scary, step of letting go and focusing on the journey.

In the start-up phase of any company, it is easy to listen to the few key voices of your business. It's just you, your customer, and your product. It's easy to have a dialogue with your key customers. Yet, as a company grows, the actual effort of connecting with these key voices takes a more formalized, bottom-up strategy.

WHAT THIS MEANS TO YOU

Think about your customers. Do you know who the trendsetters, trend translators, early majority, late majority, and traditionalists are? For most industries and companies, the trend translators or opinion leaders have the key voices. Usually, the thoughtfulness in the trend translator's decision-making process is an important part of their psychological makeup. It is important to them that their peers see them as diligent and trustworthy but also progressive and forward thinking. Think about your customers. Can you identify the key voices? What would make someone in your community a trend translator? Is it their age? Their income? Their usage pattern?

Once you have identified who the trend translators might be, search for them. Where would they hang out? What would they do? What Web sites might they visit? Make them a part of your team in the mission to understand their worlds. They are your tour guides. Also, think about creating a community space for them. Can you create a place on your Web site for them?

Start a dialogue with them, as individuals. Who are they? What do they do? Invite them to bring their peers into the dialogue. Just be sure to pay them well, respect their time and opinions, don't burn them out, and always keep listening. Your company will gain a large strategic advantage over your competition if you can engage the key voices in your community in the context of your bottom-up strategy.

6

STEP TWO
Get the Story

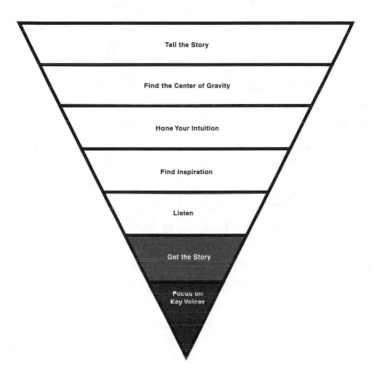

*The human story does not always unfold like a mathematical
calculation on the principle that two and two make four.
Sometimes in life they make five or minus three; and
sometimes the blackboard topples down in the middle of the sum
and leaves the class in disorder and the pedagogue with a black eye.*
WINSTON CHURCHILL[1]

There is a story about "coolhunting" that has become an urban legend. Coolhunting, of course, has become a popular research methodology for companies, particularly when trying to make sense of the youth market. One sporting goods company is reported to have hired a well-known coolhunter to find the hottest trend for working out among teens. The coolhunters hit the streets of Los Angeles and started talking with teens, asking them who among their friends was cool. One name kept coming up; let's call her Rachel. The coolhunters approached Rachel and asked what "cool" things she was doing. Rachel wasn't entirely sure, however. She saw herself as a pretty normal girl. Then, after a few minutes of thought, she offered, "I do jump on my parents' trampoline every once in a while. . . ." That was it, the coolhunters decided: trampolining is the next hot trend. Soon the coolhunters had convinced their client that trampolining was set to storm the youth market. So, advised that it should focus its energy on designing and developing trampolines and trampoline-based workouts for teens, the client did so. Several months and millions of dollars later, the sporting goods company discovered that there was, in fact, no real business—teen or otherwise—in trampolining.

Coolhunting can be enlightening in a superficial way, but too often it doesn't go deep enough to understand the underlying assumptions of people's lives, behaviors, and actions. Such an understanding really drives bottom-up strategic thinking. Only at this deep level can the useful context and meaning behind outward actions and behaviors be understood. This understanding is also the primary source for new ideas and product innovation. The only way to get to this level is by investing a lot of time and energy engaging in real conversations. To participate in these, you've got to go to the source—out on the street—and get the story.

Many models can be used to aid our thinking about the relationships that exist in any community or ecosystem and how they might inform a bottom-up strategy and prompt real innovation. One such model is the ecological term *ecotone*. An ecotone is a place where two different, distinctive ecosystems meet, such as where a forest and a wetland meet. In this zone, the ecosystem is neither a forest nor a wetland but has all of the attributes of both. Ecotone is used to describe a place where evo-

FIGURE 6.1 *Opportunity Ecotone*

lution happens, where a natural dialogue is occurring.[2] In the business world, all brands live in an ecosystem made up of many components. An ecotone from this perspective can represent the opportunity that lies within the overlap of a business or brand and its market (see Figure 6.1).

The bigger the ecotone—the more overlap between the two ecosystems internally and externally—the deeper the dialogue and the greater the opportunity for the business. For most companies, the ecotone exists at the fringes of the organization, and all growth in understanding and meaning happens here. This is also true in natural systems, where an organism or ecosystem expands at the fringes. The key is to be sure that all of the growth happening at the fringe, where customers are constantly interacting with your associates, is communicated throughout the whole organization. Too often, the learning taking place at the fringes never gets communicated to the core, where senior management is making the strategic decisions of an organization.

At Radar, many of our customers needed help in guiding the team that interacts with customers on the fringes to tell their stories in a powerful way; this narrative is essential to presenting information in such a way that senior managers, at the core of the company, can be inspired to pursue new directions. Only at the core of a company do changes to its soul or philosophy really happen. Chapter 11 will help you under-

FIGURE 6.2 *The Ecosystem*

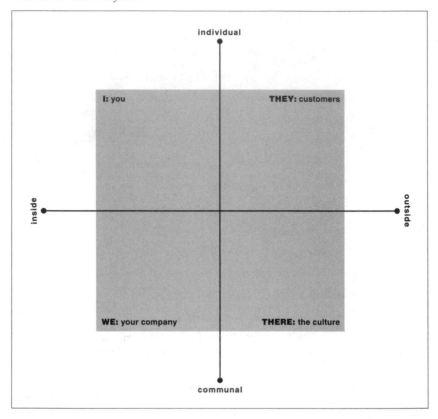

stand how to tell these powerful stories after they've been gleaned from the streets.

Before your storytelling can begin, you've got to lay the groundwork; you have to *get* the story. Doing so through a dynamic and integrative approach will provide valuable insights to your bottom-up strategy. We work and live in a very complex world. It is essential to take a complex approach when trying to understand and obtain information from the overwhelmingly vast number of relationships that we all participate in, both consciously and unconsciously. These relationships determine how a dialogue is conducted, and it is important to take some time to think about what each group brings to a dialogue.

In all of our businesses, we live in an ecosystem that is a complete system of all the participants and relationships that make up a community. It is essential to understand all of these. The two-dimensional map in Figure 6.2 is a place to start understanding the scope of an ecosystem and the interactions that take place in it that can form the foundation for a successful dialogue.

This four-quadrant approach can be used to look at each of the ecosystems in which your business or brand exists. The upper quadrants represent individuals. The upper-left consists of *I:* you and your team and what you individually bring to the relationships and interaction in the ecosystem. The upper-right quadrant consists of *They:* your customers or your potential customers, individually. The lower quadrants represent the communities that make up the ecosystem. The lower-left quadrant is *We:* your company or brand and the other partners or suppliers that make up an internal team and have the goal of delivering a product to customers in the ecosystem. The lower-right quadrant is *There:* the outside culture where customers exist. This is the culture in a broad sense, including cultural issues, competitors, the political environment, etc.

This map can also be looked at left to right, the left side representing internal participants and the right side representing external participants. When laying the groundwork for a successful dialogue, it is important to think about the participants in all four quadrants and how they interact. An understanding of all of these relationships goes a long way toward facilitating a deeper dialogue.

A BOTTOM-UP STRATEGY

The goal in an integrative approach is to find the ecotone, or center of gravity, where the participants from all quadrants exist in a place of common understanding. From this starting point of common understanding, a journey through dialogue can expand the common ground and help to satisfy everyone's needs. Certainly, this is a moving target.

To explore and more deeply understand the intentions and needs of each participant in every quadrant, a good starting place is Abraham Maslow's Hierarchy of Needs. Many other models can later be substi-

FIGURE 6.3 *Maslow's Pyramid*

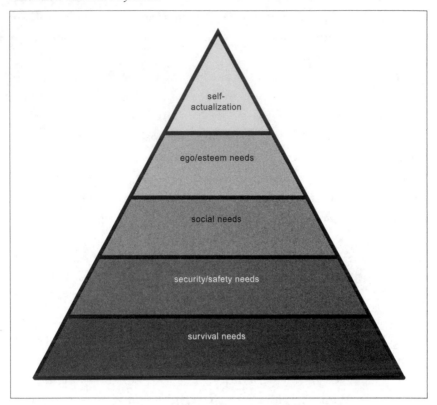

tuted; using a few different models will deepen the understanding, and thus the quality, of the dialogue between each quadrant.

Many of us remember Maslow's model from our Sociology 101 classes (see Figure 6.3). Maslow, a humanistic psychologist, developed a hierarchical theory of needs in which all the basic needs are at the bottom and the needs concerned with an individual's or an organization's highest potential are at the top. The hierarchic theory is often represented as a pyramid, with lower levels representing the most basic needs and the upper point representing the need for self-actualization. Each level of the pyramid is dependent on the previous level. A person or organization does not exhibit the signs associated with the next need until the demands of the first have been satisfied. People, companies, and cultures slide up and down the hierarchy as both internal and external factors change.

The five levels of needs are:

1. *Survival needs.* These needs are the most basic and can be biological for a person or financial for a company. These needs are the strongest because, if deprived, the person or company would perish.
2. *Security/Safety needs.* These needs can be satisfied by stability in the overall ecosystem and are stable except in times of emergency or periods of disorganization in the social structure.
3. *Social needs.* Both people and companies have the need to be liked and feel a sense of belonging.
4. *Ego/Esteem needs.* People and companies need a stable, high level of self-respect and respect from others to feel satisfied, self-confident, and valuable. If these needs are not met, feelings of inferiority, weakness, and helplessness can be exhibited.
5. *Self-actualization.* This stage is an ongoing process. Self-actualizing people and companies are involved in a cause outside themselves. They are devoted and working at something that is a calling or vocation to them. It is about more than money. It is about *wanting* rather than needing to do something.[3]

Historically, the social sciences tried to embrace the more objective, "harder" paradigm of the natural sciences. As David Boyle says in his book *Why Numbers Make Us Irrational,* "Numbers do a wonderful job of telling us an answer. But did we ask the right question?"[4] Without asking the right questions, we will not get our answers, no matter how good the quantitative information is.

Qualitative tools for getting the story, such as focus groups, when used to better understand customers, have become more about prediction and justification (validating existing hypotheses, rubber-stamping and confirming decisions) than discovery. Overall, this drive to quantify business in general has given us a more sterile and generic world. It has made managers rely more heavily on numbers to justify their decisions instead of stories to illuminate their intuition. The context of the conversation and the lives of people have been stripped away in the process

FIGURE 6.4 *Research Spectrum*

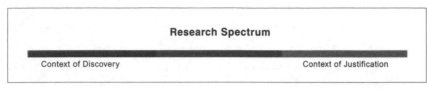

of finding the "right" answers. There are, however, ways to overcome some of some of these shortfalls.

INFORMATION SPECTRUM

At the ecotone, or center of gravity, it is necessary to take information beyond knowledge and even insight and move it into the realm of intuition, inspiration, and innovation. Intelligence to support a bottom-up strategy is usually done along a spectrum from discovery to justification (see Figure 6.4).

One of the important things to assess is where along this spectrum intelligence is being gathered. If, for instance, you are trying to understand the future potential of a product category, you need to use different tools than you would to test a couple of print ads. Unfortunately, focus groups have become the one-size-fits-all solution for gathering intelligence for many companies. You must know at which end of this spectrum you are operating. Too many times, we've seen clients who think they want to justify something that they've already developed, when in fact they are looking for intelligence to discover the potential future of their product.

TOOLS FOR GETTING THE STORY

The tools we use at Radar for getting the story and forming bottom-up strategies are taken from the world of investigative journalism and anthropology. They are simple tools that are often overlooked, yet they can help anyone locate the deeper human inspirations that can drive new ideas. While there is no one right way, we like to use a dynamic and eclectic approach. We call it *anthrojournalism.* This term was first used in 1985 to describe the pursuit of journalism that went beyond the traditional journalistic questions of who, what, when, where, and why to examine issues. Anthrojournalism sees journalists and cultural anthropologists as workers in related fields, seeking different goals but sharing similar tools.[5]

The focus of anthrojournalism is on the systemic nature of human relations and the cultural fabric in which these relations are embedded. The goal is to find and report on commonalities in the human experience crossculturally, giving participants new and deeper insights that drive innovation and inspiration. We, at Radar, define anthrojournalism as the combination of the following:

- *Anthropology.* A discipline that seeks holistic understanding of human experience, past and present
- *Journalism.* The style of writing characteristic of material in newspapers and magazines, consisting of direct presentation of facts or occurrences with little attempt at analysis or interpretation

The aim of anthrojournalists is to develop deeper understandings of the communities they report about; they are willing and able to investigate human events and issues in a comparative, holistic, and culturally sensitive manner. Anthrojournalism draws on anthropology's understanding of culture and its personal, face-to-face approach to data through participant observation and ethnographic methods. It borrows journalism's communicative skills and its ability to synthesize information, understanding of the cultural context of issues, and methods of allowing events to be widely shared. The overall goal is to use a tool that seeks context *and* perspective in understanding human interactions—with not only each other but with their cultures, including the products that they use. In his book *The Turning Point: Science, Society, and the Rising Culture,* physical anthropologist Fritjof Capra suggests that

> . . . in the future, journalists will change their thinking from fragmentary to holistic modes and develop a new professional

ethic based on sociological and ecological awareness. Instead of concentrating on sensational presentations of aberrant, violent, and destructive happenings, reporters and editors will have to analyze the complex social and cultural patterns that form the context of such events, as well as reporting the quiet, constructive, and integrative activities going on in our culture.[7]

Companies can learn to use these anthrojournalistic tools to help them gain a deeper perspective in the context of the community when gathering intelligence to inform a bottom-up strategy.

To better understand how to use anthrojournalistic tools, here are seven principles to remember:

1. Being aware of context.   Unless you understand the context, you can't get the meaning. At Radar, in the spirit of journalism, we call the key voices we interact with our "reporters." We give them many assignments that include interviewing their peers and giving us a tour of the context of their lives.

Toni was one of our reporters for a project we did recently about women. She was 20 years old and thinking about pursuing a career as a designer. At first glance, Toni was a party girl. The things she showed us were all about having good time. When she wrote in her "diary" for us, she talked about hanging out with her friends, going to parties, and enjoying herself. She sent us pictures of herself drinking and even taking bong hits with her friends.

Only after spending several hours with her to better understand the context of her life did we discover the underlying angst that really drives her. Toni's parents emigrated from Vietnam. They own a small company and have been pushing her to become a part of the family business. She wants to go to design school to become a designer. To make matters worse, she lives at home. Toni feels trapped. Her reality is actually one of longing and despair.

Only after we spent a great deal of time with Toni, through several interactions over several days, was she willing to let us see her deepest thoughts. These insights and inspirations cannot be gained by shortcutting the process. Only when a customer can trust you enough to be vulnerable will you learn their real needs and desires and really get insight into the context of their lives.

2. Insisting on eyewitness perspectives. You have to go there—be where it's happening, when it's happening. You have to observe and ask questions until you understand the meaning from the point of view of those involved. We did some work for a clothing company to understand the value segment of the blue jean business. One of the goals was to understand how to change their specialty store strategy and address the mass-merchandiser market. Currently, Wal-Mart's Faded Glory brand sells more jeans than anyone else, and our client realized that, to continue to be a significant player, they have to understand how to play in the value arena.[8] The stories that you hear on the street, however, can be counterintuitive.

Susan lives in Pueblo, Colorado, and is a mother of four. She is recently married and lives in a new development east of town. We had engaged Susan in a dialogue through a series of various interactions over a three-week period. These interactions included Susan participating in an online survey, interviewing friends, keeping a diary about her shopping habits, taking pictures, and participating in a group discussion at a friend's house. The final interaction was a joint shopping trip that we went on with Susan. It wasn't until she was pulling into her driveway at the end of the shopping excursion that Susan explained that she would never buy clothes at Wal-Mart because that was where "*those* people shopped." During the discussion, we realized that Susan was referring to people on welfare. She went on to say that buying her kids the "right" kind of clothes signifies her ability to stay off of welfare and is a source of immense pride to her. She reiterated her point by saying, "Image is everything."

Only when you get out on the street and spend time with someone do you really get to know them. Susan would never have opened up about her personal fears regarding welfare without our spending time with her in her world. It begins with honoring people and spending time with them in the context of their lives, which then helps foster the intuition that drives innovation.

3. Holism.   Before focusing in on the details, you need to look at the big picture—the whole experience within which a particular behavior makes sense. We recently worked with a technology company to understand the future of the PC. After a couple of conversations, it became clear that our client's internal team was speaking a totally different language than their customers.

This client has a history of focusing on superior functionality with a premium on speed. But when their customers started to talk about their PCs, they talked about how ugly they were. The customers were talking about the holism of their lives and how computers fit into them. Our client had a much narrower view regarding computer usage. The reporters talked about their computers being so ugly that they wanted to keep them in the home office and not in their living rooms. Conversely, when they talked about the Apple iMac, customers talked about how beautiful it was. They also discussed seeing an iMac in the living room right alongside the family's stereo and TV. While our client saw a computer only in terms of its functionality, their customers saw them for their form.

When you are developing your bottom-up strategy, you have to be able to think about the lives of your customers in whole, not just from your perspective.

4. Dynamism.   You must seek to understand a living, evolving process—not a static snapshot. People do not lead simple lives. Likewise, their relationships with brands and products are dynamic, not static. A bottom-up strategy understands the dynamism of the world and accepts the reality that there is more than one best way.

5. Descriptiveness.   God is in the details: the story and its meaning are embedded in the concrete, particular details of what people actually do and say. This is "ecological validity"—keeping the level of abstraction low enough to keep the story honest. Sometimes the story is obvious, but it must be described in the context of your organization listening to be understood.

During customer conversations about a Web site and its well-known New York news organization, it became obvious that the biggest strategic issue for the online venture was the pricing policy. The Web site subscription was too expensive. Customers felt that financial information had become ubiquitous and, therefore, was not worth as much. The internal team working on the Web site felt the same way but had been unable to convince the company's senior management that lowering the price was the right direction.

When the discovery was shared with the management team, the chief marketing officer (CMO) kicked off the meeting by saying, "The pricing question is off the table." During the meeting, several customers were introduced, through videotaped interviews, into the bottom-up strategic conversation. Many voiced the sentiment that they *would not pay* for a subscription to the Web site. The message was so clear that at the end of the meeting, the CMO said, "We need to rethink our pricing structure." An honest description of the voice of the customer—or that voice itself—must be presented in the context of the company's culture.

6. Rigorous subjectivity. Anthropologists and journalists are only human. It is, therefore, their responsibility to know their own biases well enough to keep them from interfering with telling the story in a fair and accurate way.

Recently, we were doing some work involving teen kids and sports. One of our staff was facilitating a group discussion in which the conversation focused on the topic of sports heroes. As she led this discussion, she noticed that one of the guys in the session had a Washington Wizards jersey on. The jersey had the number 23 on it. The facilitator asked the guy whose jersey it was. There was a lot of laughter in the room as he explained that it was Michael Jordan's jersey. Instead of being embarrassed, she launched an amazing discussion about why Michael Jordan was still a significant hero to these teens.

We all bring our own lens to the work. This lens includes our beliefs, expectations, values, history, and unwritten rules—as well as our ignorance, at times. It's impossible to get rid of our lens. What's more important is to recognize what we bring to the table and put that aside, to be as open and simple as possible.

7. Appropriate interpretation. While all human interactions involve interpretation, companies have become so sophisticated in their strategic research that they can filter and interpret *too much*. The anthrojournalist's job is to give an audience enough direct inspiration to allow them to come to their own conclusions and point of view. Because of the context, much of the most important inspiration is ignored simply because it comes out of the consumer's mouth first or because we've heard it before. We tell each other, "They always say that." Many listeners are so educated and so busy looking for the golden nugget that lies at the center of an interaction with a customer, they lose sight of what's going on right in front of them—especially when sitting behind a one-way mirror.

As active listeners, people who are there to learn, it's important that clients not preoccupy themselves during an interaction. They shouldn't wait for the "experts" to offer their interpretation of inspiration, completely out of context from the customers.[8]

GETTING THE STORY: THE RADAR FUNNEL

While there is no one right way to inform a bottom-up strategy, it's important to have a simple process that gets the story from the streets and makes meaning in the context of the strategic question being asked. It is also important that the process have enough space so that one can be creative. In that spirit, here's how we approach the anthrojournalistic process to getting the story.

Part of using a simple process, such as the Radar Funnel (see Figure 6.5), is that it allows you to interject dynamism, which helps you to go beyond just looking and actually develop a new way of seeing. When you really see something, you see its potential, without limitations. By this, I mean the ability to understand the broader context of how strategic questions fit into a larger environment. If simply *looking* is to view things in the context of their limitations, then *seeing* is noticing the limitations themselves, bringing a new awareness of the broader context. In fact, most of the time, the limits are ones that we have placed on a

FIGURE 6.5 *The Radar Funnel*

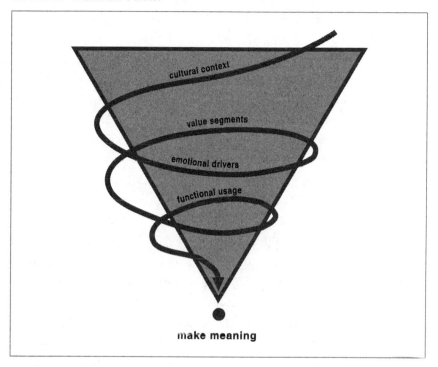

cultural context

value segments

emotional drivers

functional usage

make meaning

situation by the mere act of observing. When starting to use the Funnel, think about this difference between looking and seeing. Concentrate on seeing.

Second, it's important to remember that you are entering a new culture to get the story, and the very process of entering into this culture alters its context. Culture in itself is not anything a person does but what people do with each other, interacting as a group. As groups of people interact, culture is formed and transmitted through human communication. Remember that a listener and speaker have the ability to understand each other, not because they have the same knowledge about a subject or because they have a common understanding, but because they both know how to have a conversation. The journey through the Radar Funnel starts with a conversation.

The anthrojournalistic process should be viewed as a funnel. This process gives you the ability to ensure that your conversations in the community follow a system and fit into a structure that leads to finding the center of gravity. The five steps of the process include:

1. Recognize cultural context. Many people who are trying to understand a culture start way too far down the funnel. They want to jump immediately into the functional usage and explore the way their product or marketing is being perceived. It's great to be excited about going out and getting the story, but without going slowly enough to understand the cultural context, things can go wrong very quickly.

I experienced such an example just the other day. I was getting out of the water after my morning surf session in the small Mexican town where I spend a great deal of time. That morning, I was surfing with a friend who had been in the film industry for a long time. It was still early, and the light was beautiful. We looked around and saw a photo shoot in progress. It seemed intriguing that such a thing was happening in our small fishing village. The large group of folks included a couple of photographers, a make-up artist, an art director, the director, some assistants, and several models. As we walked over and inquired what the photo shoot was for, a tattooed woman looked at us with disdain and said it was for The Buckle, a teen retailer in the United States. For an instant, it felt like we were in Los Angeles. It was obvious that The Buckle's creative team decided to be sure their photos were authentic— so they jetted the team off to Mexico to enjoy a little of this authenticity.

As we watched, the photographer directed a male model jumping around with a surfboard in his hand. The photographer was yelling, "Rub the surfboard! Rub the surfboard!"

During the action, my buddy said, "Watch this." He quickly strolled over right behind the producer and said very quietly, "The surfboard's upside down."

All of a sudden the producer started yelling, "Stop! Stop! The surfboard is upside down!" which sent everyone scrambling.

The creative team for The Buckle thought that they could prove an understanding of the culture by spending a ton of money on a Mexican surf experience. The problem was that the team didn't know anything about surfing. Obviously, they thought surfing was cool, so it became the theme for this year's catalog. But they could have been much more authentic by really understanding the cultural context of surfing, driving to one of the amazing beaches in Southern California, and hiring real surfers as models. They would have saved The Buckle a lot of money in the process—but missed a nice Mexican vacation on the client's dime.

2. Discover value segments. Once you understand the context of the lives of the people who are helping you get the story, the next step is to go deeper to understand what they value. Is it true companionship? Independence? Belonging? If you look at an investigation in the context of an iceberg, it's at the level of people's values and attitudes where the most inspiring stories can be found. Do you remember Tina from earlier in the chapter? If you haven't spent a lot of time with Tina, you'll miss the values that her parents have instilled in her and how she is conflicted by them. You've got to dig deeply, taking nothing at face value.

3. Uncover emotional drivers. Once you understand a person's values, it's time to explore the emotional drivers that make them choose to act. What makes someone *emotionally* want to buy a certain type of car? For instance, suppose you go out and ask young men about their relationship with their cars. They might talk about the independence that their cars give them. For most young men, a car is their first taste of freedom and the first environment that is theirs to do with what they want.

While all of this is probably true, it is not the only way to look at these guys' relationships with their cars. How would your perspective change if you rode around with them for a couple of days? You might notice that when they get to a stoplight, and if there is a pretty woman in the car next to them, they might rev their engine or accelerate quickly once the light turns green. In this case, one of their emotional drivers has nothing to do with the experience of freedom or the power of their own environment. Instead, it is all about showing off, power, and sex. Only in the environment can the emotional drivers be observed in action.

4. Evaluate functional usage. When people are trying to get a story, most of the time they start here. They want to show their customers a few samples or ideas that they might have, in an efficient manner—say a focus group—and move on. As we discussed earlier, if you are trying to conduct your investigation in the context of justification, instead of the context of exploration, then this is where you might start.

There are lots of great ways to understand functional usage. Probably the best is observational research. That means getting out in the field with a video camera and shooting lots of footage of people using your product. We've worked with a German research company that does automobile research and has a very sophisticated way of tracking where a driver is looking while he or she is driving. It was frightening watching some of the video, with a pointer indicating where the driver was looking. In one instance, a driver looked at the dashboard for over six seconds while speeding along the Autobahn. But it's an incredible tool for thinking about how to design car interiors.

5. Make meaning. Many companies outsource their conversations with their customers to agencies. Often, the agencies are also in charge of making meaning of the work. While it seems efficient to let the "experts" make meaning, they cannot understand your company's needs like you do. The stories that you discover must always stay in the context of your company and its heritage. If you are a clothing manufacturer and the story says you should get into something very different, such as cars, you probably need to dig a little deeper. Once you understand the story in a deeper way, what does that mean to your company and brands? How does it inspire an answer to a strategic question?

Keep in mind one important caveat when using these types of tools: There is simply no substitute for spending time with your customers, getting their story. There is no shortcut. Once you begin this journey of listening more deeply, however, a strengthened intuition can greatly enhance efficiency.

WHAT THIS MEANS TO YOU

Many models can help our thinking about the relationships that exist in any community, marketplace, or ecosystem and how they might inform a bottom-up strategy, leading to the co-creation that drives innovation. One such model is the ecological term *ecotone*. In a business context, the ecotone represents the opportunity that lies between the overlap of a business or brand and its market. Do you know where the ecotone lies between you and your customers? Is there a way to communicate the stories from the street through the organization?

Think about the four-quadrant approach I talked about earlier. How well does your company know the members of the quadrants: I, They, We, and There? Remember, an understanding of the relationships between the participants in each of the quadrants goes a long way toward facilitating a deeper dialogue.

The goal in any integrative approach is to find the center of gravity, or ecotone, where the participants from all quadrants exist in a place of common understanding. How much of a common understanding do you have with your community? Think about the anthrojournalism principles described above: being aware of context, insisting on eyewitness perspectives, holism, dynamism, descriptiveness, rigorous subjectivity, and appropriate interpretation. How might they help you think about the way you interact with everyone in the community, especially your customers?

Don't forget that the Radar funnel gives you the framework to ensure that the conversations we are having in the community—with the goal of getting the story—follow a system. They also fit into a structure that leads to finding the center of gravity. Do you currently use any of the Radar funnel framework: recognize cultural context, discover value segments, uncover emotional drivers, evaluate functional usage, and make meaning? Can you enhance your ability by using any of these tools in a new and different way? For instance, instead of jumping right down to functional usage of a product or marketing message, such as a television ad, think about ways to move back up the funnel to understand the cultural context, value segments, and emotional drivers that feed functional usage.

7

STEP THREE
Listen

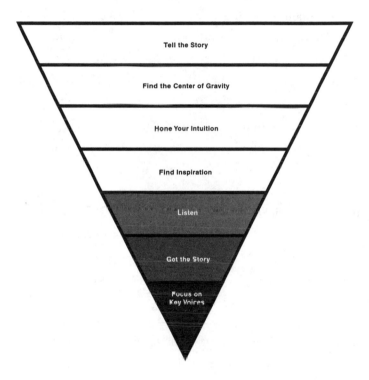

A good listener is not only popular everywhere,
but after a while he gets to know something.
WILSON MIZNER[1]

I bought *Women's Sports & Fitness* magazine in 1990. At the time it was just emerging from bankruptcy and was teetering on the edge of existence. We knew we had to do some serious triage. I opted to follow the typical market research path: I hired a research firm and started running focus groups. After a couple of focus groups, I was horrified. These were definitely *not* our readers. Most were professional focus group participants who had been recruited from a database that the marketing research firm used on a regular basis. I was also shocked by the pseudo-scientific process of sitting behind a one-way mirror, examining the participants as I might in a clinical psychology experiment.

We immediately stopped doing focus groups and launched our own organic version of market research: We started hitting the streets and really listening to our readers face to face. We went to the sports events in which our readers were actively participating. We found ways to be with them and spend time with them in their worlds, within the context of their lives. By listening to the words and inspirations of our readers, we realized that what they really wanted was a magazine that spoke to their needs as athletes.

Following this deeper connection with our readers, we repositioned *Women's Sports & Fitness,* cutting the circulation in half to focus on the core of the market and changing the voice so that it represented the authenticity of our readers' voices. Over an eight-year period, the magazine went from the brink of bankruptcy, with a loss of 30 percent of its revenues, to becoming the leading voice for athletic women in the United States, growing revenues 300 percent. Its new position in the marketplace allowed us to broker a profitable sale of the magazine to Condé Nast in 1998. The innovative process that we followed in nurturing the magazine was driven initially by the insight gained through conversations with our readers—insight that came not only from the conversations themselves but also from observing our readers interacting with each other.

What we discovered was that the core of the relationship with our readers depended on trust. This trust is necessary in any relationship, be it between a mother and her child, two friends, a boss and an employee, or a brand and its customer. Think about your own relationships. Don't you feel most comfortable with those who take the time to really listen to you? When you feel as though someone is listening, you feel important and empowered. Trust is a product of active listening.

These same dynamics are very much in play for companies and their customers. Think about a product that you enjoy using and the company that produces it. For me, this is my Apple G4 PowerBook. I always feel as if someone at Apple has been listening to my questions—before I've even asked them. My PowerBook has empowered me to be more creative with my photography and to use music in a whole new way with my iPod mp3 player (unlike the Neistat brothers, mentioned in Chapter 3, my batteries haven't died). It has shifted my personal computer paradigm and given me the ability to be much more creative, with exciting results.

Now think about a product that you've felt sure could be just a little better, yet when you asked the company for help, they were unresponsive. This always happens to me with shoes. I'll have a problem with something, like a seam blowing out. When I call the company, I can't get through to anyone. Nobody wants to listen. When I eventually do get someone on the line, I'm made to feel as though it's my fault the seam ripped. No matter how much I liked that pair of shoes, I'll do anything to find a comparable pair from a company who appreciates my business and wants to listen to my problems.

In one of my business school classes, a professor shared an interesting statistic that has stuck in my mind and continued to be a big motivator for me. He said that when someone has a good experience with a product, they will tell 30 people, on average; when they have a bad experience, they will tell approximately *300* people. Part of having a good experience is feeling that someone is listening. Many times, even when a customer is initially unsatisfied with a product or service, they can walk away from the situation a satisfied customer—but only if they feel that someone has actively listened to them.

When you really listen, good things happen. Could it be that the traditional branding process is getting in the way of listening to your customers? A successful brand is all about listening in your customers' native environments.

Jake Burton Carpenter is the founder and CEO of Burton Snowboards in Burlington, Vermont. Burton spends nine months a year traveling the world with his snowboard in hand, living the sport that he helped to create. In the mind of a 15-year-old snowboarder, Burton's lifestyle is a dream come true. For the average CEO of a $365 million company, it seems more like a pipe dream. Yet being on the road is Burton's primary objective as CEO.

Jake Burton has embodied the sport of snowboarding since the 1970s and is considered to be the sport's patron saint. While many consider Burton the "inventor" of snowboarding, Burton's inspiration came from the Snurfer, a department store toy that allowed kids to "surf" on snow. After graduating from college and going to work at an investment company in New York, he was still haunted by his memories of snurfing. In 1977, he quit his job, moved back to Vermont, and launched Burton Snowboards.

After a couple of years, the company was struggling. Burton had to take on other jobs to fuel his dream. Through it all, he focused on having a "sport-first" mentality, which became integral in creating a market for the sport of snowboarding. This attitude was reflected in early Burton ads and catalogs and was instrumental in giving a voice to a generation of snow sport enthusiasts. The early ads never overtly mentioned the company but instead focused on the sport of snowboarding. With this positive, sport-first attitude, both the sport and the company began gaining momentum.

As the company grew, it fought many battles to win acceptance. For many years, snowboarding was not even allowed at ski areas. But Burton's grassroots support of local riders and its snowboard-first philosophy inspired a whole generation of winter athletes, who were tired of playing by the rules imposed by their parents' sport—skiing. To move the snowboarding industry to the next level, Burton lobbied hard for local areas to open their lifts to snowboarders. In the early 1980s, he succeeded in convincing Stratton Ski Area to give snowboarding a chance.

Soon the rest of the ski industry followed. Now, after years of 50 percent growth, the company is becoming more mature. At 27, it is significantly older than its average customer. While the company constantly works at redefining itself as it matures and the growth of the sport inevitably slows down, Burton is still out there, riding his snowboard all over the globe with his customers.

There is a method to his playing. "I watched skiing lose its youth culture," he said. "When I was a kid, skiing was cool. But the ski industry totally lost that, and as long as I'm around, we won't make that mistake."[2] Burton doesn't use conventional forms of market research, like focus groups. He gets his information directly from the slopes. There are no filters between him and his customers.

What would happen if more CEOs spent 100 days a year living with their customers? Real listening starts at the top of the organization. In today's dynamic environment, CEOs of companies must focus fanatically on understanding what their customers want. The senior executives of a large home improvement retailer must be passionate about home improvement. They must be able to walk into any home improvement store, whether it's theirs or their competitor's, and know intuitively what the store feels like in the context of their customers' lives. They must know what tools and materials it takes to build a deck and know how a customer wants those displayed. That seems like an awful lot to ask for executives who are trained to run businesses and communicate with shareholders. Yet it all starts with one simple step: listening.

START BY LISTENING

Listening is a very difficult skill to learn. Asking a provocative question is one thing; listening well to the answer is quite another. Really listening depends in part on making yourself innocent again. Within any company, learning by listening means divesting yourself of all the baggage a brand has acquired over the years. It's so easy to hear something a customer says and quickly respond, "We've heard that before," without really *listening* to what that particular person is trying to tell you.

Listening does seem incredibly basic. Yet the reality is that all of us are often distracted and don't bring all of our skills or faculties to a listening situation. Have you ever left a meeting and wondered, "*What* did they just say?" When you are out listening to your customers, the first thing to remember is to clear your mind and enjoy the very human process of listening. This is difficult for most of us. The overall goal of listening is to see patterns where others see chaos and to make meaning that is well grounded in both experience and intuition. To achieve this goal, you have to capture the *vox populi,* the voice of the people. Here are six things to remember.

1. *Concentrate.* It is very difficult for companies to concentrate. There are spreadsheets to fill out, sales to be made, and the bottom line to look after. How can anybody take the time to concentrate on listening with so much to do? Yet concentration is absolutely essential to effective listening.

2. *Free yourself from anxiety.* This is, possibly, the hardest thing for a company to do. As a businessperson, you know how hard it is to not focus, always, on the bottom line. It is hard not to be anxious about getting a product or service to market. Likewise, it is also hard not to think about accomplishing specific goals when you are talking to a customer. Being free from anxiety, however, is the only way to hear clearly and so have a successful dialogue.

3. *Imagine.* Aren't all great companies started by someone with an amazing imagination? Look at Apple: Steven Jobs and his imagination created the personal computer that fueled a revolution. Likewise, Nike's Phil Knight spent his first few years selling shoes out of the back of a station wagon. They were both out there with their customers, listening and learning. They were imagining ways to solve problems, whether for computer users or runners. Every great company has a heritage of myth and imagination surrounding its start.

4. *Empathize.* At the foundation of most great companies is a group of people who embody the passion and commitment of their customers and have a vested interest in doing things right. In essence, empathy can be defined as the ability to relate to customers in an intuitive manner. The most straightforward way to attain empathy is to be a passionate user of your company's products.

5. *Understand.* Understanding is not about simply downloading a bunch of numbers and statistics, then analyzing them from behind a desk. In this context, it means feeling an impact in the heart and soul. True understanding comes from experiencing what's really happening.

6. *Love.* While many businesspeople might laugh, this is the start of great listening. Great companies don't just like their customers—they love their customers, and their employees, too. Look again at Nike and Apple. Both companies are on crusades with their customers to change the world. And their customers can feel the love. They recognize that these companies really care about them and want to spend time with them. It's all about letting people talk and tell their stories without any screens or interruptions. It's about slowing down enough to engage people in a passionate dialogue while in the context of their lives.[3]

Use More Than Your Ears

Scientists suggest that 70 percent of human communication is nonverbal. If that's true, then it is especially important to learn to listen with your eyes. Visual listening is critical to understanding what the market is saying through the stories of the street. Just as there is body language, there is market language. To hear and understand this language, it is essential that not only your eyes but all of your personal senses—and your company's senses—be engaged, to understand fully what is happening. Shunryu Suzuki, pioneer of Zen practice in the United States and founder of the San Francisco Zen Center, called this ability to look at the world with fresh eyes and an open spirit the "beginner's mind."[4] When you have the open spirit of a beginner's mind, you are more excited to participate creatively in the learning process as a journey, allowing the exploration to take you where it is going.

Cultural anthropologists use the iceberg as a metaphor for the layers involved in getting to know someone. Above the water line, at the tip of the iceberg, are all of the observable artifacts of a person or culture. Just below the surface lies what a person says they value—the information that might be learned from a quick interview or survey. But the underlying assumptions of people's lives reside at a much greater depth. At this depth is where the context and meaning behind outward actions and behaviors can be understood. Underlying assumptions are also the primary source for new ideas and product innovation. The only way to get to this level is by investing significant time and energy.

A friend told me an interesting story about traveling with two co-workers to New York. One of her colleagues was in marketing, and the other was a designer. The three of them walked into a shop full of very creative and unusual toys. The marketing person grabbed one interesting toy off the shelf, took it over to a salesperson, and started asking questions: "Do these sell well? How do they compare to their competition? Who buys them?" You can imagine the multitude of questions a marketing person might ask. At the same time, the designer was sprawled on the floor, surrounded by a half dozen toys. He was interacting with them and trying to figure them out. Every once in a while, he'd ask a kid that walked by, "Do you know how to make this work?" Usually, the kid would sit down with him, and they'd rap for a few minutes about the toys. The designer was interested in going on a journey, wherever it might take him. At the same time, the marketing person was only interested in the actual destination. She wanted to get her answer and then move on.

Listening needs to be a journey, not a destination. To really hear what is going on, you must be open to any experience that comes along and be ready to know it with a beginner's mind. The first step is to recognize markets as dialogue.

UNDERSTANDING MARKETS AS DIALOGUE

One of Radar's clients, an automobile company, recently needed help in resolving an internal conflict. Their Japanese design team was convinced that SUVs were no longer popular and that their next utility vehicle should be a "station wagon on steroids," much like the Audi Allroad and the Volvo Cross Country. The U.S. team, on the other hand, was convinced that the true SUV still had a place in people's lives. To get an inside perspective on the issue, we hired 15 SUV owners to help us understand SUVs in the specific context of their lives—all made over $250,000, owned a vacation home, and were willing to take two days out of the middle of the week to drive to those vacation homes to meet with us.

A large team from the car company joined us as we spent time with these people, rode with them in their SUVs, hung out in their vacation homes, and shared new design concepts with them. Watching the designers, many of whom didn't speak English, interact with the people was an amazing process. For instance, to observe how they dealt with space needs, people were asked to unpack and repack their SUV. And the designers watched carefully how each different person sought to customize their SUV driving experience—by adjusting their seat and mirror or allocating a specific place for their cell phone. Instead of gaining intelligence using traditional focus group strategy, assembling drivers around a table and asking them *hypothetical* questions such as, "How might you adjust your mirror?" the team actually experienced the drivers moving the mirror and making adjustments in the context of their *actual* driving experience.

After spending a couple of days having substantive conversations with real SUV drivers, executives at the company were able to formulate a new consensus regarding the strategic directions the company ought to take. The company used this knowledge to design a line of new SUVs that are significantly better at addressing their customers' needs.

Of course, having one cathartic experience getting out of the office and participating in the market conversation is great, especially when it leads to insightful, positive changes in your operation systems. But this process needs to happen consistently in the context of a bottom-up strategy, and it needs to be an ongoing priority. It's all too easy to get caught up in the day-to-day activity of work demands and lose sight of the real world that exists outside company headquarters.

Currently, most companies employ complicated metrics or very limited qualitative methodologies to do their listening. As the world becomes a much more complicated place with a lot more white noise, new, dynamic listening skills are needed. We certainly must go beyond the *intention* of slowing down and listening to the market. Many individuals inside companies have discovered this fact and have come up with their own organic, ad hoc methods of listening. Regardless of how listening happens (once the need for it has been recognized) and assuming that humanistic tools have been successfully used, the bigger issue becomes having the structure to communicate your findings across the company: You have to focus on both *getting* and *telling* the story.

It is often very difficult for those at the core of a business, who are in charge of making strategic decisions, to hear for themselves what is happening with their customers. But these are the very people who most need to listen to their customers. If they can't (or won't) listen firsthand, then the information has to be carefully and accurately translated for them by other members of the team. If the team can successfully understand their markets as dialogue, their participation in the collective conversation with customers will be more rewarding, and the results will be easier to understand and communicate throughout the company.

It's critical to recognize the importance of the relationship between you and your customers as people. Nathan Schwartz Salant develops this idea in his book *The Mystery of Human Relationships*.[5] Salant proposes that what you know of another person is really not that person at all but rather a third entity: the relationship itself. This idea comes from the world of psychotherapy, in which therapists are cautioned not to project their own biases onto a patient. Projecting biases while listening to feedback only muddies the waters. It is imperative that listening be done with an open mind, that we both know and account for the particular lens through which we interpret reality. We can't completely remove our lens. It is, however, essential that we know the biases that we bring to any conversation.

While listening to the key voices of your community is a challenge, there are amazing examples of companies using ingenious methods to listen, even in difficult circumstances. One such company is Hindustan Lever, Ltd., the Indian subsidiary of Dutch giant Unilever, the world's largest consumer products manufacturer. While the company has successfully built a distribution system that moves its products to every corner of the country, it has recently started to focus on a new group of consumers: the rural poor. How does one of the world's richest companies understand some of the world's poorest people? Simple: They listen in the context of their customers' worlds. That means that every Hindustan Lever management trainee starts their career by spending six to eight weeks in a rural village. They not only listen to but actually live with their customers; they spend real time eating, sleeping, and talking with them in the context of their worlds. People in the marketing department continue to make regular trips to low-income areas, to make sure that listening continues to happen.[6]

If Hindustan Lever employees can live with their rural customers in India, you can certainly leverage today's tools, including the Internet, to listen to your customers.

LISTENING ONLINE

In Chapter 3, we talked about the power of the Internet and how it has changed the way that people share information with each other about brands and companies. Brands can also use the Internet to facilitate going native and listening deeper.

Case Study: Procter & Gamble

Procter & Gamble, a company for whom branding has been almost everything, is a great example of a company that is using the Internet to listen to customers and become more attuned to their needs.

"We've been voted the best marketer of the 20th century [by *Advertising Age* magazine]," says Greg Icenhower, an associate director of corporate communications at Procter & Gamble. "But that's because we were the biggest shouters. In the 21st century, we want to be the best listeners."[7] Icenhower has led the effort to make PG.com a vital community, where customers and the company can participate in a dialogue about Procter & Gamble's products and the underlying problems those products are developed to solve. P&G is utilizing the Internet as a device for listening to its customers and, in doing so, has developed a unique virtual marketplace where it can experiment with its products and brands.

The maker of such products as Folgers and Tide, Procter & Gamble has always been considered a secretive company. Today, P&G is taking steps toward creating a new openness to listen to their customers in more productive ways. Its Web site, http://www.pg.com, is a clear example of this new accessibility. On the Web site, customers can review information about the company, including its history, structure, and operations. Users can also link to "tips and resources" on family, household, and personal care products. Another aspect of the Web site goes the greatest distance in developing P&G's listening skills: Customers take an active part in the company's product and marketing development by getting involved in product testing and feedback.

Historically, Procter & Gamble has focused its energies on communicating with customers through traditional means, especially television advertising. The Web site lets them lose the media—which acts as an intermediary in their relationship with their customers—and gain a more direct connection. To accomplish this, PG.com was designed to be highly interactive. When Icenhower was put in charge of the redesign of the Web site, he urged his team to experiment: "I told them that we wouldn't get everything right, but that by making mistakes, we would start learning lessons immediately."[8] One new feature, which the team developed specifically to promote a more intimate conversation, includes Try&Buy. The site's most visited section, here customers can purchase new products *before* they are launched in the supermarket or drugstore. Another new feature is Help Us Create, where P&G conducts virtual test markets in which consumers can tell the company which kinds of new products it should make or how it might improve existing products.

One of Procter & Gamble's ancillary Web sites, http://www.tide.com, offers features like the Stain Detective, a tip sheet on how to remove almost any substance from nearly any fabric. The main goal was to build resources for fabric-care advice and make the information readily available to consumers. Today, customers can even download the Stain Detective to a handheld device. In the course of developing these strategies for both providing resources and listening to their customers, P&G has found that they entered into a deeper dialogue with customers based on the strength of the Tide brand, ultimately giving P&G the opportunity to listen to new input and increase profits by attracting more loyal customers.

P&G has also learned that a successful strategy for engaging in dialogue is a two-tiered approach, where branding and listening work together. "We have massive expertise behind all of our brands," says Icenhower.[9] By using the strength of its brands—like Tide or Pampers—to make initial contact with customers, P&G can take the next step and let those customers provide the voices behind the brands. Pampers.com has become a community of users sharing information on a variety of pregnancy and parenting topics. Carefully listening to those consumer conversations allows Procter & Gamble to tailor both new and existing products to fit their needs. Like the local shop owner, P&G is going beyond listening, becoming at one with their environment and going to the center of the communities in which their brands live.

For Procter & Gamble, fostering two-way communication between the company's R&D teams and its 2.5 billion customers is a great place to start. To be successful in this venture, they must be open to both constructive and positive comments, and allow those with negative comments to express their concerns and be taken seriously. P&G has exemplified clearly how companies can actively and effectively use the Internet as a listening device and a vehicle for information, and it has taken the critical next step for any company: using the knowledge gained from that listening to make marketing and product development decisions.

When you open yourself up to listening to your customers, you cannot go part way and only make time for the voices that say what you want to hear. Many of us have a difficult time listening to voices that offer dissenting viewpoints. But it is critical that you grant equal access to both positive and negative feedback. If you try to control this access or choose to ignore negative comments, you are doing the company a disservice, and the company will ultimately suffer the consequences of limiting its vision.

WHAT ARE YOUR CUSTOMERS REALLY SAYING?

Real listening means facilitating real understanding. Have you ever had "experts" talk about your customers in a way that just didn't seem connected? They might truly believe they're saying all the right things—all the things they want you to hear—but much information can become lost in their "expert" translation. When you start to eliminate the intermediaries and do your own listening, you'll develop a gut sense whether the information you're getting is lacking something, out of touch, or just plain wrong.

Some friends once shared a similar story about a market research "expert" whose job was to go into the field and offer insight into what was happening with boys and the outdoors. A couple of months and hundreds of thousands of dollars later, this market researcher convened a meeting with 60 people in the company. She started to weave a wonderful tale regarding her findings, and the audience was hanging on her every word. About a third of the way through her presentation, the expert stated, "Boys are really into rappelling." The only problem was that she mispronounced the word *rappelling*, meaning a way to descend a rock face when climbing. Nearly everyone in the room was well acquainted with this term. They reacted to her obvious lack of understanding by immediately ceasing to listen. Suddenly, everything she had said and was about to say was called into question. She had instantly lost her "expert" status.

The problem is not industry experts themselves. Much can be gained by listening to people who know a lot about any given subject. But, if we put too much emphasis on their individual opinions, perspectives, or views, we're giving them way too much power. Remember the old saying, "Don't put all your eggs in one basket?" Don't be too quick to put all your trust in any one "expert."

Interpretations of the marketplace can be compared to the neck of an hourglass—if the neck moves even slightly, the flow of the sand is dramatically altered. When anyone interprets what's happening in the market, they often bring their own biases to the process, perhaps only looking at a static portion of the market. Every company has to interpret or at least make some sense of the knowledge gained from the marketplace. It is not good to relinquish this important process to a third party completely. Assigning someone else the job of listening for your company is a lot like hiring a translator; you are not always told exactly what was said. Your translator is really telling you what they *thought* was said. You need to trust yourself, your team, and your company to do at least some of your own listening. Start small and work your way up to doing most of it. Later, when you get really good at it, call in the occasional "expert," just for fun.

HAVING A DIALOGUE WITH YOUR CUSTOMERS

What happens when you start listening? Well, listening is really the start of a dialogue. And a dialogue is the basis, or beginning, of a relationship. So, if a relationship is what a brand is trying to establish with people, then how do you create a dialogue? It is all about give and take. It is about active listening: Not listening for the sake of getting your point across and not just waiting for your turn to speak. It's about listening for the sake of learning. Learning is all about destroying old concepts and preconceptions. For companies, learning is also about growing. It is about extending a philosophy that goes beyond the production paradigm. Just like individuals, brands that tend only to talk and are unwilling to listen and learn have a very difficult time growing. The act of offering silence is what makes your customer's voice powerful. As the apostle Paul said, faith comes from listening. Brands must have faith that their customer's voice is important and will help them succeed.

Listening involves promoting an outside-in or open system. A closed system does not have the necessary semi-permeable boundaries for information to come in and go out. By definition, a closed system cannot be a learning system, and eventually it will die from sucking its own exhaust! All new learning also involves disequilibrium, a letting go—perhaps an unlearning, or moving out of the status quo for a while—then finding new balance. As Robert Kegan so elegantly explains in *The Evolving Self:* "Every new balance represents a capacity to listen to what I could only hear irritably, and a capacity to hear irritably what before I could not hear at all!"[10] How could you ever learn anything if you spent all your time talking?

Listening is a journey with neither a start nor an end point. To grow, it is essential to think about a brand as a set of experiences and relationships. Those experiences and relationships must supersede accomplishments. It's easy for brands to get stuck in the rut of relying on a historical path of accomplishments. Instead, there needs to be a constant balance between exploration and accomplishment, and that balance point will always be shifting. It will never be an either/or proposition. Both must happen, and can happen, but not if a company is unwilling to fail or to try anything new, for fear of not living up to past accomplishments. Great relationships often involve taking risks, going places that you've never gone before, trusting in the unknown, and trusting in the relationship itself. When your company can look at itself and its brand this way, your journey will begin.

Most listening in an organization really happens at its extremities, where people inside the company actually interact on a daily basis with their customers. At the core of the company, the furthest away from such interactions, lies the heart of the strategic process. The greatest opportunities for learning and listening, then, are at the edges of the organization. In Chapter 11, we'll talk more about how to communicate that learning to the core of the company.

Synchronicity

One goal of active listening is to be in sync with your customers. In *The Natural History of the Senses*, author Diane Ackerman asks an interesting question: If a red apple falls from a tree and nobody sees it, is it still red? Ackerman's answer is no; the color red is dependent on the light that is reflected off of the apple and onto our retina.[11] But most other animals see the world in black and white. Likewise, most of us see the world with at least slightly different perspectives. Unfortunately, many companies have actually become divorced from the world around them. They don't have a shared perspective at all. They must find a way to reconnect with the world before they can hope to listen to their customers. The key is first to get in sync with their surroundings.

If synchronicity is the magic formula, then how do companies reconnect and become consistently synchronized with their customers and their environment? When humans enter REM sleep, our bodies operate at a frequency of 8 to 13 hertz. The earth's natural rhythm is 10 hertz. We seek synchronicity and, organically, we find it.

Companies can achieve synchronicity by going beyond the old model—of us and them, producer and consumer, company and customer—and developing a more organic, albeit more complicated, model of the relationships that people inside a company have with people outside the company. Concentrating on these relationships means thinking about the dynamics of any organic system of give and take, ebb and flow—a system based on dialogue. As we discussed earlier, if traditional branding is all about searing the name of the company into a consumer's mind, then bottom-up branding is all about slowing down enough to listen to the people on the street. When I say listen, I mean *really listen.* Listening is much more than hearing. It is listening with our ears but is also about watching, thinking, learning, and actively participating in a dialogue from an acknowledged subjective point of view. It is about a journey of learning rather than the accomplishment of finding the "right" answer.

To understand how to start a dialogue and where things should go next, it is helpful to understand what an ideal relationship is. Here's one way to think about it: Esho Funi, a central tenet of Japanese Buddhism. It means that a person is at one with their environment, actually becoming indistinguishable from their environment. Nichiren Daishonin, the 13th-century Japanese sage, expressed it in one of his writings: "Environment is like the shadow—and life, the body. Without the body, there can be no shadow. Similarly, without life, environment cannot exist, even though life is supported by its environment."[12]

The principle of Esho Funi suggests that we are not simply conditioned by our environment, including our customers and the marketplace. We are actually compelled to live our best within it; because there is no essential difference between our lives and our environment, our lives actually affect our environment and vice versa. Think of it this way: How do you feel when you walk into a favorite store—do you feel like you've entered an environment synonymous with the store's focus?

I have a good friend who owns a bike shop. Every morning he goes for a ride; for the rest of the day he sits outside the shop and personally greets all of his customers. He is their first point of contact, before they even enter the store. He's not just a random part of the cycling environment—his shop is at the center of the cycling community and *is* the environment. Can you and your company be at one with your customers and the marketplace? Can you *be* the center of your community?

We typically regard the environment and the individual as two separate phenomena. We even see ourselves as having an "inside" and "outside," with our skin as a kind of dividing line. But, if we really think about it, we know that human existence is impossible to sustain without a supportive environment. An individual without food, water, and air will die. Similarly, human beings can either support and protect the environment or damage and pollute it. Although we tend to see self and environment separately, in reality they are clearly, intimately connected.

We often blame people and situations "outside" our control for the circumstances in which we find ourselves. But the principle of Esho Funi shows that, because the individual and the environment are inseparable, both the *causes* and the *solutions* to our problems are not "outside" but, rather, lie within us. Esho Funi teaches that we don't have to wait for anyone or anything else to make change. It starts with us. Any change in the environment is a manifestation of a simultaneous change taking place within individuals.

The poet Federico García Lorca provides another perspective on synchronicity. In his book *In Search of Duende,* Lorca describes Duende as the place where a performer and an audience are in the same moment. He talks about Duende as being a deep connection and intense emotional involvement with music, song, and dance. "Duende is a power and not a behavior, it is a struggle and not a concept. I have heard an old master guitarist say, 'Duende is not in the throat; duende surges up from the soles of the feet.' Which means it is not a matter of ability, but of real live form; of blood; of ancient culture; of creative action."[13]

If you are passionate enough in what you do and remain open to feedback, your customers will sense your attitude and be excited by it. They will realize at a deep level that they are witnessing more than just a showy display of branding; they are hearing an authentic voice based on a deeply rooted understanding that comes from listening and being a part of the culture.

Even big businesses can attain this understanding. Think about a company like Intel, which has achieved its position through their unwavering passion around computer chip design. Great branding is based on real understanding, which is gained from the insights and inspirations of existing in the context of your customers' lives.

Everything we're talking about here is based on trust. Webster defines *trust* as a firm reliance on the integrity, ability, or character of a person or thing. Nothing can undermine a relationship between a brand and its customers more quickly than a lack of trust. In any relationship, trust is the essential prerequisite for success.

Trust is not something that exists only at the beginning of a relationship. It's certainly not something we can assume or take for granted. Developing trust is an active and dynamic part of developing synchronicity. Trust can only be built and sustained by keeping our promises and commitments—by having integrity. Deep trust can be developed that is also sophisticated and responsive. The key to creating such trust is listening, being willing to be honest, and sometimes even bringing uncomfortable subjects into the open.

Case Study—Doctors Are Listening

Like some companies, doctors have a reputation for not listening to their customers. Think about it. For most of us, the image an empathetic, caring doctor might only be a figure from our memories of childhood visits. Unfortunately, technology has become a religion for most doctors these days. Doctors rely heavily on diagnostic tests and the latest medical advances, not so much on intuition or instinct.

I recently got a postcard from my doctor, who recommended that I go to the lab for a blood test to have my liver enzymes checked. It freaked me out one day as I sifted through my mail, and there was the card: no call, no human contact. I did remember that I had had my blood checked several months before, but for the life of me I couldn't remember why. So I went to the lab and had my blood taken. I asked the lab tech about the test I was getting. She said it was somewhat rare and she wasn't sure why my doctor wanted it. I called the doctor's office a week later and talked to the nurse about my results. She said that she couldn't find them but would call if it were "anything serious." Anything serious!

Whatever happened to the good old days when you'd sit down with the doctor and have a real conversation?

Even with significant advancement in diagnostic tools, many experts believe that over 80 percent of any diagnosis is in the patient's story. The problem is that doctors are insufficiently trained to listen. This fact has inspired medical schools to begin to teach listening skills as what they call "narrative medicine." Like business people, medical students need to learn to pay close attention to what their customers or patients are saying and to understand the way their own emotions affect their diagnoses and perceptions.

"No medical school can train students in empathy," said Dr. Charon, a professor at the Columbia University College of Physicians and Surgeons, who has both an M.D. and a Ph.D. in English, "but we have a duty to equip them with the ability to see, to articulate, to grasp and comprehend the position of the patient."[14]

Many courses in medical school now focus on narratology, the study of how stories are told, the effects of point of view and structure, and the way in which storytelling can sometimes suggest cause and effect. Teaching listening is also helping doctors be more sensitive to ethical issues.

But the real revolution in medicine is that the act of listening may help patients achieve a higher quality of life—not just a longer life. Recently, my 92-year-old grandmother passed away. She was an amazing woman. All my life, I heard her say, "I'm going to live until I am 92." When she finally reached 92, she was ready. Her body had worn out, and she was basically being kept alive by lots of medicine. When she consulted with her doctor about what to do, he never asked or listened to what *she* wanted—he just prescribed more medicine. This continued until she decided to talk with a doctor at the local hospice. Slowly, over a couple of months, she stopped taking the various medications. She later died in her sleep, at home, and with her family by her side. It was a beautiful thing. I admire her ability to take control of her own life and not put false hopes in doctors who refused to really listen to her. When doctors choose to listen to their patients and understand what quality of life really means to them, medical care will improve for all of us.

Likewise, when executives can really listen to their customers about the quality of life and how their brands can support that—instead of thinking about the quantity of product a customer can consume—they will begin the journey of a deeper and more profitable relationship. Building these relationships will transform their business, driving profitability by increasing the number of engaged, loyal customers and decreasing their sales and marketing costs.

WHAT THIS MEANS TO YOU

How well does your company listen to the *vox populi*, or the voice of the people? When you do, remember to keep these steps in mind: concentrate, free yourself from anxiety and greed, imagine, empathize, understand, and love. Encourage your key customers to talk and tell their stories, without any screens or interruptions. Slow down and engage people in conversation, interacting with them while in the context of their lives. Also, remember that 70 percent of human communication is nonverbal. So, you must also listen with your eyes and engage your other senses. Does your company listen with an active and open mind?

The ultimate goal of listening is to get in sync with your key customers, creating an ongoing dialogue to support co-creation. It starts by recognizing that listening is more than hearing. It is about watching, thinking, learning, and actively participating in a dialogue. It is all about a journey of learning rather than discovering the "right" answer.

Think about how listening currently happens within your company: Do people get out of the office and get a chance to spend time with customers in their worlds, or is all of the "listening" done by studying secondary data about customers and the marketplace? Try setting up a trial. Find a local customer and ask if you can visit. Don't worry about answering any specific question. Just go find out about that customer *as a person*. Think about the context of that person's life. Are they married? A parent? Where do they live? What is their profession? Be sure to take one of your coworkers along. After you've listened to the customer, talk with your coworker about what each of you heard and saw.

The only way to understand your customers requires listening to what they really have to say, face-to-face. Are there people in your company having human, ongoing conversations with your customers? Can you join in?

8

STEP FOUR
Find Inspiration

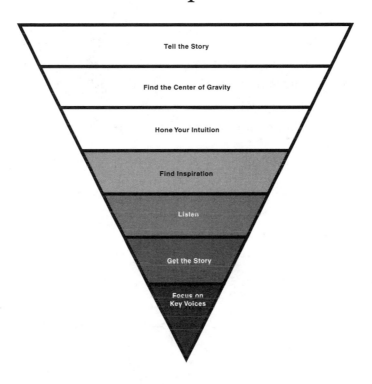

A rock pile ceases to be a rock pile the moment a single man contemplates it, bearing within him the image of a cathedral.
ANTOINE DE SAINT-EXUPERY[1]

Radar conducted some work last year for a cell phone company. The company's primary goal was to examine early adoption of instant messaging (IM) technology. Typically, when looking for early adopters of IM technology, companies focus on students and businesspeople. However, as we found out in this project, it's really important not to get trapped in the practice of looking in just one place for inspiration.

In our search for the right people to engage in an IM dialogue, we stumbled across a group of six women in the Atlanta area who were couponers—all committed to collecting coupons and shopping aggressively for discounts. For instance, these women knew that the best time to buy Campbell's soup was in January—so they would buy a year's supply then. Likewise, many had found such good deals on diapers that they bought enough to keep them from ever buying another pair for their children who, in some cases, were years away from being potty trained.

This group of women had met each other on a couponing Web site and had formed their own community. Prior to our conversation, they had only communicated via instant messaging online. They had never met each other and only knew each other by their IM names. Unbeknownst to them, they were at the cutting edge of IM technology. Their anonymity allowed them to share much more than just information about couponing. They also shared all of the thoughts and concerns someone might share with her best friend—without the fear of that information getting out.

After spending a few weeks exploring and reporting on their respective worlds through taking pictures, keeping diaries, and conducting peer interviews, these IM reporters came together for the first time at one reporter's house for a morning of talking about instant messaging in the context of their lives. The cell phone team joined us and took turns holding babies, petting dogs, and engaging in a dialogue about instant messaging. The cell phone team was inspired by the fact that the market for IM technology was much broader than they had initially thought. Sometimes, looking in places that are well beyond your periphery can bring unexpected insights and inspiration.

LOOK TO YOUR PERIPHERY

Once you've identified the key voices in your marketplace and begin listening to them, the next step is to find inspiration. Typically, inspiration comes not only from those key voices but also their friends and peers, their social networks, and their environments. We've all been on a treasure hunt for information: we remember hearing something that could enhance a current project we're working on but just cannot remember *where* we heard it. When this happens, you go on a treasure hunt. You think to yourself, "Who is most likely to have the information I need?" Obviously, you start with whomever you think will be the most likely source—or key voice. After interviewing them, you discover that they don't have what you want but do know where you might go to find it. You've now entered your social network and are beginning to explore its periphery to find what you need. It always amazes me that, after three or four of these conversations, I can always find what I need. Welcome to the world of networking.

SOCIAL NETWORKS

For good or ill, the way that information about a company's product is communicated will determine the fate of that company. To understand what's going on, you have to go beyond the key voices you've identified and become a part of their network.

By understanding and utilizing social networks to identify valuable customers to talk with, you can get ahead of a trend and introduce a new level of strategic awareness that can drive profits in a profound way. Think of social networks as an early warning system and the key voices as your entry point.

Historically, social networks have been associated with the phrase "six degrees of separation," popularized by a 1990 play of that title and a later film, both written by John Guare.[2] The idea is that any human on earth is no further than six relationships away from any other per-

son. Guare attributes this notion to Guglielmo Marconi, who supposedly said that wireless telegraphy would so contract the world that any
two people could be linked by a chain of 5.83 intermediaries. Stanley
Milgram put this "small-world hypothesis" to the test in a famous experiment in 1967. Packets addressed to a stockbroker in Boston were given
to 300 volunteers in Nebraska and Kansas. Each volunteer was directed
to pass the packet along to any personal acquaintance that might get it
closer to its intended recipient. Instructions within the packet asked
each person who received it to follow the same procedure. Surprisingly,
100 packages reached the stockbroker, each passing through the hands
of an average of 5.5 people on its journey.[3]

A popular example of networks is the game called Six Degrees of
Kevin Bacon.[4] This example can help show the way that people are connected in a network. The game reached iconic status in a 2002 Visa ad
featuring Kevin Bacon. Its premise is that all actors in Hollywood have
been in a film with someone else who is only six movie roles away from
Kevin Bacon. Because popular movies are a small universe, the structure of this Hollywood network, with Bacon in the center, can be deter-
mined in detail. By using the Internet Movie Database, scientists have
found a total of 355,848 actors, who have appeared in 170,479 films, all
with some connection to Kevin Bacon.

There is even a Web site (http://www.theoracleofbacon.com) that
keeps track of the Bacon network. This Hollywood network includes exactly one person with the number 0—Kevin Bacon himself. Another
1,433 people have Bacon number 1 (those who have acted with Bacon
directly); another 96,828 have Bacon number 2 (those who have acted
with someone who has acted with Bacon), and 208,692 have Bacon number 3. Scientists have found that, because the number of actors is finite,
the network around Bacon cannot continue expanding. At Bacon number 4, there are 46,019 actors, then 2,556 at distance 5, and 252 at Bacon
number 6. Finally, just 65 actors require 7 intermediaries to be connected to Kevin Bacon, and 2 exceptionally obscure individuals have a
Bacon number of 8.

In 2002, Duncan J. Watts, author of the book *Six Degrees: The Science of a Connected Age,* replicated Milgram's small-world hypothesis experiment using e-mail. Researchers asked 61,168 participants to deliver messages to 18 targets ranging in location and occupation from a Norwegian veterinarian to a Siberian student. While only 324 chains were fully completed, those chains averaged 5 to 7 steps, the same as in Milgram's findings. Even though participation was low, the researchers suggested that college educated participants felt more confident that they could reach their target and, hence, had a higher chance of doing so.[5]

British psychologist Richard Wiseman decided to test the effects of confidence on networkers by targeting events planner Katie Smith. Ten packages (out of 100) reached Smith, in an average of just four steps. Wiseman found that senders who considered themselves lucky got packages to Smith more often. This finding supported Wiseman's belief that people who consider themselves lucky cultivate larger networks.[6] These people expected success and were more motivated to continue the chain. Positive people who feel they are lucky can be a tremendous asset to you in finding inspiration in a network.

So, that's all pretty cool. But what does it mean, and how can you use it? Well, it turns out that networks don't much care whether they're made up of people, computers, companies, or power lines—they exhibit similar behaviors. So, if all of these networks are also "small worlds," this has far-reaching practical consequences. For instance, a small-world Internet is efficient but also vulnerable to hackers. A small-world electricity network delivers power well but also enables minor faults to cascade into catastrophic blackouts, as happened in August 2003 across the northeastern United States. Networks can combine robustness with sometimes surprising fragility. For good or bad, networks exist. What's important is to understand them and leverage their use to inform your bottom-up strategy.

There are two things to take away from the study of networks. First, by using key voices to start a process of social networking, you can better understand the social context of the inspiration that you are looking. Second, by utilizing these social networks, you can find much more (and more useful) inspiration that can drive category-shifting innovation in both product design and marketing.

A great example of using the principles of networking is some recent work we did for Merrell. Once just plugging away as an old-school hiking boot company, Merrell has stepped into the core of the outdoor industry by developing a dynamic, bottom-up strategy, tapping into the kind of network that can ensure they never lose the ability to hear their customers. You've probably seen Merrell's Jungle Moc. It's the comfortable slip-on shoe that nearly everyone wears and many companies have copied. After Merrell introduced it, the Jungle Moc became a cultural phenomenon that literally doubled the size of Merrell's business. Unlike so many other companies who stumble onto some real innovation that resonates with the market, only to ride the trend into oblivion, Merrell wanted to find a way to continually fuel innovation. With Radar's help, Merrell set up a global network of people, all trend translators, who could consistently give them quick and vital feedback. To develop this network, we used the principles of networking to find the right key voices that could offer the best inspiration to Merrell.

The resulting network has been used for feedback on both tactical and strategic questions. Merrell has used it to get global inspiration for innovative point-of-purchase displays; they have also used the network to understand how Merrell's entry into a new category of business would be received. Most of the time, companies get this kind of feedback only after it's too late, when ideas have already been conceptualized, dollars have been spent, and egos are on the line. This all too typical path amounts to finding inspiration in the context of justification. And that just doesn't work.

With a preexisting network, on the other hand, Merrell can answer questions in the context of *discovery* well before anyone is committed to a specific idea, either financially or psychologically. This is precisely how Merrell has gone from being a small hiking boot company to a global force in both the fashion and outdoors industries, picking up *Footwear News'* 2001 Brand of the Year award along the way.

Another easy and fruitful way to find inspiration by connecting with a network is to visit one of the many new Web sites that have built upon Milgram's small-world hypothesis.

Case Study: Friendster

You may have heard of Friendster (http://www.friendster.com). It's a popular social networking Web site that has assimilated real-life social groups into a large virtual network. Friendster, launched in March of 2003, expanded at a rate of 20 percent a week in its first year of existence. By the end of 2003, it had over four million registered users.

So, what is Friendster? The basic idea behind Friendster and other social networking sites was launched in a 1997 site called SixDegrees .com (http://www.sixdegrees.com). SixDegrees.com patented a process to connect people on the Web but failed because too few people were online at the time. Jonathan Abrams, a 33-year-old dot-com survivor, first conceived of Friendster as a dating site, but people's social curiosity turned it into a place where everyone becomes the center of a connected world, only six clicks away from anyone else.

The service works on referrals and helps users find dates, new friends, or social and business contacts by referring people to friends, or friends of friends, or friends of friends of friends—á la six degrees. When a new user signs up, they can post a picture of themselves and a list of their interests, but the key is that they are also asked to provide a list of their friends and their e-mail addresses. If their friends also sign up, they are asked to confirm their relationship to the inviter. Once these social links are established, users can traverse the entire web of contacts, finding people they'd like to meet and sending them messages. When people feel less connected in the physical world, there is a frenzy to get connected—through Friendster and other services. This network has grown rapidly due to the use of referrals as a method of promoting trust.

Friendster has even gained enough social momentum to become part of the lexicon. Much like *googling* has become synonymous with an Internet search, *friendster* is now used to describe a person who someone meets or knows through the Net. It has also spawned a number of variations: pretendster, fakester, and enemyster, to name a few. Although Friendster is the most popular social networking Web site, it is only one of many, including Everyone's Connected (http://www.everyonescon nected.com), Ryze (http://www.ryze.com), Ecademy (http://www.ecad emy.com), and LinkedIn (http://www.linkedin.com).

To demonstrate the power of connecting people through Friendster, San Francisco programmer Dave Coleman built a virtual, interactive model of his network stretching across the globe (http://blogosphere .headmap.com/friendster/dav.html). Coleman's map of his own global social network shows thousands of people, represented by points, with whom he shares a social connection. The most interesting thing about Coleman's social map is that it is interactive. If you select the "Show One Hop" button, a single point in San Francisco is shown, representing Cole-man himself.[7] Then, just as in any other network graph, when you select the Two-Hop, Three-Hop, or Four-Hop buttons, a map of the world quickly fills in with friends, their friends, and the friends of their friends.

While Friendster is a great way to meet new people, there is still a question on what effect it will have on live relationships. A human relationship develops in a social context; it doesn't just flow through a network as if it were made of pixels. But these sites *can* be a powerful place to go to understand the power of networks and how you might use them to answer your strategic questions.

ENTREPRENEURS AND MANAGERS

Beyond looking to Friendster and other social networking Web sites to learn how to build your own network and facilitate inspiration in your business, it's important to find successful examples of people who consistently use networking for inspiration. A network gives you the ability to move incredibly quickly when using a bottom-up strategy to find inspiration. Such speed can give you an advantage in the dynamic world in which we live. One of the best networkers I've ever met is Tinker Hatfield, the VP of Innovation Design for Footwear at Nike. At the foundation of Hatfield's incredible ability to network is his natural curiosity. He has a deep desire always to look around the corner and explore the unknown. This is a characteristic of all creative entrepreneurs—being willing to take risks and possibly fail in the quest of acquiring valuable insight.

That curiosity is what makes most designers such important people in any business. I've seen it play out in my own community of Boulder, Colorado, a community of 100,000 people. Boulder became one of the hubs of the dot-com economy in the late 1990s. Between 1998 and 2000, a handful of companies raised over $600 million dollars in venture capital. Today, all of those companies have been shut down. What a crazy ride for a small town! One of the most fascinating things that happened in this mania is that people started to get confused about the role they should play in business: managers began to imagine themselves as creative entrepreneurs, and entrepreneurs began to think of themselves as managers. This misunderstanding of roles added significantly to the destruction of these businesses.

A creative entrepreneur, or a group of them, traditionally starts a company. They have a keen sense of intuition and can see beyond the horizon. Remember Apple and Steven Jobs—he invested the creativity and imagination that launched a personal computer revolution. Phil Knight at Nike spent his first few years selling shoes from the back of a station wagon. They shared their passions with their customers and got out there to listen and learn from them. They sought to collectively solve problems and create relevant products for computer users and runners. They were acting as creative entrepreneurs.

The problem is that, as companies grow, they need to have the controls in place to get the work done and actually deliver products to their customers, on time and at the right price. Usually, when an organization grows, the "creatives" begin to leave and the managers take over, although there are some exceptions. Typically, as the managers start to exert control over a company, the imagination and mythology of the creativity of the founders is squeezed out. The managers become so busy working that they don't have time to connect to the networks that the creatives have built. It's essential to maintain a balance, to be able to listen to the network the creatives have established, and to hear the inspiration.

What makes creatives so good at networking? One of the ways to divide the business world is into camps of static people and dynamic people. Most creative people are dynamic. Look around you. Isn't the *world* dynamic rather than static? Yet many business processes, as taught by business schools, are static. They try to take the dynamic world we live in and turn it into static data points to understand it. While that might work well in fields like finance and accounting, it's not a great way to find inspiration. Such a point of view proposes that there should always be a "best way" to do things—yet this notion is increasingly irrelevant in a decentralized and dynamic world. To find inspiration, companies must embrace a fluid world of creativity and discovery. Finding inspiration in a dynamic world demands a dynamic mind-set for everyone in the company, managers and entrepreneurs alike.

Many businesses, inspired by their communities, have begun to put in place strategies based on design. Recently, there has been a democratization of design and an evolving expectation of aesthetic quality. But historically, function was everything, and design was an afterthought. Amazingly, some companies still have this perspective. More companies, however, are responding to the demand for a new emphasis on the power of design and creative thinking. People assume a high level of functionality in everything from a disposable razor to a new car. The resulting plethora of highly functional, look-alike products in most markets means that relevant, carefully designed products and messages— ones that find their inspiration in the context of people's lives—have a better chance at success.

Smart companies like Target have used a combination of design and network to drive inspiration in a deep way. Design and creativity have a new power in business that makes finding inspiration easier. Not since the late 1960s and early 1970s has design been so powerful. Today, this power can be seen everywhere you look: in fashion, furniture, and household products. Design has taken on a life of its own and has inspired a new level of consumerism. With so many products available today, design must play a more significant role in defining each product. Look at many of the most popular products: computers, cell phones, personal organizers, digital cameras, designer pharmaceuticals, and information such as software programs. These complicated products have a real need to be designed in a humanistic way. A big part of making them successful is the power of design and inspiration translated from the streets. The more contextual the design, the better their chance of succeeding.

The power of design is as Marshall McLuhan saw it in the 1960s: The medium is the message.[8] The actual design of a product or message connects it to its user, and design plays an equal role in the functionality of the product. Weaving function and form together is much more difficult than focusing only on function. Hence, finding inspiration that drives a design point of view is the only way to ensure differentiation in today's crowded marketplace. The key task in finding inspiration is to make it a strategic goal at the core of the way you do business. It's finding the philosophical balance between the infrastructure, systems, and bureaucracy needed to get things done on the one hand, and being flexible enough to listen to the key voices in your market and navigate their network to find inspiration on the other.

Case Study: LVMH

The fashion conglomerate LVMH is an interesting example of a company that has worked hard to find the balance between commerce and creativity. Bernard Arnault, LVMH's CEO, was one of the first investors to realize the commercial potential of a multibrand fashion group. Arnault started building his empire by acquiring Christian Dior in 1984 and a controlling interest in Louis Vuitton in 1989. The com-

pany has since grown to become the world's largest luxury-goods conglomerate, housing over 60 luxury brands and showing revenues of over
$14 billion. The group includes fashion and spirit brands including
Fendi, Givenchy, Donna Karan, Pucci, Dom Perignon, Moet Chandon,
and Hennessy. Arnault has succeeded where many have failed—balanc-
ing the discipline to run such a large company with the creative freedom
to find contextual inspiration in the world of his customers, navigating
the razor-thin line between commerce and design.[9]

Arnault has found this balance by giving complete freedom to his
designers to design haute couture, the high end of every brand, continually pushing back the edges to discover new inspiration. The LVMH
team then takes the haute couture designers' ideas and translates them
into more affordable, commercial products. By having such a philosophy, Arnault has created a company that can be intimate to both the
core and high end of the market. By designing based on the right inspiration, LVMH still serves the economic needs of the company's customers at the middle and lower ends of the market. By doing this, LVMH is
able to stay relevant to all of its customers. The key is finding the right
management team to work with such a design strategy. While managers
have to be very organized and precise, designers have to be allowed the
freedom to find inspiration.

Although Arnault gives LVMH's haute couture designers the ultimate say in creating their lines, he likes to stay involved in the creative
process himself. Unlike many CEOs, who feel most comfortable focusing on the technical aspects of running their businesses, Arnault sits in
on brainstorming sessions and is involved in understanding the inspiration from the marketplace. By staying involved in this way, Arnault is intimately in touch with his business. LVMH has gotten their whole team,
from managers to designers, in the mode of finding inspiration together. Getting the different parts of your company engaged in finding
inspiration can make your bottom-up strategy that much more powerful.

SIX STEPS TO FINDING INSPIRATION

The companies that thrive on the inspiration that the market provides them, and can interpret it into something real, have ingrained this approach into the philosophy of the company—it goes deeper than any individual. These companies all share some common attributes based on good listening to their key voices and understanding how to leverage the networks that exist in their markets. Companies that strategically find inspiration time after time—from Apple to Intel—follow these six steps.

1. *Be curious.* Have you ever spent time with someone who always knows what the next trend will be? The biggest factor is usually their curiosity. Companies, as well as people, can be curious, but static systems stifle curiosity. Reintroduce curiosity to your company by changing your world view to a more dynamic perspective. Instead of focusing on controlling the outcome when developing new product and marketing ideas, focus instead on thinking in dynamic terms and accepting many possible outcomes. Such an outlook, in and of itself, will go a long way toward making your team more curious.

2. *Be keenly aware.* Part of finding inspiration is being keenly aware of subtle changes in your surroundings. Companies that are good at it spend a lot of time deep in their market's network. Only by getting out of the office and living within the network participants' worlds will you be able to notice the subtle changes that magnify inspiration. Remember Jake Burton? What makes Burton Snowboards so dominant in its market is that they are intimate with every aspect of the marketplace and know what network to tap into to find inspiration for new product and marketing efforts. As we discussed, at Burton it starts at the top, and that means that Jake is snowboarding 100 days a year. When your CEO is that well connected to the marketplace and keenly aware of the subtleties

of the market, always knowing where to find inspiration, it's hard for your competitors to keep up.

3. *Use your imagination.* I'm always amazed by the imaginations of my two little boys. They really started talking around Halloween last year. One of the first full sentences both of them could say was, "Oh, no! Ghost coming! Scary!" After saying it, they would run around the house, laughing and laughing. One of the things that strikes me most by having small children around the house is that we, as adults, have lost our imaginations. The world is a serious place, whether it's business, world affairs, the economy, or, for that matter, our entertainment. People took the Chicago Cubs's loss in the 2003 National League Championships pretty seriously—seriously enough to phone in anonymous death threats to the poor guy who made the Cubs's right fielder miss a foul ball catch. Likewise, companies can take things way too seriously. It seems that in today's business environment, which is recovering from a recession, a lot of underlying stress is making everyone more serious. One of the key ingredients to finding inspiration is to have an active imagination. We all have imaginations but, like a muscle, you've got to use it or lose it. Turn on your imagination by doing creative things. Get your team together and have some fun. Do things that encourage people to find inspiration through the use of out-of-the-box thinking. When you support this kind of thinking by not criticizing it, new inspiration will really start to flow.

4. *Have a human touch.* I've been on some explorations with clients where some team members are so focused on accomplishing the task at hand, they act more like robots than humans. When looking for inspiration, it's essential that you use a human touch. When you're out trying to explore newly formed network connections, you've first got to gain the trust of those in the network. If you're only there to complete your business task, your focus is obvious and doesn't engender trust at all. Being human means taking the time to really care about the *people* from whom you're trying to gain inspiration. That requires sharing a part of your-

self. Being more human means being more vulnerable, and that's a very hard thing to do—especially in the context of business.

5. *Be patient.* The most important thing to remember about finding inspiration is that it's a journey with neither beginning nor end. As with trying anything, most of us can't find real inspiration the first time. The first time you see someone, you're not going to ask them to marry you, are you? Well, I guess it does happen . . . Finding true inspiration is something that you've got to spend every day doing, a little at a time. Probably the most important way to find inspiration is by integrating the search into your daily schedule. Read magazines you don't usually read, go to new restaurants, stay in a different hotel each time you travel, and most importantly, talk to new people. It's one step at a time.

6. *Always stay connected.* Apple is firmly connected to the creative graphics community, Nike has a support system of athletes, and Patagonia is connected with outdoor adventurers. With whom are you connected? Are you networked intimately enough to your group of trend translators that you can call or e-mail at any time to explore a couple of new ideas? Do you know them well enough that, if they don't know where to find the inspiration you're seeking, they will turn you on to their network? Not only are Apple, Nike, and Patagonia connected, but they have each become a vital part of their network's community, allowing them to find inspiration for both products and marketing consistently and much faster than their competitors.

WHAT THIS MEANS TO YOU

Once you've identified the key voices to heed in your marketplace, the next step is to find inspiration. Typically, inspiration comes not only from those key voices but also from their social networks—their friends, peers, and environments—and that means using your peripheral vision. How well do you know the social networks of your community? Remember, information about your company's product can be communicated in subtle ways that will determine the fate of the company. Think of social networks as an early warning system and the key voices as your entry point.

Finding inspiration in a dynamic world demands a dynamic mindset. Does your company have one "best way" of doing things, or is your strategy decentralized and better at understanding the dynamic world? Do you embrace a fluid world of creativity, discovery, and competition? Do you embrace the dynamic world we live in? Can you find more inspiration that leads to innovation by being curious, being keenly aware, using your imagination, having a human touch, being realistic, and always staying connected?

Think about a burning strategic question you have. Go out and talk to a few key voices and ask *who influences them* when it comes to your question. By doing so, you can enter the dynamic network of your marketplace and start discovering new places to find inspiration.

Gather your team together and brainstorm creative ways to find inspiration in your dynamic marketplace. Think about how your company can become more curious, more keenly aware, more imaginative, more human, realistic, and connected. Try to bite off small, manageable goals that fit into the context of how your company does business today. It's always better to try and fail at a small level, learning from your mistakes, before you take on systematic changes. After you come up with a few good ideas on how to find inspiration, cut the list in half. Prioritize and then cut again until you end up with two or three things that you can do *today,* without making them into new strategic initiatives.

9

STEP FIVE
Hone Your Intuition

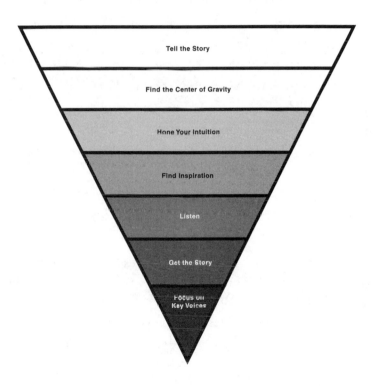

Information consists of differences that make a difference.
GREGORY BATESON[1]

A couple of years ago, Radar was working on a car project and needed to get a point of view before getting started. We hired one of our reporters, Nate Sherwood, to talk to his friends about their cars and their lives and videotape the conversations. What came back in a couple of weeks was a brilliant, inspirational video of Nate and his buddies hanging out in cars, drag racing, and jumping over cars on their skateboards. In the videotape that Nate delivered, he included clips from a video game, Gran Turismo, interspersed with footage about real cars. Nate and his buddies also produced a rap song called "Gran Turismo" to go with the video. When we talked to Nate about his video, he explained that each of his friends owned *two* cars: the one that they actually drove and the virtual car they drove on Gran Turismo. What stood out above all was the fact that Nate and his buddies thought of their real cars and their virtual cars as having the same importance.

We were very excited about this reality-versus-virtuality inspiration and looked forward to sharing it with our client. But when we assembled the client's team in the conference room and played the tape, there was a general sense of disbelief. Of the 20 people present, only 1 had ever heard of Gran Turismo (although at the time, it was the number-one selling video game). Nonetheless, the client soon came to grasp and embrace the opportunity that seemed to present itself—namely, to start testing the relevance of new car concepts *in virtuality*. Not only would this approach be more intimate, but it could be conducted at a much lower cost than more conventional testing. The video game world would be a place where our client could have a deep enough dialogue to understand exactly what their customers and potential customers really thought, in an uncluttered and cost-effective environment.

The dynamic environment in which your customers live demands that your company's tools evolve. Today, risk taking and creativity are rewarded more frequently; in many markets, innovation has become a winner-take-all game. In this environment, you need to reduce the time it takes to make good decisions. One way to do that is to increase the level of emotional intelligence or intuition. Intuitive brands show a superior ability to adapt to and capitalize on a rapidly changing and often unpredictable environment. Conversely, many aging companies have fallen on hard times because they have been unable to innovate and renew themselves. Renewal is an act of creativity. Something has to die—irrelevant products, brands, or tools—for something else to thrive. Using your intuition can fuel this creativity and renewal.

WHAT IS INTUITION?

Most businesspeople are scared of the word *intuition*. They are usually not anxious to admit that they use their gut in many of their decisions—especially when those decisions have a good chance of being reviewed by their boss, their boss's boss, the board, or even the company's shareholders. No one wants to admit that a strategic choice "just feels right" or that they relied on something as unscientific as intuition in shaping important decisions. Some, in fact, are reluctant to admit it even to themselves. In the field of medicine, quantitative studies can tell you whether one illness is more serious than another or that you have a 90 percent chance of recovering with no long-term side effects. But all a patient really wants to know is how to *feel* better. It usually takes a doctor with a highly developed sense of intuition to dispense comfort along with a cure.

Many people prefer the term *value judgment* when talking about intuition. Either way, not using your intuition—like the man who drowned in a lake with an average depth of six inches—can get you in trouble. Still, many are reluctant, when exploring the market for innovation, to be more organic, to get out there and really understand the dynamism of a customer's world. It is said that, after you've done something the same way for two years, you should look it over carefully. After five years, look at it with suspicion. After ten years, throw it out and start over. It's certainly time to get out from behind the desk, get out on the street, and start using your intuition.

To be clear, let's define intuition further. By intuition I don't mean instinct or primal drive. Instead, I mean intuition rooted in reality. It must be based on logic, knowledge, and most importantly, experience. Gary Klein, author of *Intuition at Work,* defines intuition as the way we translate our experience into action.[2] You must marry the rational with the emotional. Intuition has been called the nose of the mind, an especially powerful tool in developing innovation where there is little or no recorded experience to draw upon.

There is a difference, however, between personal taste and true intuition. Personal taste can lead to disaster in the marketplace, while using intuition can be the final touch in developing a successful innovation. I'm also talking about a very specific type of intuition. This intuition is oriented directly to the market and its needs.

Intuition is a creative act that takes over at the edge of knowledge. It can assemble previously unrelated facts and experiences into a new judgment about an untried solution. It is also an individual process as opposed to a committee act. As John Steinbeck said, intuition resides "in the lonely mind of a man." People who are intuitive always seem to have a healthy respect for facts, but they don't hold them sacred. They recognize that, many times, facts turn out to be little more than the judgment of another individual, or an idea that was incompletely researched or considered. Often you see scientific research at the cutting edge of many fields later debunked due to a calculation error. Someone just forgot to do the math properly.

People who know how to use intuition get a feeling of unshakable conviction and compulsion with it. We all know someone like that. A friend of mine, Ken Gart, is a master at retailing sporting goods. He participates in most of the sports for which he sells equipment, but the thing that separates him from the rest of the retailers in the business is that he also cares passionately about his customers. Recently, he gave me a tour of his new 25,000-square-foot Bicycle Village store in Denver, Colorado. Just by walking into the store, you could tell that it had something for everyone. What impressed me the most was that Ken intuitively knew how to organize this huge bike shop in a radically new way—by price point. Ken knows that the person buying a $5,000 road bike wants to feel special, so Bicycle Village has a special pro section. Likewise, when a family is coming into the store to buy their kid's first bike, it's easy to locate the sign hanging from the ceiling displaying their price point.

For most people, bike shops can be horribly confusing. First, most shops tend to hire ex-bike racers whose first priority is going riding with their buddies. Second, the bikes are usually arranged by brand, so that someone looking for a certain price point bike has to go back and forth across the showroom floor. Shopping can be an overwhelming and frustrating experience. Ken's simple idea of arranging bikes by price has resulted in a huge lift in sales, yet he didn't read it anywhere or hire a consultant to figure it out. Ken just knows his customers very well. He knows what they need and want when shopping for bikes, and he uses his intuition to drive his decision making.

Intuition is what really separates those who are good at innovating products and marketing from those who are great. It's the ability to weigh options and take a stand—even if the evidence points to a different solution. People using intuition must also have the courage to put their reputation on the line in defense of their opinion.

For a while, psychologists have recognized that intuition is a valid way of thinking, often producing better results than a more rigorously analytical approach. The reality is that timing is often the most critical element in the decision-making process. Also, in particularly high-stress situations, the typical business approach of evaluating options, collecting data, and choosing an alternative doesn't work very well.

That's not to say that intuition always works. But in a dynamic world, failure is an important part of learning. In fact, the reluctance to be intuitive and meet a risk head-on can often do more damage than the risk itself. A lack of courage can lead to a lack of confidence, which everyone in the community will notice. Such timidity is also a powerful obstacle to growth. It causes a progressive narrowing of a company's vision and prevents exploration and experimentation.

The bottom line is that, if you want to keep improving and learning, you must keep risking failure—all your life. There is a lesson to be learned from children, who are comparatively free from the fear of failure. Their questioning innocence can be of value in decision making: They constantly experiment. They come up with unique responses and solutions to difficult problems. Yet many businesspeople who are most in need of unorthodox approaches shy away from ideas that challenge fact-based conclusions. They allow their fear of risk and failure to override opportunities for success.

As with Ken Gart, the key lies in your ability to place yourself, intuitively, in the shoes of your customers and potential customers. In their place, would you buy the product? How much would you pay for it? How would you use it? The good intuitive brander can gauge market acceptance well by identifying mentally and emotionally with the customer. He can predict with some degree of accuracy how the customer will feel and react.

USING YOUR INTUITION

One of the most important factors in developing a bottom-up strategy is the ability to understand a large scope of information quickly. The evolving world in which we live demands that we innovate more quickly, so we must use our intuition. Each of us has the ability to be more intuitive, but we all need practice to get better at it. Some people practice a lot more than others.

One of my favorite sports—surfing—has taught me a lot about intuition. In surfing, everything is about timing. Unlike many other sports, the environment is dynamic. Surfing is all about intuitively understanding the environment and being able to move with it, rather than through it, using the power of a wave to propel you. When you are learning to surf, it's easy to be in the wrong place at the wrong time. Either you are too far out in the ocean to accelerate fast enough to catch the wave, or you find yourself too close to shore, with the waves crashing on top of you. When you finally find yourself in the right place at the right time, you are rewarded by riding along with the power of the wave for a short while, getting an intuitive glimpse of its power and beauty.

Surfing is especially hard to learn because every wave is different. The only way to become a surfer is to get out in the water and use your intuition to figure out where to be and when to be there. It is a lot like business. Intuition gives you the ability to be consistently in the right place at the right time in a dynamic world.

The only way you can learn to do this is to get out in the environment and practice. To start practicing, you must first forget what you've been taught about making decisions. Business schools have done a disservice to today's executives by downplaying the need for intuitive thinking, instead encouraging students to frame problems, formulate alternatives, collect data, and evaluate the options.

You always hear the business myths about those who have used their intuition and grown grand businesses: Bill Hewlett and David Packard in their garage starting HP or Fred Smith getting a C in his economics class on a paper describing his idea for an overnight delivery service (Smith later founded Federal Express). Likewise, Starbuck's Howard Schultz found his inspiration drinking coffee in a coffee shop in Milan, Italy; he knew a chain of such shops would work in the United States.[3]

Researchers are now recognizing that the most brilliant decisions are intuitive, driven by instinct rather than rational thinking. The idea that intuition is an important part of the decision-making process is not new, yet research from economics, neurology, and cognitive psychology is starting to bring it more respect. What scientists have discovered is that intuition is a real form of knowledge. It may be irrational and hard to get in touch with, but it can process more information on a more sophisticated level than other types of thinking.[4]

As we discussed in Chapter 3, one of the foundations of economics is the idea that people make rational economic decisions. The use of intuition certainly calls such a theory into question.

Some behavioral economists believe that intuitive logic is hard-wired into us as humans; it is the product of millions of years of dealing with the demands of hunting and gathering, instead of making rational decisions. While computers excel at doing deductive and inductive calculations, humans excel at adductive thinking. Adduction is less like reasoning than inspired guesswork.

To understand the differences, let's look at each. Deductive thinking would suggest that all fish swim—this is a fish; therefore it swims. Inductive thinking, on the other hand, goes like this: These animals are all fish; these animals all swim; therefore, all fish probably swim. Finally, adductive thinking: All fish swim; this animal swims; therefore, it is probably a fish. Adduction jumps to conclusions by connecting a known pattern—fish swim—and a specific situation—this animal that swims must be a fish.

While computers excel at doing lightning fast calculations, people are great at recognizing patterns. Psychologists believe that much of what we call instinct is simply pattern recognition taking place at a subconscious level.

Antonio Damasio, head of neurology at the University of Iowa's Carver College of Medicine, has done some very interesting work in pattern recognition. Damasio found that his subjects could recognize patterns physically much more quickly than they could verbalize them. He theorizes that emotions start the decision-making process, presenting the conscious, logical mind with possibilities. Damasio believes that without intuition the decision process would never start.[5]

As suggested earlier, neither by-the-facts rationality nor pure intuition is right all the time. The best approach when trying to inform a bottom-up strategy is somewhere between these two extremes. The trick is to find out how much of each is needed. There are all types of problems, but they can be broken down into five major categories to help you think about when and how to use intuition.

1. *A scarcity of information.* It always seems that we have to make decisions critical to a new strategy without having all of the information we would like. When talking to customers, we often feel that it would be better to spend time with more of them in more locations. When we are back in our office trying to construct the

strategy, it's easy to feel as though we've forgotten something. This is where finely tuned intuition comes into play.

2. *A short timeline.* I don't know if this happens to you, but with every project we work on, we could always use more time. In many cases, it feels like the strategy would be much better if only we could go back out and do more interviews, but the schedule won't permit it. The discipline of a timeline makes you work harder and rely more on intuitive leaps to inform and develop your strategy.

3. *A complicated environment.* To understand a complicated community, you need to understand the quantifiable aspects of the market. How big is it? How many customers are there? Is there potential for an innovation? What innovations have been embraced? It's important to understand fully the *how* and *what*. Intuition plays a role in defining the *why*.

4. *A complex environment.* In this area, intuition takes on some quantifiable methods. Just too much is unknown. Most complex systems cannot be understood through a method of "take it apart and see how it works," because the system is in flux and anything new, including your presence, changes it. In complex marketplaces, it is important to look intuitively for patterns in the dynamic system.

5. *A chaotic environment.* This is another situation where intuition can produce better results than rational analysis. Some parallels can be drawn from the chaos theory, which suggests that, beyond a certain point, increased knowledge of complex systems does little to improve one's ability to extend the horizon of predictability. The only thing you can do in a chaotic marketplace is to jump in, using your intuition to know where to start, and try to make sense of the environment. This trial-and-error method is the most successful in today's typically chaotic marketplace, especially because customer relationships have become dramatically more complex. You just have to admit that you don't know the answer and go with your intuition.

Using and relying on your intuition may well feel uncomfortable at first. The fact is that no one likes uncertainty, and it's going to be hard to explain to your boss a hunch you can't really articulate, even to yourself.

Even if you rely on quantitative data, however, it's important to recognize that it's much more subjective than you think. Remember, you had to choose how to define your study in the first place. Most of the time that's guided by your hunch, isn't it? Do you remember David Boyle's comment from Chapter 6? He says in his book *Why Numbers Make Us Irrational*, "Numbers do a wonderful job of telling us an answer. But did we ask the right question?"[6] You are already using your intuition every day—now slow down and trust it.

Gary Klein, one of the foremost authorities on intuition, only became interested in it after his research on the way firefighters made decisions wasn't yielding the results he expected. Klein's hypothesis was that, when firefighters arrived at the scene of a fire, they would identify a couple of options and weigh them against each other. What he learned when he actually interviewed experienced firefighters was that they would start with only one option. In fact, the firefighters told Klein that they didn't really consider anything first—they just acted. They knew where to start and would take that course of action until it didn't work, then move on to the next idea. They were using their intuition.[7] Have you ever been with someone who's really good at exploring the market? They know how to find amazing inspiration—but they could never describe a logical process for it.

Case Study: The Marines

Even an organization like the U.S. Marine Corps, known for its orderly, logical decision making, is starting to embrace intuition. In 1995, retired Marine Corps Lt. General Paul Van Riper was trying to improve the decision-making process that takes place in wartime. Van Riper found that, in the intensity of war simulations, let alone real combat, rational decision making using the classic checklist system didn't always work.

Inspired by Klein's work with firefighters, he took a group of Marines to the New York Mercantile Exchange to try trading—a situation that he felt was similar to a war room. The traders routed the Marines, which was perhaps unsurprising, given the fact it was their turf. But when Van Riper then invited the mercantile traders to play a simulated war game, to the Marines's surprise, the traders won just as handily. The fact was that the traders were better at using their intuition to sort through all of the disparate information and take quick action. This so impressed the Marine Corps that their current official doctrine now reads: "The intuitive approach is more appropriate for the vast majority of . . . . decisions made in the fluid, rapidly changing conditions of war, when time and uncertainty are critical factors and creativity is a desirable trait." That sounds a lot like today's business environment.[8]

Case Study: Songbird

What would happen if someone from outside your industry thought intuitively about the problem that it solves for its customers and was able to flip the paradigm from a custom product to a disposable one? That's a potentially scary concept, isn't it? Today it's happening in the hearing aid market. Songbird Hearing has developed a digital hearing aid that lasts for just over two months. Once it stops working, the Songbird's customer tosses it in the trash and reaches for a new one.

Historically, the hearing aid business has been a custom-fit business, like many in the medical industry. Typically, an audiologist had to customize a hearing aid to fit individual ear canals and tune the acoustic circuitry to match the patient's level of hearing loss. As the electronic components in hearing aids have become more sophisticated, customized costs have continued to rise. Today, the cost of a digital hearing aid can range from $1,800 to more than $4,000. In contrast, Songbird's disposable hearing aids sell for $79. While at least 22 times less expensive,

Songbird's hearing aids share the same basic electro-acoustic components as those featured in conventional digital hearing aids. While most of the parts are similar, the Songbird uses nonreplaceable batteries. Their units come in over 25 models to fit the physical and auditory requirements of different people.

So, how did Songbird accomplish such an amazing feat? The transformation of an expensive, customized product to a disposable one started by using intuition to develop a fresh perspective. No one on the Songbird team had hearing aid experience, but they were experts in battery design and intuitively understood that their knowledge would suit the requirements for hearing aids perfectly. The Songbird design team had two goals at the start of the project. First, component manufacturing had to use automated assembly to lower costs. Second, the hearing aid had to satisfy customers' needs by offering superior sound quality. What good is a cheap hearing aid if it doesn't work?

The biggest issue for most traditional hearing aid users is the size of the batteries. Have you ever tried to change the tiny batteries in a hearing aid? I helped my grandmother change hers periodically. I had a difficult time picking up the miniscule batteries. There was certainly no way that my grandmother with her stiff fingers could complete the operation on her own.

Songbird's disposable hearing aids are cheaper both in the short and long run for their customers. For instance, a five-year supply of Songbird hearing aids costs about $2,050. That's only a little more expensive than the *cheapest* digital hearing aids, and the sound is as good as the best custom models available. The other advantage that disposability affords Songbird is that they can constantly improve their technology and get it to their customers with their very next pair. Disposability also freed Songbird's designers from many design restrictions. Songbird was able to develop a microphone that is seven times larger than the microphones in traditional hearing aids. By supersizing the microphone, the designers were able to reduce noise significantly and improve sound quality. One of the reasons the designers could develop such an improvement was that the disposable device didn't need a battery door.

While disposability allowed designers more freedom, it also imposed discipline on the team to keep the hearing aid cost below $80. To accomplish this, Songbird designers integrated many of the individual hearing aid components into a few subassemblies. They also found ways to automate much of the manufacturing process.

Disposability also meant that Songbird had to custom design many new components and find suppliers such as Texas Instruments, Energizer batteries, and Star Micronics willing to push their own design envelopes. The key to both disposability and quality sound required a thoughtful battery design with low power—the Songbird hearing aid uses less than one-fifth the power of a traditional digital hearing aid. By figuring out how to manufacture hearing aids at such a low cost, Songbird gained the ability to produce a high volume of units. The company now makes five million hearing aids each year, more than twice the rest of the global market.

Songbird's designers intuitively knew that the real success of the hearing aids would hinge on the unit's ability to fit a range of individual ear canals and hearing-loss characteristics. To make sure that the hearing aids fit properly, the designers made hundreds of impressions of ear canals. This extensive research revealed that manufacturing only four sizes of tips would allow the hearing aids to fit most adult ears. To solve the variety of hearing-loss characteristics, Songbird designed ten "acoustic formats," instead of custom programming hearing aids to each patient's hearing loss. With a range of different models available, Songbird hearing aids can fit 80 percent of adult ears and can be fitted and dispensed during one appointment.

It is amazing how Songbird has been able to flip the hearing aid industry on its ear (so to speak) by asking simple strategic questions—how do we make hearing aids better and at a lower cost for hearing aid customers?—and using their intuition to drive a completely fresh perspective. Every industry has a Songbird moving around in its underbrush. Only by understanding their customers intimately, and using intuition to drive a fresh perspective toward innovation, will current industry leaders avoid being caught by the riptide of a paradigm shift.

DEVELOP YOUR INTUITION

When businesses are under increased pressure to be more creative, more quickly, in an uncertain environment, it is paramount to develop better intuition. Here are six considerations.

1. *Practice makes perfect.* All of us can be intuitive; we just need more practice. Start integrating intuition into your decisions by asking yourself, "What if . . . ?" Remember that intuition is a form of pattern recognition. It's a bit like playing chess. The more you practice, the more patterns you recognize. When you do use your intuition in a way that adds to your decision-making ability, think about what happened. Why did your intuition work so well? Did you recognize a pattern in your work and use adductive thinking to understand what to do next? Can you use it again in a similar way?

2. *Tell more stories.* As we'll discuss in Chapter 11, when you are meeting with your team, instead of just presenting data or analysis, start putting the information into stories. Think more creatively; change the setting of the problem. Talk about it as if it were an article in a magazine: explore how the problem makes you feel and what your gut is telling you to do. Consider the possible endings of the article. Keep the stories short, so that others can share theirs as well.

3. *Encourage others.* Using your intuition can be inspiring and contagious. Encourage others to flex their intuition by asking them to dig deeper into how they *feel* about information in a meeting. Remember that intuitive feelings are hard to express and can be accompanied by a lack of confidence. Encourage others to verbalize their stories. Help make sure that intuitive thinking is supported but not overanalyzed. It's easy to get an intuitive spark, only to throw doubt on it by overthinking. Be positive and welcome out-of-the-box thinking.

4. *Listen more.* People can develop all kinds of reasons why they should ignore their intuition. Focus on what your gut is saying. It's not only listening to yourself, it's listening to the subtle signals in the market that highly intuitive people tend to recognize before others do. Also, listen to what your team members say about their own intuition. Ask them how a situation made them feel. Ask them to think about their feelings instead of the facts around a situation.

5. *Rely on experience.* The best way to grow your intuitive abilities is to get out and have more experiences in the market. Intuition is like a muscle; you can't sit at your desk pounding away on the keyboard and expect it to get stronger. You've got to get out of your chair, get into the market, and start using your intuition. Start building mock scenarios around your experiences. Ask yourself the meaning of the things you experience. At first you'll make wild guesses, but after a while, with more experience, you'll become more accurate.

6. *Integrate intuition into your process.* An interesting apparent dichotomy is that many of the companies that embrace and encourage intuition are also very process driven. Nike or Patagonia innovate constantly, yet have product development timelines and processes that are quite rigorous. Yet, by embracing intuition and creativity, and building room for intuitive decision making as *part* of the process, these companies set up two seemly opposing forces to enhance each other and add value.

WHAT THIS MEANS TO YOU

Why use your intuition? Well, when you really get to know your customers and use your intuition, your ability to co-create and beat your competition to market with breakthrough innovation can be greatly enhanced.

What is intuition? Intuition is what separates those who are good at innovating products and marketing from those who are great. It's the ability to weigh options and take a stand—even when the evidence points to a different solution. Intuition is a creative act that takes over at the border of knowledge. It assembles previously unrelated facts and experiences into a new judgment about an untried solution.

Remember, there are all types of problems, but they can be broken down into a few major categories to help you think about when and how to use intuition: a scarcity of information; a complicated, complex, or chaotic environment; or a short timeline.

It pays to develop better intuition when businesses are under increased pressure to be more creative, more quickly, in an uncertain environment. Think about how you can practice using your intuition, tell more stories, encourage others to flex their own intuition, listen more, and rely on your own experience.

Think about your company's decision-making process. How intuitive is it? Can you react to rapid changes? Does your gut tell you something is right only to be confirmed weeks if not months later, after in-depth analysis? Try implementing a few of the tools mentioned above. Start by getting out on the street and getting experience in the dynamic community. Instead of taking the same route to work, try a new one. Turn off your rational mind and let your intuition guide you.

Likewise, at work, think about starting a new format for meetings that allows creative thinking and intuition to be a part of each meeting. Instead of making meetings a time to share progress reports, interject some questions that make people use their gut. Support people's creativity. Once you feel comfortable with your intuition, get out in the market and start using it with your customers.

C *h a p t e r*

10

STEP SIX
Find the Center of Gravity

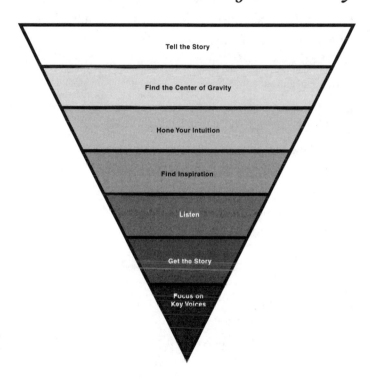

Tell the Story

Find the Center of Gravity

Hone Your Intuition

Find Inspiration

Listen

Get the Story

Focus on
Key Voices

At the center of your being you have the answer;
you know who you are and you know what you want.
LAO-TZU[1]

A few months ago, we were working with a technology client to develop new tools with the goal of enhancing their product design process. We had just finished a project focusing specifically on their marketing and were curious about how they integrated the voice of the customer into their design process. Did they have a bottom-up strategy in place, we asked. Our contact said no. In fact, he said, the company believed that their customers couldn't tell them what they wanted anyway, so why involve them? Instead, he told us, the company had a team of futurists that he called "the freaks," who sat around and dreamed up ideas. He continued by saying that they came up with some really crazy stuff, but that as a marketing guy he didn't get too involved with it, because it was rare that the ideas the freaks proposed ever reached the market. They were just too radical.

We think it's great that our client has a team of futurists looking around, actively trying to divine the future of technology and how their company can take advantage of various advances. But we would suggest that the company might be better served by involving both the "freaks" *and* their customers, by stirring up all of the perspectives and trying to make meaning of it all. For innovation to move forward, a company must make meaning out of all of the intelligence that it gathers—in the context of who it is as a company. It is important that, as you begin to make meaning, you also seek the center of gravity of the community. From there, you can move forward—using all of the intelligence you gather from your bottom-up strategy—to better inform your innovation process.

At the core of finding the center of gravity is another dialogue. This dialogue happens between you and your internal team regarding what you have learned from the intelligence you've gathered from the marketplace. Having partners in learning and action is important. All companies, like individuals, have cultural filters and assumptions that, over time, harden into mental models of the world. These models determine our horizon of expectation, what we accept as valid in our own worldview. Large organizations embed these mental models into their structure, dividing the world into categories. From this vantage point, it becomes very difficult to see and act upon opportunities that lie be-

FIGURE 10.1 *Finding the Center of Gravity*

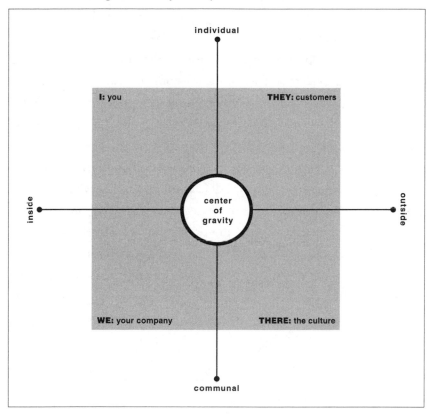

tween and across categories. New tools have to be used to break down the old paradigms.

There is an important dynamic between the left and right sides of a bottom-up strategy map (see Figure 10.1). What we do on the outside (e.g., listen, collect stories, and have dialogues) must also happen inside, if anything is to come of the intelligence we gather. At the core of this dynamic is the highly interactive activity of listening. Intent listening is the first step in creating a deep dialogue and finding the center of gravity.

As I said, the goal of a bottom-up strategy is to find the center of gravity, or sweet spot, where the participants from all quadrants of the map exist in a place of common understanding. When I was beginning to rock climb, finding my center of gravity and being fully aware of it as I moved up a rock face was the hardest thing for me to learn. To be able to climb well, you have to be able to climb from your core, or center of gravity. If you decide that you need to move your foot in an awkward way, stretched far to your side at the height of your shoulder, you cannot move any further up the rock until you can stand on that foot, moving your center of gravity over it. Rather than a physical place, when I climb, I've found that my center of gravity is more of a philosophical point. I can always find it when I feel in tune with my body and the rock wall that I am climbing.

Likewise, when your company finds its center of gravity, it can move smoothly through the marketplace. It is in tune with its environment, or has accomplished Esho Funi, as discussed in Chapter 6. From this starting point of common understanding, a journey through dialogue can expand the common ground and help to develop a bottom-up strategy. Certainly, this is a moving target. A brand or company must frequently check assumptions and characteristics, through a continuing dialogue, to make meaning of and fully understand the center of gravity.

DIALOGUE

While many people view *discussion* and *dialogue* as the same thing, they are not. Discussion leads people to hold separate points of view, while dialogue can lead to shared meaning. David Bohm, the British physicist, suggested a concept of dialogue as the glue that holds a community together. He describes the nature of dialogue by saying:

> I give a meaning to the word *dialogue* different from what is commonly used. The derivations of the word suggest a deeper meaning. *Dialogue* comes from the Greek *dialogos. Logos* means the word or the meaning of the word. And *dia* means "through"— it doesn't mean two. A dialogue can be among any number of people. The picture or image this suggests is of a stream of meaning flowing among and between and through us. This will make

possible a flow of meaning in the whole group, out of which will emerge some new understanding. This shared meaning is the glue or cement that holds people and societies together.[2]

So, why is dialogue so important? Well, the reality of living in a dynamic environment involves greater complexity than living in a more stable world. Today, as evolution is happening so quickly in most markets, one of the issues that must be addressed is that the thought and energy to develop an innovation has to be increased to understand the outcome of the innovation itself. Only through dialogue can you and your team start building plausible scenarios that can inform your search for the center of gravity and fuel future innovation. While some tools may help you guess the future, only through dialogue—in the context of a bottom-up strategy—will you gain the ability to allow many different points of view to survive and instigate learning.

At the center of the dialogue process is listening. As Bohm said, "When you listen to somebody else, whether you like it or not, what they say becomes part of you." Listening is at the core of all human interaction. Through focused listening, in the context of a relationship, dialogue develops. Hence, dialogue cannot exist without both humanity and humility. There is always a certain amount of vulnerability. Again, Bohm said, "An idea must be vulnerable—you have to be ready to drop it, just as the person who holds the idea must be vulnerable, I think. He should not identify with it. Dialogue, as the act of communally learning, can break down if those participating lack humility."[3]

This humility is a trait that is sometimes hard to come by in business. Many people have been taught, especially in business school, the fine art of discussing and arguing to support their point of view. We need to shift to an understanding that it's not about winning an argument; it's about learning what the market needs. Someone who cannot acknowledge themselves as an equal of everyone on the team, no matter the title or experience, will have a hard time participating in a dialogue. Only when people are ready to learn more than they already know will they be able to participate. Paolo Freire said, "Faith in people is an *a pri-*

ori requirement for dialogue; the 'dialogical man' believes in others even before he meets them . . . . Without this, dialogue is a farce which inevitably degenerates into paternalistic manipulation."[4]

What skills are necessary to use dialogue to find your center of gravity? To fully participate in a dialogue, people must first discover what currently limits their own learning. Second, they must uncover the assumptions and beliefs that contribute to these behaviors. Once these behaviors are recognized, they must be evolved. These behaviors are usually recognizable by others: depend on your teammates to help you discover your own limits to participating in a dialogue. Asking for feedback is also a great way to become more vulnerable and humble. The very act of asking for help can go a long way toward developing a dialogue. Through this process, a new level of trust can be found, promoting deeper cooperation.

Furthermore, there is certainly a link between cooperation and productivity. Through dialogue, you and your team can attain a higher level of concentration and be more efficient in reaching your center of gravity, thereby making your innovation process that much more productive. In turn, productivity creates more opportunities to have more frequent dialogues and through them create shared meaning.

For change to occur in a company, a team must have a shared framework and a common understanding of its center of gravity. Many companies are in such a rush, subject to "the tyranny of the urgent," that they cannot slow down to go faster. It is a commitment to understanding: once people have really listened in the dynamic outside world, they need to spend time listening in dialogue with each other to create a shared understanding, out of which aligned action and commitment grow. When companies truly listen and have a dialogue around the inspiration that they've discovered in the conversations with customers, there is an opportunity for real innovation. Customers can sense when a company is internally aligned around a central point of view. These companies tend to have brands that are much more intimate with their customers.

FIGURE 10.2 *Shared Meaning and Internal Alignment*

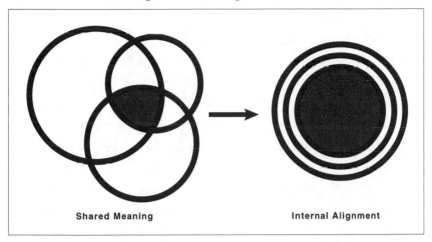

Shared Meaning   **Internal Alignment**

People are bound together not only by shared stories and information but also through shared understanding, or meaning making. Once a team finds its center of gravity and has a shared meaning, derived from the stories captured from customer conversations, they can drive inspiration and innovation. When there is shared meaning about a problem or opportunity, there is internal alignment (see Figure 10.2).

To find shared meaning, storytelling is the key. It is the most ancient form of sharing information known to humankind. It carries our hopes, dreams, and values. It is also a goldmine for anthrojournalists, because a good story will stick in the mind forever. In the future, companies and individuals will find meaning and thrive on the basis of their stories and myths instead of data. The key will be to create products and services that evoke a deep emotion. Products will actually be as important as the stories they tell. True stories inspire action, and true branding is authentic storytelling. Listening, storytelling, and dialogue with your internal team connect you to humanity in the fullest sense: through intuition, creativity, and innovation. By going slowly in collecting the stories from customers and having a deep dialogue about them with your team, you can develop the intuition to go much faster in implementing any kind of innovation.

THE FORMATION OF CULTURE

When companies listen well and have internal alignment based on shared meaning, they can find their center of gravity and become more than just participants in their marketplace. They can become drivers in the formation of culture. Nike is a great example. When they expanded into the golf market in 1995, adding golf apparel, balls, and equipment, they called upon their successful formula of participating in a market at a level of deep understanding. It took Nike four years to find their center of gravity, but by 1999, they got all the pieces put together and became the leader in a very competitive marketplace. Nike entered the market quietly. They first developed a deep dialogue with club pros and top players, highlighted by the $100 million sponsorship of Tiger Woods. Once they had the right relationships in the market, Nike went on a learning quest. They not only wanted to get to know the players but also their needs on a deeper level.

Things started to click in 1999, when the winner of the British Open won the tournament in a pair of Nike shoes. Next, in 2000, Tiger Woods dropped his relationship with Titleist and played very successfully using Nike's new golf balls. The final piece fell into place when David Duval won his first major tournament in 2002 using Nike's new clubs.[5]

All of the hard work and deep dialogue around the needs of golfers began to pay off, as Nike became a resounding market leader in a short period of time. Nike does more than participate in the sports marketplace; they understand their center of gravity as a brand so well that they actually help form the culture of sports. Like Nike, companies that can successfully communicate their understanding of their own center of gravity are usually industry leaders. Think about your industry. Does one company within it understand itself, the marketplace, and their customers so well that it dominates the competition?

Sometimes, however, internal cultures get in the way of listening and creating shared meaning. You've probably seen it in your company. Two vice presidents disagree on a course of action. Instead of getting together in a room, resolving their differences, and moving on together, often one will encourage the project while the other subtly tries to put the brakes on it.

Just like individuals, all organizations have their own filters and assumptions that, over time, harden into mental models of the world. These models act as a lens, or filter, that alters the way an individual or company sees the world. Factors that contribute to such a lens include our individual expectations, beliefs, assumptions, values, history, and unwritten rules. The reality is that we all have them permanently attached. There is no way to remove them. We cannot walk away from our own childhoods and life experiences and their effect on the way we view the world.

Likewise, a company cannot forget its own history. Ironically, the most successful companies often have the thickest lenses. Their own success has told them that the world works in a specific way. Hence, when the paradigm shifts, they may be the last to notice. Successful companies must invest a great deal of effort to understand their lens and how it alters their perceptions of reality in the marketplace.

Gaining a deep understanding of each participant you work with is helpful in developing your company's bottom-up strategy. This includes individuals on your team and throughout your company and the filters each brings to any interaction. To spark further thinking and dialogue regarding how individuals might act within the context of the community, consider asking yourself a few contextual questions (see Figure 10.3). Keeping each participant in mind as you answer some key questions can help give both your team and company members greater context, which in turn provides you with a better understanding of how they may interact with each other in the quest to find your center of gravity.

Our lenses can be helpful in determining our horizon of expectation and what we will accept as valid. However, large organizations often embed these mental models into their structure, dividing the world into categories. From this static perspective, it can become very difficult to see or act upon opportunities that lie in the open space between and across categories. In rock climbing, finding the center of gravity is about knowing your environment and yourself well enough to predict how the

FIGURE 10.3 *Contextual Questions*

Participant _____

1. Their world view is:

Egocentric   Ethnocentric   Worldcentric

●——●
   1   2   3   4   5   6   7   8   9   10

2. They are more oriented toward:

Numbers and figures   Faces and names

●——●
   1   2   3   4   5   6   7   8   9   10

3. Customers are perceived as:

The core of the company   A necessary evil

●——●
   1   2   3   4   5   6   7   8   9   10

4. Who is right most of the time?

Company   Outside Experts   Customers

●——●
   1   2   3   4   5   6   7   8   9   10

5. Their listening is guided by:

Instinct   Facts

●——●
   1   2   3   4   5   6   7   8   9   10

6. They are:

Thoughtful   Spontaneous

●——●
   1   2   3   4   5   6   7   8   9   10

combination of the two will best interact to accomplish your climb. Likewise in business, finding the center of gravity not only means understanding the world around you but also the internal world of your company.

The real goal in finding your center of gravity is to innovate. Innovation is always an act of courage, conviction, and passion. Having a firm grasp on your center of gravity and the internal alignment of your team will help engender these essential traits.

INTERNAL ALIGNMENT

With internal alignment around its center of gravity, a company can evolve its interactions in the marketplace and drive real innovation. In Chapter 6, we talked about the ecological term *ecotone*. In a sense, an ecotone is a natural center of gravity. Do you remember how an ecotone is a place where evolution is happening at a quick pace? Likewise, the center of gravity is the place where things are changing quickly, yet if you are centered, this change doesn't feel out of control. Remember, an ecotone is a place where two different, distinctive ecosystems meet: In this case, it represents the external ecosystem of the marketplace and the internal ecosystem of your company.

Too often, the learning at the center of gravity never gets fully communicated to the core of a company. And only at the core can significant changes to the soul or philosophy of a company really happen. The key is to understand and communicate inspiration throughout an organization in a powerful way.

THE GRAVITY OF CREATIVITY

When I'm climbing and having a difficult time finding my center of gravity, many times I try to change my focus and think creatively about the situation. In climbing, it's easy to get overly focused on the goal of completing the climb, instead of slowing your mind down enough to think about the more immediate situation. In some cases, the only way to the top is to go sideways or sometimes even down to find a creative solution to the problem. Sometimes, it means trying to use your body in a new way, like hooking your heel on a hold above your head and using your hamstring as a bicep, pulling the rest of your body up, thereby finding a new center of gravity.

Similarly in business, creativity must be employed to get a sense of the center of gravity. By creativity, I mean getting away from the preciousness of getting everything right. It means getting everyone on the team to start thinking about finding the center of gravity more as a process than a goal. Corporate annual reports routinely proclaim a commitment to creativity and innovation, yet these traits rarely show up anywhere in the company. In some companies, creativity and innovation are philosophical concepts, rather than practical direction. Too often, creativity and innovation are sought out but never understood and never incorporated into a working, evolving strategy. Conversely, innovation can also be so incremental and predictable that it isn't really innovation at all. I'm talking about going beyond just encouraging creativity, about developing a process that makes creativity an active part of the bottom-up strategy you follow in finding your center of gravity. Here are ten ideas to spur creativity in the pursuit of the center of gravity.

1. *Encourage conflicting viewpoints.* The first step in implementing creativity is to expose the people you work with to a variety of conflicting perspectives. It's important and valuable for people to realize there are many ways to look at a problem.

2. *Get people on your team who have a talent for raw ideas.* Get in the habit of bringing radical new ideas to the table. Every time you get your internal team together, take five minutes and ask for the most creative idea, no matter how crazy. Support it with a rotating award.

3. *Use fewer resources.* Try giving your team fewer resources and see what happens. Be sure to give them more time to do things themselves. Instead of hiring someone else to lead a meaning-

making session in the quest of finding your center of gravity, experiment with doing it yourself. It's okay to make mistakes and get frustrated with the process. That's all part of the game. The key is that you and your team are learning.

4. *Facilitate an institutional memory.* In your quest to find the center of gravity, make sure that the process is documented and shareable. It's important not only to share the findings and inspiration but also the process. For a company to be positioned on the center of gravity, it must have the capacity to learn as an organization. Remember to facilitate the ability of your team to share their experiences through stories. We'll talk more about this in Chapter 11.

5. *Allow for experimentation.* Another key to making meaning is to allow the process time to explore mistakes and dead ends. Too many companies are looking for the right answer instead of being open to seeing the environment as it is. As we discussed earlier, it's the difference between *looking* and *seeing*.

6. *Use short-term mentoring.* Some people in the company probably have a wealth of experience in meaning making in the context of the environment that you are exploring. Seek them out. Let your team use them as short-term mentors. Short-term could be a one-hour dialogue or a couple of days of learning.

7. *Don't be a slave to research.* How many times have you heard, "Well, that's what the research says," when you know that it just doesn't feel right? When you feel this way, take the time to dig deeper. If your gut tells you something is lacking, just "off," or just plain wrong, trust your instinct. Don't take anything at face value. Go slower and farther in locating the *real* center of gravity. Then you can go faster in your innovation process.

8. *Participate in dialogue, not discussions.* Earlier, we talked about the difference between dialogue and discussion. While discussion usually leads people to hold separate points of view, dialogue can lead to shared meaning, the first step on the road to finding the center of gravity.

9. *Change environments.* All too often, teams get in the habit of a weekly meeting, holding it in the same room, using the same agenda, at the same time every week. While that's an efficient way to have a meeting, it's probably not the best way to inspire meaning making. Try to keep the creativity flowing by changing things up. Alternate the team member who runs the meeting weekly. Let them develop the agenda. Infuse creativity.

10. *Offer your time and energy.* In any company, whether it has 10 people or 10,000, it's critical that the leaders of the company and of individual teams are accessible and have the willingness to give of their time and energy. Developing a culture of such generosity will yield enormous benefits in laying a foundation of trust, where creativity can flourish on the road to finding the center of gravity.

Evolve Your Language

How does your team talk about what you've learned from your bottom-up strategy? You can find out a lot about a company by the language people use to describe how they engage with their customers and the marketplace. Do you use the latest business jargon, or is it an organic language grown out of the evolution of your company? The language of a company pursuing an evolved strategy, not surprisingly, reflects its immediate environment. For instance, Nike uses the language of sports, while Intel uses the language of technical innovation. The language must also be a tool to promote creativity in the pursuit of the center of gravity. Here are five examples of language styles that can help promote creativity.

1. *Raw.* Conversations in the pursuit of creativity and the center of gravity need to be honest and rugged. They also need to be in context. Too many times, I've seen executives holed up in a four-star hotel, their every whim being catered to, while focusing on

finding the market's center of gravity. If you're trying to explore teens, get to a place where they might hang out. Invite a few of them to the meeting. Also, the rawness can come in when you let go of the corporate hierarchy in team meetings. This is a *team* in search of inspiration—not a couple of VPs, a couple of directors, and some marketing people. In that situation, everyone sits there waiting to agree with one of the VPs. Make it accessible. Make it raw. Make it real.

2. *Contradiction.* The world is full of contradiction. Yet many companies would rather actively avoid it or pretend it doesn't exist. Support contradiction by exposing people to as many real perspectives as possible. To get to the center of gravity in a dynamic world, you need to understand the contradictions. Some of the best bottom-up strategies have subtle contradictory parts. Contradiction is a valid part of our lives and has a place in every process.

3. *Collaboration.* I've found that company leaders, especially founders, can set the tone for how people behave toward one another. One important element of collaboration is generosity. Creating an atmosphere where ideas can be shared freely results in people being unafraid that someone will "steal" their ideas. Instead, they will engage with each other in a deeper dialogue.

4. *Dialogue.* As we discussed earlier, dialogue is a powerful tool. So many companies use either argumentation, having a power struggle between factions, or discussion, a tool used in the classroom under the supervision of a professor, in the pursuit of the center of gravity. Dialogue, on the other hand, focuses you on the journey and not the destination by promoting collaboration and rewarding collective effort. Dialogue is not a way of clubbing an idea to death. Instead, it's about moving the idea forward in a conclusive way. Many people in business situations confuse dialogue and discussion. The goal in a dialogue is for everyone to be in a different place when it is over. It's about evolution. The goal of a dialogue is to reach a place where no one

asks a question to which he or she already knows the answer—a place where ideas move in one direction only: forward.

5. *Storytelling.* It's important to get your team together in a casual setting and swap stories. When telling stories, think about creative ideas that succeeded and failed and unique solutions to especially difficult problems. Share everything from breakthroughs to breakdowns. The real purpose of such a gathering is to perpetuate institutional memory and knowledge.

Companies with no knowledge of their own oral history tend to borrow one to answer their own strategic questions. That's one of the reasons so much advertising today is interchangeable. Storytelling can be fostered by the design and flow of an organization's social and community habits, like its informal gatherings. Stories are a way of communicating. They offer a way of keeping the company true to its center of gravity.

FINDING THE CENTER OF GRAVITY

Finding the center of gravity means that you yourself are on a quest for the genuinely new, and that if you achieve that quest, you will immediately start searching all over again. There's no goal when trying to understand your center of gravity. There's not meant to be one. It's a journey. Once you find the center of gravity, it usually moves, unless you are standing still. It's all about evolving and exploring new terrain. Here are five ideas to help you along your journey.

1. *Get out.* Whether it's to hang out with a customer, see a retailer, or have a meeting, try getting out of the office and into the field so that you are in the same context as the dialogue you're having. It's always important to continue to reframe the dialogue by changing the environment.

2. *Flex your intuition.* As discussed in Chapter 9, really flex your intuition. Encourage people to think about blue-sky scenarios. A

good exercise is to start creating group stories. One person starts a story, and everyone else helps finish it.

3. *Hire the right people.* The first step on this journey is to teach people inside a company to think about who the customers are as people, then hire people who fit this profile. Many of the best young companies, for instance, Nike, Patagonia, Burton, and Microsoft, have an innate, intimate knowledge of their customers' needs and preferences, because they have taken the time and steps needed to relate to their customers. Beyond a certain point, company and customer come to share common values, sometimes deeply.

4. *Discover a corporate sage.* Some people have a natural intuition. Usually these people are artists with a keenly developed sensuality. A prime example would be Tinker Hatfield, Nike's renowned designer mentioned in Chapter 8. Hatfield is a great natural listener, and when you spend time with him, he has a natural ability to broaden the frame of the conversation. He is always asking, "Why?" Perhaps it is not surprising, then, that inside Nike, Hatfield has become a sage. Every company needs to find people with the natural ability to be intuitive and to help them become a corporate sage.

5. *Evolve your philosophy.* Michael Jager, creative director of the Jager, DiPola, Kemp advertising agency, sees the world differently than most. JDK operates with a "manifesto" at its core. It's called The Consciousness of Chaos.® This manifesto describes how the world is changing and becoming incredibly fragmented. To respond to these rapid changes, Michael envisions a state where managing in the context of this chaos can be built upon "embracing fluid thinking without fear."[6] Evolve your corporate philosophy so that it captures the center of gravity of the marketplace.

Case Study: Volkswagen

Once a company successfully finds its center of gravity, a newfound intimacy happens with its customers. People rarely love a brand itself as much as the products and ideas *behind* the brand. They love the relationship they have with "their" products and, hence, the company. Today, with so much marketplace noise, customers are always testing their relationships with companies. Unless a company puts a lot of energy into those relationships with people, love can be a fleeting thing.

One company that clearly understands the value of an intimate relationship with its customersand knows its center of gravity is Volkswagen. Volkswagen's Beetle transcends the typical relationship people have with a car—it achieves an intimate personal relationship. Many people consider their Beetle a part of the family that just happens to live in the garage.[7] Based on their success in the 1960s and 1970s, the Volkswagen team understood that most people relate to cars in the deepest emotional recesses of their minds. For Volkswagen to reenergize their brand in the mid-1990s, they had to find a way to transcend the typical relationship people have with cars. The results of this sensitivity and attentiveness to the feelings of their customers were apparent.

Typically, automotive companies have focused more on an engineering perspective—the statistics of the car. How fast does the car go from 0 to 60, how big is the engine, how many people does the car hold, and what are the possible seating arrangements? Instead, Volkswagen understood that it is essential to go beyond the benefits that a brand offers and connect to people on an emotional level. They not only reinterpreted the original Beetle design that was such a cultural icon of the 1960s, but they also revealed their intimate knowledge of their customers' lives by including things like a flower vase on the dashboard. I'm sure the accountants at Volkswagen were scratching their heads when a designer proposed the vase! Yet these little touches acknowledge the humanity of the Beetle. The problem with focusing only on the practical benefits of a product is that it is a one-way conversation all about the company, outside the center of gravity. The goal is to have the kind of shared meaning and internal alignment that, in turn, will create more intimacy and balance.

Case Study: Disney

Although Disney has recently suffered from declining profits and management turmoil, it is still another great example of a company that has understood the power of its reputation and the importance of knowing its market's center of gravity. Some would say that Disney has an advantage attaining their high level of intimacy, because their customers come to their theme parks every day. Certainly, it is an advantage to see the world automatically through your customers' eyes on a daily basis, yet this viewpoint is essential to all companies.

Disney also has some other advantages in creating deeper, more intimate relationships with its customers and understanding, intuitively, its center of gravity. First, Disney is more than a brand. It is a great story. Walt Disney, its founder, is a household name. Disney understood the power of tapping into the human need for stories. A plaque at the entrance of Disneyland, dedicated in 1955, reads: "Disneyland is dedicated to the ideals and dreams that have created America . . . ." Walt's vision has now grown to a global level, with theme parks and movies reaching a worldwide audience.

The company has thrived by telling great stories with the same Disney magic. From classic stories like *Fantasia, Sleeping Beauty,* and *Snow White* to the more recent incarnations of great mythological stories such as *The Little Mermaid* and *Mulan,* storytelling continues to be at the core of the company. Being a good storyteller, Disney fully understands the power of myth in the characters it has created, from Mickey Mouse to Ariel, the little mermaid. And not only does Disney tell great stories, it also understands the importance of repeating each story through many venues, from movies to toys to clothing.

Beyond storytelling, Disney has been built with the vision of understanding the center of gravity of its marketplace. The company strives to engage in a dialogue with all of its customers' senses. Visually, it engages its customers with amazing animation and architecture. Acoustically, Disney utilizes the power of music. Lastly, the sense of touch is incorporated into the toys that represent many of the Disney characters.

Volkswagen and Disney work hard to stay balanced over the center of gravity of their marketplaces and, hence, stay intimate with their customers. Some companies, however, have forgotten the importance of the market's center of gravity and have put themselves at the center of their worlds. This arrogance has caused many CEOs to lose their jobs in the past few years.

When companies are intimate with their customers, truly listening and having a dialogue with them, there is an opportunity for real innovation. People can sense when a company knows its center of gravity. This understanding is the foundation for every company's long-term success.

WHAT THIS MEANS TO YOU

For innovation to evolve, a company must make meaning of the intelligence that it gathers in the marketplace. It must also do this in the context of the company's own personality and culture. The real goal, however, is to translate the meaning into finding the center of gravity of the environment. Once this is accomplished, you can move forward—using the intelligence gathered from an evolving, bottom-up strategy—to inspire innovation.

The foundation of this process is dialogue. Do you have a dialogue, not a discussion, with your internal team about the intelligence you've gathered in the community? Remember that when companies listen well, they have internal alignment based around shared meaning, and they find their center of gravity. You can become more than just a participant in your community. You can start contributing to the formation of the culture of the community. Are there companies in your industry that play that role currently?

Think about your company's lenses that have altered the way you see the world. Remember that the factors that contribute to a lens include our individual expectations, beliefs, assumptions, values, history, and unwritten rules.

To overcome these obstacles, creativity can be used to get closer to the center of gravity. How well does your company encourage creativity by: encouraging conflicting viewpoints, getting people on your team who have a talent for raw ideas, using fewer resources, facilitating an institutional memory, allowing for experimentation, and using short-term mentoring?

Think about the kind of meetings you tend to have around your customers. Are they dialogues or discussions? Is there shared meaning and internal alignment around the customer's point of view? Do you have a sense of the center of gravity in the marketplace and the direction it is moving? How can you get your team to become more focused on the customer's point of view and what meaning it might have for your company?

Try to discover areas in your company that have a large ecotone with your customers and the community. Can you feel the center of gravity there? Think about why a product or brand is particularly connected with its customers. Do the team members who work on the brand or product have a deep connection to each other, the community, and their customers? Is there a way to duplicate and implement these insights within your team?

Remember, finding the center of gravity is one of the most critical issues for any company's adaptation and survival in the face of in this economy. Such an environment demands that participants seek efficiency in using intelligence gathered from the community and creatively use it in co-creating and driving innovation forward.

11

STEP SEVEN
Tell the Story

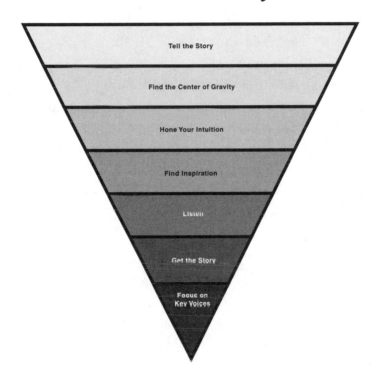

When we dream alone, it is only a dream. When we dream together, it is no longer a dream but the beginning of reality.
BRAZILIAN PROVERB[1]

One of our clients at Radar experienced a drastic business shift following a single phone call. The new executive at an automotive company had decided to bid out every new car interior project, rather than maintaining their longstanding partnerships with our client and a handful of other car interior design companies. After recovering from the initial shock, our client approached Radar to develop a customer-inspired design process that would help them win several new car interior projects.

Our process started by identifying nine groups of people who represented potential car buying segments. Those segments included, for example: Goldilocks—young women who needed a car that was not too big or small, Dominators—guys who are all about testosterone, Mid-America—families with three kids and needing lots of room, plus six more segment profiles. Our team went out on the streets to connect with these people and listen to their stories. The reporters did lots of creative exercises, including collages about their lives, timelines of significant events, and photography of their homes and cars. Following these creative exercises, we conducted videotaped interviews with a number of the participants so that they could personally tell their stories.

Once these stories were compiled into nine separate collections, one for each segment, the designers went to work and started to think about how to meet the needs of each segment. When our client's team presented their ideas, the videos of their potential customers were at the center of their presentation. By making these customers the stars of their sales pitch, team members were able to bring a sense of reality and deep understanding to the presentation. Best of all, they secured new business.

Storytelling is the most ancient form of sharing information. Stories carry our hopes, dreams, and values. They arouse our curiosity and invite us to wonder. They are also a gold mine for anyone trying to gain deeper knowledge. Told well, they stick in one's mind forever. Julie Taymor, the designer of the *Lion King* play, said, "It's how you tell the story that makes it new. That's what artists do. They let us look at the world from a different perspective. They let us look at birds in a way that makes us never see birds again in the same way."

WHY STORYTELLING?

Telling stories? That doesn't sound very businesslike. It does seem odd, doesn't it? Especially when the typical way that most corporations look at their customers is through the rigid paradigm of analytical thinking. You know the drill: analyze the customers, fix the systems, reengineer the products. Everything can be laid out on a graph or a chart. Companies develop plans into which they try to fit an individual customer's needs as mechanically as they would analyze a computer bug. Step one . . . step two . . . step three. They then build elaborate mechanics to share the information, usually via the dreaded PowerPoint presentation. The reality is that traditional PowerPoint presentations are obscure, mechanistic, and lifeless. Charts and graphs communicate something very different from pictures of living things. Who hasn't sat through an awful PowerPoint presentation?

A couple of years ago, I was at a conference where one of the featured speakers got up and clearly demonstrated the potential problems of using PowerPoint. The speaker was a well-known marketing strategist and author who specialized in teens and all things hip. When she first showed up, she sat near the door of the conference room, taking calls on her cell phone, while the speaker at the podium had to repeat several sentences to be heard. To make matters worse, the obnoxious speaker opted to dress like the teenager she was scheduled to talk about, by wearing what looked like a size four miniskirt—when she really needed to be wearing a size ten. When she finally took the podium, she looked awkward in her very tight dress and disheveled blonde hair. Then, instead of engaging the audience, she used her forefinger to twist her hair while she chewed on it. Her presentation, created in PowerPoint, consisted of white slides with over 150 words on each in Times 12-point text. She proceeded to read her slides verbatim for the next half-hour, looking up from the screen of her laptop only long enough to chew a few more strands of hair.

It didn't take long before most of the audience was dedicating their time to doodling or moving toward the door to find the restroom.

After the mechanistic analysis that businesses have applied to their strategic questions, the format used to present them isn't always much help. The problem is that these presentations don't deal with the complexity, mess, clutter, and confusion of the reality and living inspiration from the customers. Analytical presentations rarely succeed in persuading companies to change in a profound enough way to find the market's center of gravity.

At the root of this analytical approach is the education many of us received at business school. When I was attending business school, there wasn't a lot of room for stories. Instead, the focus was on statistically verifiable analysis. Statistically based tools poorly express the complexities of human needs in an easily understood fashion. Instead of speaking in the context of the corporate language, stories insist that we speak from human experience, allowing humanity into the strategic thinking process. Where the typical presentation about customers seeks to isolate and reduce, the story expands and encourages. Stories help exercise our imaginations.

Despite this apparent ignorance of narrative, storytelling is pervasive in all of our lives. Storytelling creates dialogue and brings a sense of continuity to our lives. It is an integral part of human communication. In fact, many scientists feel that our brains are structured around storytelling at the most fundamental level. Everything we do and experience as humans involves telling and listening to stories. Think about good movies: Movies, television, and the other mass media have been so successful because they are vehicles for storytelling. They transfer relevant information in a very fast and efficient format. When done well, these stories can become myths. I recently saw the movie *The Lord of the Rings: The Return of the King*. I was surprised by how many people took the effort to dress in costume to come to the theater. *The Lord of the Rings* is a great story that resonates deeply and has become a myth through people's sharing it. Stories serve the purpose of helping us put information and experience in context. Great stories become myths by deeply resonating with their audiences, becoming the source of our thinking and culture.

Historically, stories have also been the most successful way for people and societies to store their most important information. Since ancient times, cultures have shared the meaning of human existence through stories. Likewise, companies remember their own cultures by the stories that are told and retold in the company's hallways. Think about powerful stories that are told inside your company. Is there a founding story? Is there a story of a brilliant strategic move? Stories bring context and meaning to the work we all do. They resonate deeply in our souls. One of the reasons that stories are so successful is that they mirror the way our minds work. They have always been at the center of our evolutionary communications and have been the main mechanism for passing on our values and principles from one generation to another.

So, if stories work so well at communicating complicated information, what kind of stories are the most successful in communicating inspiration from a company's center of gravity? The most successful stories do have certain characteristics. They are told with a single voice. They explain a strategic question in a way that can be easily understood across the company. The story must not only answer this strategic question but must also be familiar to the particular audience. You've got to know your audiences and tailor the story for each one. Lastly, the story must capture the imagination of the audience by sharing some magic, while at the same time it must be believable, so that it feels like a premonition of the future.

Inspirational stories must also be simple and as concise as possible. It's more important to spark new stories in the minds of the listeners, which they can invent in the context of their own environments, instead of sharing the details of exactly what happened in your intelligence gathering.

Last year, we worked with a client on trying to decipher their customers' behavior and how those customers might react to the launch of their brand into a new channel, at Wal-Mart. After we spent several weeks with a handful of customers, one individual began to epitomize the prototypical customer and the challenges that the company would have in launching their product in Wal-Mart. During the investigation, this customer, Heidi, began to represent the center of gravity. We started asking each other "What would Heidi think?" when we had a dialogue with our client regarding its strategy. The final presentation to senior management was a series of stories about different customers and their lives. Most prominent among these stories was Heidi's. To ensure that everyone would grasp not only the story itself but also deeply understand the context of Heidi's life, we used a great deal of video. As with many of our projects, Heidi was videotaped in her daily context: showing us her home and closet, driving around town, talking with others at a friend's house about their lives and their shopping experiences, and, lastly, shopping. In the final presentation, we were able to immerse the senior executives in the context of Heidi's life. Today, when a strategic issue needs to be discussed in regards to Wal-Mart and the brand's customers, people still ask themselves, "What would Heidi think?" The strategy is always compared to the center of gravity that is represented by Heidi.

It's always good when stories also have a happy ending. This makes it easier for listeners to make the leap from the explicit story, the one being told, to the implicit story that will move the company forward.

The reality is that most strategic questions are so big that they can feel unmanageable or incomprehensible. The magnitude can dwarf us as individuals, making us feel insignificant and giving the impression that we have no influence. The very size of global strategic issues can lead to feeling that it doesn't really matter what we as individuals might think. These strategic questions create their own dynamic that must be overcome before solutions can be found.

Storytelling is the best tool for dealing with the immenseness of such strategic issues, especially when trying to get the rest of the company to buy into a plan to move forward and innovate. These kinds of stories must provide a kind of plausibility, coherence, and reasonableness that enables people to make sense of the immensely complex issues that are being examined. A powerful story can hold the different elements of a strategic question together long enough to energize and inspire action. Such a story can give people the ability to make sense of whatever happens in the context of their own lives, allowing them to contribute their own input toward creating the future of the company.

For the story to be effective in sharing inspiration and driving innovation, it is more important that the story be true in the context of the company than be scientifically true. It is also important that the story be true in the sense of the narrative and the point of the story itself, with its goal of inspiring change and innovation.

When the story rings true for the audience, it allows listeners to generate a new framework in their minds about the strategic question. It is more important for the audience to be able to immerse themselves in the story than listen to the mere transmission of information. This immersion can have an impact far beyond the obvious and lead to the embodiment of the inspiration, much the way our client has put Heidi's face on their strategic quest. By becoming immersed in a story, the audience is able to participate in the journey of finding the inspiration.

Most of the time, listeners miss certain details in any presentation. In our dynamic world, the inspiration we have found by using a bottom-up strategy is not precise and is usually still evolving. This inspiration usually cannot be captured or even fully understood at a static point in time. Incompleteness of communication is a reality.

The goal of any presentation, whether dynamic or static, is to generate in the listener's mind an inspiration that will feel new and self generated. Inspiration can then become part of the way in which everyone internally sees their work. Ultimately, when people begin to form communities around the inspiration and create a safe place to extend this inspiration into innovation, a presentation has succeeded.

To accomplish this, the story must take the audience on a virtual journey to the context of the story. This is a place where the story is actually happening, on the streets or in someone's home. This transition from physical to virtual worlds must happen actively. Thus, listeners must constantly be inspired to co-create with the storyteller. Luckily, as humans, we seem to be able to slip in and out of the physical and virtual worlds with ease.

When fully engaged, the listeners can work with the storyteller to focus on generating the virtual world of the story. As the story unfolds, listeners can feel connected not just to the story itself but also to the participants in the story, the storyteller, and their fellow listeners. The listener can momentarily be transported to view the world through the eyes of those in the story. Such a story can help them reframe their world view in a profound way and become a common rallying cry around the center of gravity of the marketplace.

In contrast, when you listen to a presentation built on the foundation of static thinking instead of the foundation of a dynamic narrative, your mind is active in a very different way than when participating in a story. When (or if) engaged in listening to a presentation based on static thinking, the listener is not allowed to call upon their own experience or background to make the presentation more relevant. Most of the time, a listener has to put everything *out* of their mind and focus solely on understanding the static thinking. They are required to forget their own imaginations, experiences, and anything else that might be a "distraction."

When listening to a story, however, the opposite happens. The listener must actively participate and contribute to the context of the story and, in effect, help tell themselves the story. Such active participation promotes a common understanding, based on the experience of listening to the story, that the audience will continue to relate long after the exact details are forgotten. The listener is invited not only to listen but to live the story with the storyteller, contextualizing the story into a living experience. Part of what makes a story successful is that it provides a place for the listener to visit on their virtual journey to further nurture their own experience.

Finding the center of gravity is one of the most critical issues for any company's adaptation and survival in the face of an increasingly dissonant environment. Such an environment demands participants who seek efficiency in the use of intelligence gathered from the marketplace and use it creatively in driving innovation forward.

Stories are more efficient tools, because they take less mental energy to understand than data. To be efficient, stories must be simple, accessible, and in the proper context for the audience. When a story does its job well, the listeners' minds race ahead—they try to imagine the further implications of elaborating the same inspiration in other contexts, making the inspiration more powerful and intimate. In this way, inspiration that is based on a deep center of gravity can spread throughout a company.

STORYTELLING VERSUS INSTRUCTION

When using storytelling to spread inspiration throughout a company, you don't want to fall into the instructor or teacher mode. Your company doesn't need "teachers" who impart their knowledge to the uneducated; it needs co-creators of stories who spark creativity in their teammates. While stories can generate positive attitudes that will inspire innovation, instruction usually doesn't.

Why is that? Well, listening to stories gives participants the space to fill in the gaps of the story and imagine the missing links in the context of their own work. The meaning of the story that you are trying to convey is usually not in the story itself but instead in the meaning that the listeners help create out of it. Finding the center of gravity means finding meaning in the story in the context of the listener's own work.

One of the biggest problems with the typical corporate presentation, concentrating on hard facts and findings, is that this static way of thinking leaves most people, on the outside of the process as spectators, self-conscious. It's as though they are watching the facts being presented on the other side of a glass wall, with no way to interact. Such a presentation is a static picture with no way of making the dynamic intelligence come alive and be usable.

In contrast, storytelling and the narrative way of thinking are immersive and can be easily internalized. They demand that the listeners forget themselves and participate in the journey of finding the center of gravity. As David Abrams said in *The Spell of the Sensuous,* the explicit meanings of the actual words ride on the surface of this depth like the waves on the surface of the sea.[2]

Somehow in our corporate lives, our jobs have come to demand that we treat people as mechanical things. We've deceived ourselves into believing that we can be objective. Yet, when we are in a social setting with our friends, we treat people very differently—as humans, not as things to be manipulated. The result of the mechanical behavior in most companies is a breakdown in trust. Without such trust, not only with fellow employees but also with customers, it is impossible to find the elusive center of gravity.

In the effort to find the center of gravity and communicate it internally, the goal of storytelling is to facilitate the rearranging of established knowledge inside the company. It encourages listeners to make new connections between what they currently do and what they need to do to be centered. The ultimate goal is to encourage listeners to generate their own stories around the principals of your story. A listener hears the storyteller and, simultaneously, hears a silent voice within themselves, as their minds create a variety of outcomes to the story, built upon their own personal experiences.

Instead of playing the role of the teacher, a storyteller should allow some mental space in the story for the listeners to forge their own thoughts. A good storyteller must keep in mind the objective of having listeners invent their own stories built on the foundation of the original story. When this mental space is offered, everyone in the audience can co-create in a way that bonds them deeply to a common experience.

Storytelling can also be an incredibly useful tool for coping with complexity. As humans, we have always used the narrative language of stories as the most efficient way to communicate the nature and behavior of complex adaptive phenomena. As a description of complex systems, stories are considerably more accurate than scientific thinking. Our world is full of these systems. Look around. Anything that is important to know about—people, companies, economies, animals, plants, and weather—is a complex system. Humans have always intuitively used stories to communicate the complexity around us. This is why stories are ubiquitous. Only when we get serious do our minds lock up, our business school mind-sets take over, and we start talking in linear terms about complex phenomena and drawing two-dimensional maps of our thoughts.

DEVELOPING THE STORY

We are in the twilight of a society based on data. In the coming years, brands and companies will not thrive on the basis of their data but on the strength and meaning of their stories, creating products and services that evoke emotion. Products will become less important than the stories they convey and the way those stories are interpreted. It is a return of the ancient form of narrative. Companies need to have stories to tell—stories that inspire action. And companies must themselves embody those stories with congruency and authenticity.

Your narrative must have the following nine essential qualities.

1. *Context.* The story must be in the context of the audience's experience. You want the audience to think about their own experiences and stories and be able to see themselves in the story.

    Do you remember, from Chapter 4, the speech on storytelling I gave at an internal innovation conference for an automobile company? The audience was made up of 300 engineers. When I was setting up, one of the senior engineers walked by and said, "Storytelling! I'll be asleep in five minutes." Needless to say, I was a little nervous. After an hour or so, the audience started to get the idea of the power of stories—especially when I asked them to talk about the founder of their company and what he did to make the company what it was today. It was as if a light had gone on. People's eyes sparkled as they told stories about the founder and his intuition that drove far-reaching innovation. The ball was rolling.

I then asked them to share stories about their own cars. It was cathartic. It felt like a group therapy session as everyone shared wonderful stories about their first cars, events that had happened to them in their cars, and their lust for cars they didn't own. There was lots of laughter and some sadness. It was real.

Finally, toward the end of the session, the engineer who was so skeptical at first told a wonderful story himself. He spoke about his dream of owning a sports car, contrasted with the stark reality of having two kids and needing a minivan. He related a feeling of lost youth and the reality of maturity with a great deal of emotion. At the end, I thanked him for his story and reminded him that anyone can tell a good story, especially when it is in the context of the audience's own experiences.

2. *Simplicity.* I'm sure you've been in a meeting where someone starts telling a story that gets so complicated and long that everyone gets lost. I always try to keep each slide in my presentation to no more than two sentences. Sometimes the simplicity of one word is even more powerful. When trying to explain something like the meaning of a term, it's not necessary to give a paragraph-long explanation. Show the word and talk about the meaning. Keep your story simple and to the point.

3. *Interest.* A boring story is just that. We've all sat through presentations where it seems as though the presenter has lost their way. You can look around and see the audience mentally wander off and tune out the rest of the presentation. Engage the audience with an interesting story. If it's boring, the story will do nothing to inspire action or promote understanding. A story has to be interesting enough for the audience to register it, remember it, and tell it again.

4. *Trust.* The best stories are stories that are actually true. I don't mean true in a scientific context but true to the audience's experience. The trust is amazing when you feel the audience saying that they've been in the same situation. True stories evoke in an audience an attitude of "I can do it, too."

5. *Meaning.* A story must get across a strong message that inspires the audience to rethink something. The story is the structure or framework that adds support to the deeper message being conveyed. It's easy to get lost in the story itself and forget why you are telling it. Remember that a story is not just a way to illustrate the analysis. Rather, the story's job is to convey meaning from the analysis and act as a conduit of understanding.

6. *Connectedness.* To be successful, the story must connect the audience with the inspiration you are trying to convey and to customers with whom the audience can empathize. It is vital to get the listeners to mentally place themselves in the shoes of the customers.

7. *Magic.* A great story often violates the listener's expectations. There is a surprise. This gift is usually an action that has laid the groundwork for profound inspiration in the story. Remember to plant the seed of the idea of the center of gravity and let them invent the missing elements.

8. *Relevance.* To be successful, a story must embody the inspiration in such a way that the audience will almost intuitively know what to do with it. If the listeners are given the opportunity to co-create the story, they will believe that it is their story and will be more likely to become champions of the inspiration.

9. *Immediacy.* Stories are efficient. When the deadline is tight, it isn't possible to detail all of the data to prove your point scientifically. A story helps people to take the leap of faith necessary to innovate.

Remember, the goal of a bottom up strategy is to catalyze organizational change around the center of gravity in the marketplace. Stories play an important role in making this happen.

SHARING THE STORY

For an organization to change, inspiration from the street must find its way into the core of the company. As in any other organism, change happens at the fringes of a species. The center of the species is always the last to change, and the center of the community resists change the most. It is essential to use the intelligence found on the streets to start a revolution internally by making that intelligence as impactful as possible. Impact can come from ease of use, accessibility, insight, relevance, and beauty. But the real power resides in the presentation of the story. Also, remember that you are simply the storyteller, the illustrator of the information, and that the story itself should be the star. Your job is to be the conduit between the intelligence from the streets and the rest of the company.

Here are four considerations when you're sharing your stories to make them as impactful as they can be.

1. *Engage the audience.* While a great story can engage the audience, most of the time, the magic that makes the story engaging comes from the way it is told. Think about reading stories with your parents when you were a kid. The best stories were those about which your parents were passionate and so told with excitement. As a speaker, if you're excited by what you're talking about, chances are that your audience will be excited as well. Conversely, if you dread the story you are telling, then your audience will as well. Think about the story and how you can change it to get yourself excited about it. Be passionate.

2. *Ownership.* To motivate people through storytelling, you must master the performance of the story. By mastering the story, you can free yourself to have the flexibility to deal with even the most difficult situations. When speaking at a "Voice of the Customer" conference, I went to the podium to turn on my computer and set up as the audience was having lunch. For some reason, my computer crashed and would not turn on. A couple of days be-

fore, I had made a CD of my presentation, but in the 48 hours before the speech, I had changed the material radically. Fortunately, someone loaned me a computer. I was able to use the CD to rebuild the story in a half hour. The only way I was able to pull it off was because I knew the material so well that I could retype several slides from memory. I owned the story.

3. *Testing.* You know the saying: Practice makes perfect. There is no substitution for it. Focus your energies on the core of the story, presenting it as interesting and meaningful. Practice in front of people and get feedback. Don't be afraid to modify the story up until you're going to deliver it. I always find that, the more times I practice a story, the more small changes I make to it. The story becomes *my* story. Only then can the magic of ownership really come out.

4. *Informal settings.* I always find that if you're relaxed as a storyteller, then your audience will also be relaxed. One of the ways to make the setting more informal is to start the story off with a series of questions. Solicit participation in the story's co-creation. Every once in a while, slow down, take a breath, and ask more questions. Questions keep the audience engaged and the setting more informal. The story becomes a dialogue between peers instead of a classroom-type performance where a teacher instructs the students.

SUPPORTING AND SPREADING YOUR STORY

Your stories can be greatly enhanced with the use of strong visual and audio tools. Video—which follows the storytelling guidelines discussed above—is definitely the strongest way to share a story. On the other hand, 20 hours of bad focus group video will do nothing to support your point. Short of using video, the next best thing is photography, preferably images that are as gritty and real as possible. Remember, a quick snapshot of a real situation is always more powerful than any stock image. You want the viewer to feel as if they are there. So, document your point of view with a digital or disposable camera. To see examples of photos and video shot for a few of our projects, check out our Web site at http://www.beyond-the-brand.com.

Lastly, think about the design of your story, whether it's written or delivered as a full presentation. We've all seen PowerPoint presentations that are a nightmare, but they don't have to be. Setting up your presentation in a creative way will allow for creativity as you tell the story. My rule is never to have more than one sentence per slide. Don't talk directly from the slides, rather use them as reinforcement for your story. Likewise, when your story is written, design the document so that it feels light and inviting. Here are three things to remember when your presentation is being prepared.

1. *Create mental space.* Great storytelling creates mental space for the audience to think and co-create. Build these spaces into the presentation of your story by leaving some white space. In written form, that might mean putting only a few words on each page; when telling the story, it might mean taking a deep breath and pausing for the audience to reflect; in PowerPoint, it might mean using fewer words per slide and not trying to explain everything explicitly for every slide.

2. *Allow for co-creation.* By creating mental space for the audience, you are inviting them to co-create with you. A storyteller who solicits input, asking for participation, will also enhance co-creation. Even in a printed report, you can solicit participation with a few good questions.

3. *Be provocative.* By provocative, I mean push the envelope. Try new things. If your company's standard practice is to tell stories in a memo created in a Word document, change it up. Add some photos. Pull out some meaningful quotes and feature them in larger type or a different font. Challenge the status quo and get people to want to read your story. If you really want to shake things up, use video. I can't stress to you enough that video is the most powerful way to share stories from the street. When you tell

someone's story in a presentation, it can have some impact; if your customer is allowed to tell *their own story* via video, then you've captured the real world, allowing people inside your company to share some of this inspirational magic. Keep it real.

Case Study: Fila

A few years ago, I was asked to participate in a design meeting for Fila Footwear. Fila had just moved their offices to Boulder and had hired a new staff to run their outdoor business. There was a great deal of tension, because the senior staff from the U.S. headquarters and the CEO and chairman from Italy would be in the new offices, meeting the new staff, for the first time. A couple of designers would show their designs for the following season.

The first designer, Kevin, brought out some very nice sketches of concepts. Kevin had been designing footwear for a few years and wanted to jump right into showing his ideas to the chairman and the others from out of town. The designs were well received, but there didn't seem to be a dialogue around them.

Next up was Steve McDonald. Steve had been designing footwear for a decade by then. Not only is Steve a great designer, but he is also an amazing storyteller. Steve took the stage in front of the small crowd and then passed out little handmade books. Before sharing the design work, he said, he wanted everyone to understand exactly how he had arrived at these particular designs. Steve had made a number of books to walk the audience through what he'd used for inspiration. As Steve took us through the books, he told stories about the poem or saying on each page and why it had inspired him. Next, Steve talked about the photographs in the book. Some photos contained patterns, textures, and colors that inspired him. They included pictures of peculiar lichen he'd found on a rock on a climbing trip and the sand at sunset that he'd observed on an afternoon hike. He also talked about sports and places that inspired him. The audience was clearly excited by this journey of exploration. The books evoked images in their own minds that allowed them to be transported to places they themselves had climbed or hiked.

Next, Steve's books told the story of the materials, which came from the inspirations he had just shared, that would be used in his designs. The books had samples of the materials, giving the audience the ability to participate in the story. We could all feel and examine the materials firsthand. Finally, Steve showed his sketches. The audience was absolutely engaged as Steve discussed the designs in the immediate context of the books. His shoe designs elegantly followed through on the inspirational stories that he had shared. It felt as if the shoes had actually been discovered within the pages of the book.

The most fascinating thing about Steve's presentation was that it took no longer than Kevin's. At the end of the meeting, the senior staff from New York and Europe agreed to produce all of Steve's designs and only a couple of Kevin's. Corporately, it was the right call. Steve's inspiration was later carried into the marketing, to complete the storytelling that Steve had begun with his journeys. Because of Steve's thoughtful designs and the extension of the storytelling in the marketing, consumers intimately understood the designs, which became very successful. At the core of this success was Steve's ability to share his story with the Fila team, giving them the ability to feel as though they helped co-create the shoes.

WHAT THIS MEANS TO YOU

Finding the center of gravity is one of the most critical issues for any company's adaptation and survival in the face of an increasingly dissonant environment. Such an environment demands participants who seek efficiency in using intelligence gathered from the marketplace and its creative use in driving innovation forward.

To catalyze organizational change around the center of gravity in the marketplace, you must help your company communicate the results of your bottom-up strategy. Telling stories can facilitate creating an environment where the customer's voice is honored and involved.

Stories are efficient because they take less mental energy to understand than data, provided they are simple, accessible, and in the immediate context of the audience. When a story does its job well, listeners can imagine the implications of elaborating the same inspiration in other contexts, making the experience more powerful and intimate. In this way, inspiration that is based on a deep center of gravity can spread throughout a company.

The ultimate goal of a bottom-up strategy is to catalyze organizational change around the center of gravity in the marketplace. Stories play an important role in making this happen.

Companies must share stories that inspire action and embody those stories with congruency and authenticity. To be successful, stories need to have context, simplicity, interest, trust, meaning, connectedness, magic, and relevance for their audience. When a storyteller can weave these qualities into a story and allow the story itself to be the star, then the story will have maximum impact. By acting as a conduit between the intelligence from the streets and the rest of the company, a storyteller can successfully impart information that will transform a company in profound ways.

As you tell the story, try to make it as powerful as possible by keeping the audience fully engaged—solicit questions, pause now and then to breathe, and take ownership of the story. Tell the story in an informal, appropriate setting that encourages relaxation for yourself and your audience. And, before you set foot on the stage, remember to practice, practice, and practice again—either in front of a mirror or a colleague. The more you tell the story, the more it becomes your own.

To build your presentation in a way that encourages the audience's participation, consider using video or photography, create mental space, allow for co-creation, and be provocative.

To illustrate all of the mechanics I've talked about in this chapter, I've prepared a story that can be found on our Web site. Check it out (http://www.be yond-the-brand.com). Use it. Play with it. Make it your own. Inspire your team to tell more stories.

12

CASE STUDY
Millennials Explored©

I don't care what other people think of me.
But I do care about who they are.
Their opinion is their opinion. Mine is mine.
That's them. This is me. You have to respect that.
MEGAN, AGE 15

This chapter is a case study of a syndicated project my company, Radar Communications, completed in the fall of 2003. It offers a demonstration of the practical application of the ideas and concepts presented throughout this book and how they can be applied in the real world. The tools discussed in previous chapters should make more sense when viewed in this context. I hope that the key voices in this project will serve as a source of inspiration for you and your business.

THE PROJECT: UNCOVERING
THE MYSTERY OF YOUTH

As generations of parents can attest, teenagers have always been hard to figure out. But for today's brands, the youth market represents a greater challenge than ever. They have never been more fickle, better educated, or harder to understand and reach. Yet today's youth aged 11 to 21, known collectively as the Millennials, represent a significant, valuable segment of the buying population, and they are critical to the success and staying power of your brand. The challenge is figuring out how best to meet their needs.

Before you can meet the needs of any group, you must first understand the attitudes, perceptions, and motivations that shape their world. In other words, you have to get to know them to understand what they want, from the bottom-up, before you can co-create with them.

The Millennials are a key trendsetting group with disposable income that is targeted directly at fast-moving consumable goods. Numbering more than 44 million, they represent roughly 16 percent of the United States's population.

Radar's goal with Millennials Explored was to take a raw, illuminating look into youth culture. Using intimate dialogue and thought-provoking exercises, it engaged young people's key voices from around the country in an open conversation of what it means to be a teenager today. Through the words, images, thoughts, and feelings of these teenagers, Millennials Explored takes you into their lives and shows you the most compelling ways to connect with them. It provides insights into the youth culture and will stimulate storytelling within your organization, so that you can turn this newfound inspiration into meaningful, successful innovation.

THE BOTTOM-UP STRATEGY

Radar Communications engaged 27 trend-translating young people ranging in age from 11 to 21 to investigate their values, beliefs, attitudes, and behaviors. We explored in detail who these Millennials are in terms of what matters to them, how they express who they are, and what influences them—how, when, in what manner, and why. They were an equal mix of males and females and represented several races. These *reporters* (our term for participants involved in any Radar project) responded to a series of questions and creative exercises that were designed to elicit the meaning behind their thoughts and actions. This was followed with a videotaped, anthrojournalistic, in-home study in which these themes were explored in greater depth. Our reporters' job was to explore all aspects of their world, including perceptions of life now, thoughts on the future, opinions on products and services that affect their lives, and preferences in communication and media.

The methodology behind the Millennials Explored project consisted of two distinct parts: reporting and sharing the story. Within these two stages, we followed the seven steps discussed in Chapters 5 through 11. By reviewing the practical application of these tools in the context of an actual project, you will gain a better understanding of the methodology and a solid foundation upon which to build your company's internal strategies.

REPORTING

Radar first identified the key voices of the Millennials, then transformed them into reporters by arming them with journals, cameras, and workbooks. We then opened a personal and informative dialogue with these reporters, as discussed in Chapter 6, "Get the Story." For this project, our young reporters delivered inspiration through a series of questions and creative exercises and captured opinions from their communities through peer interviews.

Inspiration

This in-depth exploration of the youth market reveals critical insights into everything from favored brands to purchasing habits to media preferences. Key areas of exploration included:

Who They Are

- Attitudes (life, love, present, future)
- Trends (lifestyle, fashion, pastimes, what's being talked about)

- Values (environment, relationships, money, mentors)
- Beliefs (politics, spirituality, ethics)

What They Want (Key Categories)

- Food (fast food, snacks, candy)
- Drinks (spirits, soft drinks, water, energy drinks)
- Technology (wireless devices, Internet, hardware, software, etc.)
- Entertainment (music, movies, games, hot spots)
- Sports (action, outdoors, organized)
- Fashion (shoes, clothes, home, accessories, retail)
- Transportation (cars, bikes, scooters)
- Body (health, hygiene, cosmetics/treatments, tattoos/piercings)

Because of the immense amount of information the reporters have shared for this syndicated project, I have covered only selected sections in this chapter. You can find more information about this project at our Web site (http://www.beyond-the-brand.com).

Step One: Focus on Key Voices

Before we fully developed a plan to get the story and created the questions and exercises that would give us a better opportunity to listen, the first step in the Millennials Explored project was to identify the key voices of the community. At Radar, we focus our efforts on connecting with the 13.5 percent of the market who are trend translators. We have an internal team of recruiters whose primary job is to find and create a dialogue with our trend-translating reporters.

Who are these translators? They are opinion leaders and are always a little slower to make a decision about the acceptance of an idea or product than trendsetters, because they want to make a decision that is good, right, and efficient. Within the group of translators, we worked to find Millennial reporters who were good communicators and were interested in acting as tour guides within their cultures.

One of the most important things to do when searching for key voices is to network with people and start asking them which of their peers influence them. Here are some specifics about the key voices involved in this particular project.

Total number of reporters	27
Age	11 to 21 (evenly distributed)
Male/Female	50/50
Education	Completed up to current age
Household income	Middle to upper middle class
Ethnic distribution	50% white/50% other
Psychographic criteria	Culturally and socially connected. They are avid shoppers with an interest in food, drinks, technology, entertainment, sports, fashion, transportation, and health/body.
Geographic distribution	Chicago, Minneapolis, San Francisco, Washington D.C., Detroit, Denver, Los Angeles, Seattle, Atlanta, Philadelphia, Dallas, Miami, Boston, Phoenix, New York City

Step Two: Get the Story

The key to getting the stories from Millennials was to get deep enough to understand the underlying assumptions of their lives. This project was about understanding the context and meaning behind their outward actions and behaviors. Our team had to spend a great deal of time with our reporters in the very real and active context of their lives, not in a focus group facility. We invested many hours with each reporter to engage in real, two-way conversations. When we worked with these reporters to get their stories, we used the Radar funnel as a framework to ensure that we always got the whole story. The steps of the process included exploring the following topics:

- *Cultural context.* We spent time in their homes, offices, dorm rooms, coffee shops, restaurants, and all of the other places where they spend time.
- *Value segments.* We listened a great deal as our reporters talked about what they value and how those values were formed. We wanted to know how their parents and their peers influenced them. We also spent time observing their actions to see if they were consistent with what they said they valued. If not, we'd explore deeper.
- *Emotional drivers.* We wanted to know what made them happy and what frustrated them. We had them take us on tours of those things, including shopping, getting stuck in traffic, etc.
- *Functional usage.* We explored how they perceived and used the products they own. For instance, no teen would be caught without their cell phone. We wanted them not only to talk about their phones but also show us what they specifically like and dislike about their phones.

By following these internal steps in the storytelling process, we were able to inform the true goal of the funnel: making meaning. By deeply exploring and understanding each step along the way, we were confident that we would be able to understand the center of gravity of the Millennials market.

Step Three: Listen

The third step in a bottom-up strategy is about listening to the *vox populi* or, in this case, the *"vox Millenni."* It is paramount to let people tell their stories without any screens or interruptions. Remember that 70 percent of human communication is nonverbal. That meant that we had to listen with our eyes and engage our other senses when we went to get the Millennials' stories. It also meant that we had to listen with an open mind, understanding how our individual lenses, colored by our own youth, changed the way we saw our reporters' worlds.

The ultimate goal was to get in sync with them and experience their worlds by watching, thinking, learning, and actively participating in a dialogue. Part of developing a dialogue is asking the right questions that offer the foundation for insightful and inspirational answers. Here is a sample of some of the questions and creative assignments we used to develop this dialogue.

- List three things, people, places, or events that you value most. Why do you value them? What do they bring to your life?
- What do you use to express who you are? Clothes? Your body? Your mode of transportation? Technology?
- What do your clothes say about you? What's your style? Do you care? Where do you like to shop?
- What do you do for entertainment? What's important—music, movies, games? Something else?
- What types of technology do you use—computer, games, the Internet, cell phone, instant messaging, others?
- What kinds of foods and drinks do you like (fast, healthy, candy, soft drinks, water . . .)? What influences your food and drink choices?
- What's your main type of transportation? How important is your transportation to you? What would you change if you could?

Some of the creative assignments included:

- Take photos of one full day of your life. Show us where you went, who you went with, what you did, etc.
- Create a collage that shows us your take on life. What matters? Imagine your life could be exactly the way you want it to be—what would it look like?

- Find three examples of brands or things that speak to you or that you find really lame.

Step Four: Find Inspiration

After identifying the key Millennial voices in our marketplace and getting their stories in their own words, our next step was to tune into their inspiration. We needed to use our peripheral vision, not only looking to the key voices themselves for inspiration but also to their friends, peers, and environments. We needed to go beyond the key voices we identified and become a part of their network. By becoming an active part of their social network, we found much richer inspiration.

One of the critical elements in achieving this step is assigning people to the project who have a passion for the subject or the segment. In this case, two Radar team members, Katrina and Berto, led the charge. There is, however, one important caveat—you must always be aware of your own lens.

Step Five: Hone Your Intuition

One of the critical talents we utilized in exploring our reporters' worlds was our team's intuition and sense of wonder. This is fundamental when developing any bottom-up strategy. When you are out exploring the world with your customers, you have to be able to think on your feet—actively call upon your intuition. As we traveled along the Millennials Explored journey, we were always contrasting what we saw with what our reporters and their peers were saying, always looking for opportunities to deepen those conversations. Using your intuition means being creative and always peering over the border of knowledge. We were constantly looking for opportunities to assemble seemingly unrelated conversations and experiences into a new judgment about an untried solution.

Step Six: Find the Center of Gravity

While working on the Millennials Explored project was fun and insightful, it would have had no enduring value if we couldn't make meaning from the input. The goal of the project was to translate the meaning we found into understanding the center of gravity of the Millennials' community. The foundation of this process is dialogue. This specific dialogue happened among our internal team about what we learned from the intelligence we gathered and the experiences we had. To get the most out of our Millennials Explored journey, we wanted to make sure that internal alignment formed around shared meaning.

While some of the findings discussed below might seem obvious—for example, Millennials are exceedingly busy and feel stressed—think about the implications for your company. I hope you can use some of these findings to guide you toward your own center of gravity in the Millennials' community.

Step Seven: Tell the Story

One of the most gratifying parts of working at Radar is the act of telling stories. Because most of us are journalists by background, it's what we love to do. But the fact is, stories are more efficient than other kinds of presentations because they take less mental energy to understand. We tried to illuminate the Millennials' stories by focusing on making them simple, accessible, and in the context of the audience: busy marketing executives. Our strategy in telling these stories was to make the inspiration we found on the streets through our reporters more personal and powerful. We tried to create stories that our audience would want to retell. Ultimately, we hoped that the Millennials Explored story would help our clients to catalyze organizational change around the center of gravity of the Millennials' community.

SHARING THE STORY

Following is a portion of the actual text from the project. It includes a look at one of the three sections, "Self-Expression." I have also included some inspirational quotes, photos, and video captures in the next few pages. However, it is hard to tell the story completely in the context of this book. If you'd like to explore the Millennials Explored project further, please visit http://www.beyond-the-brand.com. On the Web site, you can read the stories, view the photos and videos, and, I hope, find inspiration that will inform your marketing and product development efforts.

The Bonds of the Millennial Generation—How True to Oneself Can One Be?

The Millennial Generation is coming of age in a unique time. The modes of media have multiplied. Links around the globe are as prevalent as those down the street. Influences and ideas, cultures and connections all are fluid, omnipresent, and ever changing, traveling at the speed of data on the Internet.

The Millennials represent the first generation to grow up assuming that this is the way the world operates. As such, they've developed characteristics that set them apart from previous generations. The years that span from preteens to early adulthood have always been a stage of exploration and curiosity; now, the Millennials must find ways to navigate the seemingly infinite sources of information and possibility. Both opportunities and challenges are vast for the Millennials. They know this and have responded with a depth and maturity perhaps never before seen at such a young age.

What sets the Millennials apart? Six universal truths can be found that cut across all ages of the group.

FIGURE 12.1 *Millennial Self-Expression*

To see the video, go to http://www.beyond-the-brand.com/videos/true.

1. **Millennials have a powerful and confident sense of self.** Millennials are not plagued with self-doubt in the manner traditionally associated with the teen years. Millennials determine who they are at an early age and have a resilient and strong sense of individuality. While they are exploring how to express this self, they are not at all conflicted about whether they should be true to themselves, nor do they doubt whether they are inherently good and valued.

While previous generations might have wavered in the face of peer pressure, the Millennials strive calmly and confidently to stare down detractors. It's not nirvana, though: Millennials still voice the traditional teen complaints of feeling that their parents do not understand or trust them, and poor crossgeneration communication ensues. Additionally, they believe their parents are naive about aspects of their lives—sex, for example—and don't truly understand what they as individuals are about.

All the reporters agree with the statement: "I have the freedom to determine what happens to me, today and in my future." The overwhelming majority of reporters disagree with the statement: "My friends influence how I think and behave more than anyone else." Instead they listen first to themselves, second to their friends, and then to their family.

"Who I am is very important to me. I may be 15 and typically would be confused and insecure. But I'm blessed with feeling who I am inside and being happy with myself," reports Megan, age 15.

2. Millennials value people and wholesome concepts above money and material things. Spirituality, family, education—these values are stated over and over again by the Millennials. When asked what is important in their lives, a tiny minority of reporters focuses on the trivial (clothes, CDs, coffee) or the rebellious (being different, standing apart). In fact, the shock value placed on being radical by previous generations is all but absent from this one. Instead, they appreciate their parents, and they value the support they get from family.

While they recognize the importance of succeeding in work, the Millennials say their primary goal is not to earn vast amounts of money. They shun an overwhelming attachment to material things, in this regard harking back to generations of the 1960s and 1970s and contrasting with more recent generations' goals. God and religion play a quiet but strong role in the lives of many Millennials. These beliefs are highly personal and inform many of their actions.

"I value my family because they understand and know me better than anyone. I am much more comfortable around them than anywhere else. I value my religion because I know my purpose in life from my religion," reports Taurean, age 16.

3. Millennials reflect on their actions and are aware of consequences to others. Not only do Millennials have a strong sense of self, they are able to see and place themselves in relation to the world around them. Not appearing as insular or self-centered as previous generations at this age, the Millennials engage in reflection on their own actions. Likewise, they are keenly sensitive to whether the actions of other people are appropriate or not. They sometimes believe—and just might be right—that they show greater maturity than their elders—and at times practically cry out for nothing less than common decency. They are highly aware of pain and suffering, often seemingly based on a reaction to a personal experience (divorce or bullying, for example). They express the desire to build a life that contains real meaning through helping others—a traditional young person's idealism, to a certain degree, but exhibiting less naïveté and more specifics and hard-boiled realism than previous, less savvy generations.

"I have lived in the same neighborhood all my life, and I still get funny looks when I wave at my neighbors. People don't know how to be nice anymore," reports Sara, age 14.

4. Millennials are exceedingly busy and feel stressed. Millennials of all ages feel pressured. They are pressed for time and worry about achievement. Because they don't want to cut anything out of their lives, little—or no—down time exists. In fact, multitasking is the norm: doing homework, being online, and watching TV at the same time. (The Millennials lump entertainment into their set of "must-dos," which adds to the sense of being busy.) The stress cuts across all age groups; the sources of worry just compound as they grow older. Young Millennials—roughly ages 11 to 14—count school, grades, sports, and friends as sources of time and achievement pressure. Mid-Millennials—roughly 15 to 17 years of age—add the worry of relationships and getting into college. Older Millennials, who are considered to be young adults at 18 to 21, compound these worries with getting a good job and making money.

All groups worry about family and health, taking on emotional responsibility for these issues at an early age. Talk to the Millennials, and you'd think by the perceived weight on their shoulders that they're much older than they are. Part of the problem is the recognition of long-term consequences: The grade you get in high school can affect where you go to college, which in turn will determine the job you eventually get. This equation is constantly present in the minds of Millennials, adding to their sense of stress.

"I stress out due to tests, papers, boys, friends, money or lack thereof, and probably more than I can think of right now. When two or more of these triggers occur at once, I get absolutely crazy," reports Susan, age 21.

5. Millennials believe striving for achievements is essential. Far from slacking off in school and taking their futures for granted, Millennials develop an early awareness of the importance of setting goals, developing discipline, and striving to do their best. They agree that to push oneself is essential. They're far from perfect—but they do demonstrate an ability to admit when they are becoming lazy and work toward taking personal responsibility. Their heroes are people who have done all these things and succeeded (perhaps against the odds) such as parents, close friends, or partners as opposed to people for whom good things came easily.

"I will only achieve if I push myself—that's absolutely true. In my opinion, achieving involves striving beyond one's status and abilities. It involves hard work and desire and often involves doing things you don't want to do to achieve your goals. To achieve your dreams, you have to motivate yourself. I know I have to work hard to get what I want, because there's a good chance somebody else is working just as hard as I am, and I can't be unprepared to meet a challenge," reports Nicholas, age 17.

6. Millennials view the world as interconnected and see the importance of being aware. Millennials recognize that the world is changing rapidly, fairly spinning around them. Because they can tune into many media sources, they have no shortage of avenues by which to stay informed, try out opinions, and find like-minded peers.

As they grow older, their connection to the world around them becomes increasingly political in nature. While about half the youngsters show some interest in current events, by the late teens, virtually all the Millennials believe it's their responsibility to be informed and aware. Likewise, their sense of justice—present from an early age—expands from the personal to a grander scale. Comments about personal behavior and fairness evolve into statements about war and social justice as the Millennials increase in age. They are realistic—they say its human nature to wage war, for example—but they still hope for a better way of handling conflict.

"Yes 'freedom and liberty' *are* 'worth fighting for.' But war is war. Really the same thing as 'fighting for.' People died. It makes me want to throw up. I'm one of those people who just wish for real world peace, but I know it'll never happen. And I hate it," reports Megan, age 15.

The universal bonds that Millennials share differentiate them from previous generations. They have been forced to grow up fast. They are wise beyond their years. An evolution of development and maturity is at work—many of these individuals have been exposed to complex adult concepts on a regular basis. Divorce, job loss, and war have made them evaluate the meaning of their lives at an early age. Some are reacting to what they see as their parents' misadventures down paths of self-centeredness, material gain, and disposable relationships. Others are girding themselves for what they see as tough times in a less stable economy and a world without borders that no longer feels insular and safe. They express the desire and objective to achieve a well-rounded life: a happy marriage, strong bonds with their own children, and a job that holds meaning.

The Millennials are, for the most part, wholesome, well rounded, and relatively well behaved. These are people you'd want to know. People you'd want to talk to. People with something interesting to say. How to be a rebel is no longer the question for this age group. Rather, they are concerned with how to be true to oneself and individualize within the acceptable norms of one's community of family and friends. In fact, because the very concept of "extreme" has become mainstream and mundane, the new concept of "extreme" is rather, How true to oneself can one be? For the Millennials, that is radical. That is pushing boundaries.

Self-Expression

A solid sense of self and strong belief in self-determination means that for Millennials, self-expression takes on a key role. Whereas previous generations used self-expression to set themselves apart, this generation sees self-expression as a way to be true to themselves. The challenge is how to express one's individuality while also fitting into societal norms.

Forms of self-expression vary by the life phases of the Millennials, representing a continuum of development as they age. The youngest Millennials—roughly ages 11 to 14—are inherently conservative, albeit curious. They are increasingly aware but are allowed the least amount of freedom to explore. Middle Millennials—roughly 15 to 17—are still living at home and finishing high school but are allowed increasing freedom to experiment. These teens explore with enthusiasm and openness. Because of this, lack of clarity is at its peak, but the powerful sense of self is still evident. They give off the sense that "I am in control," and "I cannot be fooled." By the time Millennials are considered young adults—18 to 21 years of age—and able to leave home, they have a clearer definition of self and focus less on exploration and more on finding the most effective ways to communicate their individuality.

Modes of Self-Expression

1. **Physical appearance.** The Millennials are very conscious of their bodies and, thus, feel that their physical appearance is a form of self-expression. While they recognize that some aspects of one's appearance are beyond their control, they are also expert at manipulating what they have to present themselves in a particular manner.

Most are hyperaware of cleanliness and general maintenance of one's body, because much of this is still new: shaving, acne control, hair styling. A "bad body day" means a bad day overall. For older Millennials particularly, diet and exercise are already largely a means to an end; good nutrition and working out are important to looking and feeling better.

Physical appearance is also considered by the Millennials for what it does not represent: Some reporters point out that they use their appearance to show that they are not bogged down by such trivial concerns as fashion or hair.

FIGURE 12.2 *Apparel as Self-Expression*

To see the video, go to http://www.beyond-the-brand.com/videos/selfexp.

"The value that I place on taking care of my body is keeping it healthy. I feel very well pleased about my body. I take care of myself by keeping fit and healthy," reports Sa Myra, age 13.

2. Apparel. Millennials look to apparel to express who they are—it's the most readily accessible and affordable option for self-expression. Yet a tension exists between being in style and not following the herd. For example, at age 11, Sam already makes a point of claiming, "I'm the one who starts styles." Millennials of all ages seek to put their own spin on fashions, to show their creative flair. Many Millennials point out that they wear what they like, even if their friends do not approve. There is a certain in-your-face element of such choice: not so much a fashion statement as a statement of security in one's own choices.

FIGURE 12.3 *Technology as Self-Expression*

To see the video, go to http://www.beyond-the-brand.com/videos/tech.

Millennials shop the gamut of stores: from thrift and vintage to specialty. Popular choices include Gap, Abercrombie & Fitch, Old Navy, Diesel, Target, and Pacific Sunwear. Their apparel choice on any particular day tends to reflect their mood and how they are feeling about themselves. They say that comfort is a priority, and they want to avoid looking trashy at all costs.

"I look for uniqueness when shopping. I don't care about the cost but, rather, the value. If I can find an awesome shirt that I'll wear copiously at a thrift store for a bad-ass price, then my life is complete for that day," reports Susan, age 21.

3. Room or personal space. A room of one's own—or apartment, for the older Millennials—is a personal haven. It offers privacy and a physical place to be oneself fully. Because the room tends to contain all the other means of self-expression, it's taken for granted to a certain degree. Some Millennials take great care in decorating their rooms to express themselves, while others passively let it become the dumping ground of everything else: clothes, computer, games, and music. Either way, all agree that it accurately reflects who they are.

"My room is a comfort zone, and I mold it according to my likes and inclinations," reports Nicholas, age 17.

4. Technology. Millennials of all ages are completely at ease with technologies that only a generation ago did not even exist. They assume and expect access to a variety of gadgets that their own parents coveted from afar only a decade ago. As quickly as technology changes and new devices are brought out, Millennials fully expect them to be a part of their lives and fit them into their modes of connection.

While they wouldn't want it any other way, this rapidly changing technology does add to their sense of being busy and stress, as they must stay on top of the latest changes to remain connected with their community of friends. Computers and Internet access are the norm and a must-have for succeeding in school, communicating with e-mail, and pursuing interests. They are also a cure for boredom, used as means of entertainment through music, Web pages, and instant messaging. To a certain degree, computers are so omnipresent that they've become "so what" by high school—the real excitement is in their cell phone.

Cell phones are considered an absolute necessity for those who have them (the vast majority) and a conspicuous absence for the few who do not. Phones are used not just for simple communication but also for entertainment with instant messaging, and they are a security blanket confirming one's popularity and connection with others. For the older teens, no phone can literally mean no friends—the phone is their social organizational tool. The phone becomes an extension of oneself, and as such it evokes particular passion and emotion.

"I just love technology for some reason, and I need to keep constantly updated. I have practically every gadget out there, and if something new comes out, chances are I will get that too," reports Matt, age 20.

"I use the Internet for e-mail, to update my live journal, and to keep track of music news. I use a cell phone to contact other people and to place food orders while I'm driving. My phone also stores important phone numbers, and I can get text messages. I also use instant messenger to communicate with my out-of-town friends and to send pictures and music files," reports Beth, age 18.

Beth lists the Internet as the thing she values most. Living in Encinitas, California, she manages a band and interns at a radio station and hopes to work in radio or magazines in the future. Technology—particularly the Internet and her cell phone—is essential to her everyday life.

5. Entertainment.   All ages use entertainment as a form of self-exploration and a way to connect with friends. As Millennials mature, they become more articulate and discerning about the specifics of what they enjoy, seeking out niches rather than going with whatever is currently popular. For all ages, however, there are "must-sees" and "must-haves." This phenomenon perpetuates the importance of remaining connected on all levels—they don't want to miss the next big thing, be it music, a movie, or television.

Entertainment becomes blurred with technology in this regard, which is necessary to remain cutting edge. The computer is an essential venue to information, downloads, and games, and game editions constantly must be upgraded.

Universal forms of entertainment are music and movies. Music is used to set a tone and mood. Younger Millennials also look to the mall, friends' homes, and cell phones as additional forms of entertainment. To that set, the mid-Millennials add videogames, and the older Millennials enjoy going out to restaurants and clubs with friends.

"I *love* movies and try to watch as many as humanly possible. Music I already mentioned, and I am always listening to something. The top of my must-have list right now is a full 5.1 surround-sound system. This way you don't just watch the movies, you experience them, because you have theater sound," reports Matt, age 20.

WHAT THIS MEANS TO YOU

What are some implications that might affect your business? Here are a few to think about.

It's a mistake to treat the Millennials as children. They have experienced pain and insight that have led to their current awareness of self—despite their age, they are not simplistic or childish in nature. The challenge is to be relevant either as a form of self-expression or a tool that's an essential and seamless part of self-expression. Opportunity is vast, as the Millennials are fearless and actively looking to put their identities on the line and out to the world.

The older Millennials get, the more opinionated they become about what they relate to or reject when it comes to advertising. They grow increasingly articulate about why something is a turn-off. Savvy at detecting patronization, they react strongly against it. A bad ad is not just ignored but incites anger and feelings of betrayal.

There's opportunity in reducing the Millennials' stress and offering escapes and solutions that fit their lives. But they don't really want to slow their pace too much. The real question is: Are you being flexible enough to fit into the multitasking world of the Millennials? Can they enjoy your company while talking on the phone, watching TV, and surfing the Net? Are you available on more than one level, and taking advantage of crossmedia opportunities?

I hope you've enjoyed this journey "beyond the brand." I have enjoyed sharing with you some of the inspiring stories I've heard and some of the tools that have proven to work so successfully for Radar's clients.

The key to getting beyond the brand and co-creating with your customers, from the bottom up, is to start with one step. Just like those individuals in Rilke's prose who have gone beyond the comfort of their corner of the room, near the window, we all must begin intuitively to feel out the shapes in the darkness.

Jim Jannard, the chairman and CEO of Oakley, has been willing to reach out and do just that. Over the years, he has become an expert at allowing his intuition to drive him into an exploration of the deep recesses of creativity and customer connection. He has learned to think unconventionally and also to allow radical change into this thinking process. Jannard started Oakley by manufacturing grips for motocross motorcycle handlebars. Soon after, he invented the category of sports glasses by being deeply connected to the athletes who used them, and he has instilled a design-driven philosophy that makes seeking out new technology paramount. This connection has driven Oakley's business. Today, Oakley has become one of the most recognizable global sports brands.

Along the way, Jannard and the Oakley team continued to stay close to their customers by using, among other things, the grassroots sports marketing efforts the company had used from the very beginning. Success can, however, cause unforeseen threats. Last year, Jannard's son, Jamin, started working for the company and immediately noticed that, as the company had become bigger and more successful, the Oakley brand had grown more mature and less cool. Most importantly, they both recognized that the brand had strayed from its core customer. While it was connected to their 35- to 50-year-old, upper-middle income customers, Jamin told his dad that the company had gotten out of touch with the real core of their market, the 16- to 25-year-olds. Like so many mature brands, Oakley had stopped communicating with its original customer.

Jannard intuitively understood Jamin and has put in place a strategy to rediscover Oakley's roots and reconnect with a vital part of the market. Today, Jamin and Scott Bowers—vice president of Marketing Worldwide, a 16-year veteran of the company and, as Scott calls himself, one of the gatekeepers—are taking the company back to the core by getting out, listening to the right customers, and beginning to co-create with them from the bottom-up. By instinctively understanding their customers' desires and needs, Oakley can deliver breakaway products that establish the next trend.

A challenge for every successful growing company is the natural tendency to take fewer risks and make "safe" decisions. Often, early "gatekeepers," who were by nature risk takers, become stifled by the growing organization. They leave to be replaced by "experts" who have little to no direct connection to the customer and are unable to make the same intuitive risks that helped create the success in the first place.

Oakley has started the reconnection process by designing products for the right market, the opinion-leading 16- to 25-year-old. The company understands that, if they capture the imagination of their core customers, the masses will soon follow. Oakley is beginning to recapture some of their brand mystique by co-creating with their core customers. The results have been reflected in increasing revenues, but most importantly, the reconnection with their customer will give the brand a renewed longevity.

Getting beyond the brand means reinventing your processes and rediscovering what made your company great. As the example of Oakley suggests, it also means leadership and risk taking.

A lot of interesting people are finding incredibly wonderful ways to co-create with their customers and facilitate this bottom-up inspiration throughout their organizations. If you've heard any good stories that you'd like to share with others, feel free to join the discussion at http://www.beyond-the-brand.com. I look forward to learning from you.

Preface

1. Judith Martin, retrieved 18 February 2004 from http://www.quo tationspage.com/quotes/Judith_Martin/.

2. *Webster's II New Riverside Dictionary* (Boston, MA: Houghton Mif-flin Company, 1984).

3. John Philip Jones, *What's in a Name? Advertising and the Concept of Brands* (Lexington, MA: Lexington Books, 1986).

4. Mark Parker, in conversations with the author 1998–2004.

5. Steve Lohr, "Big Blue's Big Bet: Less Tech, More Touch," *New York Times,* 25 January 2004.

6. Lester Thurow, "Help Wanted: A Chief Knowledge Officer," *Fast Company,* January 2004, 91–92.

7. Marie Ranier Rilke, from *The Enlightened Mind* by Stephen Mitchell (New York: Perennial, 1993).

Chapter One

1. Stephen Jay Gould, retrieved 18 March 2004 from http://www .brainyquote.com/quotes/quotes/s/stephenjay141350.html.

2. "Who's Wearing the Trousers?" *Economist Magazine,* 8 September 2003, 50–64.

3. Kalle Lasn, *Culture Jam: The Uncooling of America* (New York, NY: Eagle Brook, 1999); Thomas C. Frank, *The Conquest of Cool: Business Culture, Counterculture, and the Rise of Hip Consumerism* (Chicago, IL: University of Chicago Press, 1997); Eric Schlosser, *Fast Food Nation: The Dark Side of the All-American Meal* (Boston, MA: Houghton Mifflin, 2001).

4. Naomi Klein, *No Space, No Choice, No Jobs, No Logo: Taking Aim at the Brand Bullies* (New York, NY: Picador USA, 2000); Curtis Sittenfeld, "No-Brands-Land," *Fast Company,* September 2000, 240–248.

Disruptive technologies references:

- "A Thumbnail History of Disruptive Technologies," retrieved 12 October 2003 from http://www.businessweek.com.
- Clayton Christensen, *The Innovator's Dilemma: When New Technologies Cause Great Firms to Fail,* retrieved 10 October 2003 from http://www.computerworld.com, http://www.radioweblogs.com.
- Polly LaBarre, "The Industrialized Revolution," *Fast Company,* November 2003, 115–120.
- Joab Jackson, "Disruptive Technologies," retrieved 10 October 2003 from http://www.washingtontechnology.com/news.
- Ephraim Schwartz, "Defining Disruption," retrieved 10 October 2003 from http://www.infoworld.com.
- "Tyranny, Terror, and Technology," retrieved 12 October 2003 from http://www.ozzie.net/blog/stories/2002/09/10/tyrannyTerrorAndTechnology.html.

5. George Santayana, retrieved February 2004 from http://www.worldofquotes.com/Authors/George_Santayana/

6. John Markoff, "Low-Cost Supercomputer Put Together from 1,100 PCs," *New York Times,* 22 October 2003.

7. Wal-Mart case study references:

- Anthony Bianco and Wendy Zellner, "Is Wal-Mart Too Powerful?" retrieved 13 October 2003 from http://www.businessweek.com.
- Matthew Grimm, "Wal-Mart Uber Alles," retrieved 13 October 2003 from http://www.demographics.com.
- Charles Fishman, "The Wal-Mart You Don't Know," *Fast Company,* December 2003, 68.
- Tim Weiner, "Wal-Mart Invades, and Mexico Gladly Surrenders," *New York Times,* 6 December 2003, retrieved from http://www.nyt.com.

Private label references:

- Sally Beatty, "At Levi Strauss, Trouble Comes from All Angles," *Wall Street Journal,* retrieved 19 October 2003 from http://www.wsj.com.

- Matthew Boyle, "Brand Killers," *Fortune*, 11 August 2003, 89–100.
- Shelly Branch, "Going Private (Label)—Store Brands Go Way Upscale as Designer Items Lose Cachet," *Wall Street Journal*, 2003.
- Brian Grow and Robert Berner, "More Rough-and-Tumble for Lee and Wrangler," retrieved 13 October from http://www.businessweek.com.
- Philip B. Fitzell, "Private Labels: Store Brands & Generic Products," sponsored by *Private Label* magazine (Westport, CT: AVI Publishing Company, Inc., 1982), 27–60.
- John Stanley, "Brands versus Private Labels: Part 1: Which Is Winning?" retrieved 15 October 2003 from http://retailindustry.about.com/library/uc/02/uc_stanley2.htm.

8. Culture of fear references:

- Barry Glassner, *The Culture of Fear: Why Americans Fear the Wrong Things*, retrieved 29 September 2003 from http://www.bowlingforcolumbine.com/library/fear/index.php.
- Grant Jewell Rich, "Why Do We Often Fear the Wrong Things?" retrieved 29 September 2003 from http://www.csicop.org/si/2000-01/fear.html.

9. Chaos theory references:

- "Chaos Theory: A Brief Introduction," retrieved 21 October 2003 from http://www.imho.com/grae/chaos/chaos.html.
- Manus J. Donahue III, "An Introduction to Chaos Theory and Fractal Geometry," retrieved 21 October 2003 from http://www.duke.edu/~mjd/chaos/chaosp.html.
- Andrew Smith, "Three Scenarios for Applying Chaos Theory in Consumer Research," *Journal of Marketing Management*, 18 (2002): 517–531.
- Ian Stewart, *Does God Play Dice: The New Mathematics of Chaos*, 2nd ed. (Malden, MA: Blackwell Publishers, 2002).

10. Behavioral economics references:

- Colin F. Camerer, George Loewenstein, and Matthew Rabin, *Advances in Behavioral Economics* (Princeton, NJ: Princeton University Press, 2003).
- Stephen J. Dubner, "Calculating the Irrational in Economics," *New York Times*, 28 June 2003.

Chapter Two

1. David Ogilvy, *Confessions of an Advertising Man* (New York, NY: Atheneum, 1963); Douglas Rushkoff, *Coercion: Why We Listen to What "They" Say* (New York, NY: Riverhead, 1999), retrieved 20 September from http://www.media-culture.org.au; Dennis W. Rook, "Focus Groups Fail to Connect Theory, Current Practice," *Marketing News,* 15 September 2003, Volume 37, Issue 19, page 40; Paul F. Nunes and Frank V. Caspedes, "The Customer Has Escaped," *Harvard Business Review,* November 2003, 96–105; Jim Spaeth, "Lost Lessons of Brand Power," *Advertising Age,* 14 July 2003, 16; Douglas B. Holt, "Why Do Brands Cause Trouble? A Dialectical Theory of Consumer Culture and Branding," *Journal of Consumer Research* 29, no. 1 (2002): 1; Adam Morgan, *Eating the Big Fish: How Challenger Brands Can Compete against Brand Leaders,* 1st ed. (New York, NY: John Wiley & Sons, 1999).

2. Claude C. Hopkins, *Scientific Advertising* (Chicago, IL: Lord & Thomas Agency, 1923); Claude C. Hopkins, *My Life in Advertising* (New York, NY: Harper & Brothers, 1927).

3. David Ogilvy, *Ogilvy on Advertising* (New York, NY: Crown, 1983); Bill Carter, "Fall TV Season Is Mostly Underwhelming," *New York Times,* 31 October 2003.

4. Jonathan Nicholas, "Paradise in Plaid," *Portland Oregonian,* 15 October 2003; Debby Kennedy, "Oregon's Dreams Find Way into Branding Campaign," *Portland Business Journal,* 5 December 2003, retrieved 19 January 2003 from http://www.bizjournals.com/portland/stories/2003/12/08/editorial3.html.

5. Jim Rendon, "When Nations Need a Little Marketing," *New York Times,* 23 November 2003; Simon Anholt, *Brand New Justice: The Upside of Global Branding* (Oxford, England: Butterworth-Heinemann, 2003).

6. Peter Montoya, with Tim Vandehey, *The Brand Called You: The Ultimate Brand-Building and Business Development Handbook to Transform Anyone into an Indispensable Personal Brand* (Santa Ana, CA: Personal Branding Press, 2002); Tom Peters, "The Brand Called You," *Fast Company,* August/September, 1997, 83, retrieved 19 May 2003 from http://www.fastcompany.com/magazinc/10/brandyou.html; Randall Frost, "Me Incorporated: Your Own Magnetic Brand," retrieved 22 September 2003 from http://www.brandchannel.com.

7. Jon Gertner, "The Futile Pursuit of Happiness," *New York Times Magazine,* 7 September 2003, 42–47, 86, 90-91.

8. Michelle Krebs, "To Complete the Pregnancy Experience, Just Add Some Pickles and Ice Cream," *New York Times*, 28 September 2003.

9. Warren St. John, "Metrosexuals Come Out," *New York Times*, 22 June 2003.

10. Mark Simpson, "Meet the Metrosexual: He's Well Dressed, Narcissistic, and Bun-Obsessed. But Don't Call Him Gay," retrieved 22 July 2002 from http://www.salon.com/ent/feature/2002/07/22/metrosexual/; Mark Simpson, "Metro Daddy Speaks," *Salon.com*, retrieved 5 January 2004 from http://www.salon.com/ent/feature/2004/01/05/metrosexual_ii/index_np.html; Stephen Armstrong, "The Game of the Name," retrieved 13 October 2003 from http://www.guardianunlimited.com; Len Lewis, "What's in a Name?" retrieved 13 October 2003 from http://www.igorinternational.com.

11. Guy Trebay, "After Nice, A Return to Vice," *New York Times*, 8 June 2003; David Barboza, "If You Pitch It, They Will Eat: Barrage of Food Ads Takes Aim at Children," and "Pitching Foods to Children through Every Possible Outlet," *New York Times*, 3 August 2003.

12. *The Barnhart Concise Dictionary of Etymology*, 1st ed., ed. Robert K. Barnhart (New York, NY: HarperCollins Publishers, Inc., 1995).

13. Alvin Toffler, *The Third Wave* (New York, NY: Morrow, 1980).

14. Fashion industry case study references:

- Conrad De Aenlle, "Famous Brands Can Bring Benefit, or a Backlash," *New York Times*, 19 October 2003.
- Guy Trebay, "Is Fashion Still Cool?" and "On Global Runways, A Longing Look Back," *New York Times*, 14 September 2003.

Chapter Three

1. Mahatma Gandhi, retrieved 30 January 2004 from http://www.worldofquotes.com/author/Mahatma-Gandhi/1/.

2. "IPod's Dirty Little Secret," retrieved from http://www.ipodsdirtylittlesecret.com; Culture of copying and sharing references:

- Greg Allen, "When Fans of Pricey Video Art Can Get It Free," *New York Times*, 17 August 2003.
- Felicia R. Lee, "Are More People Cheating? Despite Ample Accounts of Dishonesty, a Moral Decline Is Hard to Calculate," *New York Times*, 4 October 2003.

- John Leland, "Beyond File Sharing, A Nation of Copiers," *New York Times,* 14 September 2003.
- Steve Lohr, "Fighting the Idea That All the Internet Is Free," and "In the Age of the Internet, Whatever Will Be Will Be Free," *New York Times,* 9 September 2003.

3. Gary Rivlin, "Leader of the Free World," *Wired,* retrieved 31 October 2003 from http://www.wired.com/wired/archive/11.11/linus_pr .html.

4. Music industry case study sources:

- Amy Harmon and John Schwartz, "Despite Suits, Music File Sharers Shrug Off Guilt and Keep Sharing," *New York Times,* 22 September 2003.
- Nielsen/Netratings statistics, retrieved from http://www.niel sen-netratings.com/.
- David D. Kirkpatrick, "CD Price Cuts Could Mean New Artists Will Suffer," *New York Times,* 22 September 2003.
- Lisa Napoli, "Think Debate on Music Property Rights Began with Napster? Hardly," *New York Times,* 22 September 2003.
- Chris Nelson, "Fighting Song Piracy the Willie Wonka Way," and "Trying to Sell CDs by Adding Extras, *New York Times,* 6 October 2003.
- Chris Riemenschneider, "Live CDs and a Fans-First Approach Keep Pearl Jam as Relevant as Ever," retrieved 18 September 2003 from http://www.startribune.com.
- Neil Strauss, "File-Sharing Battle Leaves Musicians Caught in Middle," retrieved 16 September 2003 from http://www.ny times.com.
- Neil Strauss, "Executives Can See Problems Beyond File Sharing," *New York Times,* 9 September 2003.

5. Jeff Howe, "Big Champagne Is Watching You," *Wired,* October 2003, 138–141;

Power of reputation sources:

- Virginia Postrel, "For Those Who Live by Buzz, It's Important to Know Who's Doing the Talking," *New York Times,* 9 October 2003.
- Nancy K. Austin, "Buzz: In Search of the Most Elusive in All of Marketing," *Inc.,* May 1998, 44–50.
- Nancy K. Austin, "The Buzz Factory," *Inc.,* May 1998, 55–65.
- *Zagat's Survey,* retrieved 2 November 2003 from http://www .zagatsurvey.com.

- Saul Hansell, "EBay Faithful Unshaken Despite Ever Slimmer Profits," *New York Times,* 30 June 2003.

6. Howard Rheingold, *Smart Mobs–The Next Social Revolution,* 1st ed. (Cambridge, MA: Perseus Publishing, 2002), 113–127; Reputations Research Network, online at http://databases.si.umich.edu/reputations.

7. Mark Frauenfelder, "Revenge of the Know-It-Alls: Inside the Web's Free-Advice Revolution," *Wired,* July 2000, retrieved 5 March 2004 from http://www.wired.com/wired/archive/8.07/egoboo.html?pg=3.

8. Henry Jenkins, "Why Blog," *MIT Technology Review,* March 2002, 91.

9. Nicholas Thompson, "More Companies Pay Heed to Their 'Word of Mouse' Reputation," *New York Times,* 23 June 2003; C4.

10. Erica Goode, "In Weird Math of Choices, 6 Choices Can Beat 600," *New York Times,* 9 January 2001; Dorothy Leonard and Jeffrey F. Rayport, "Spark Innovation through Empathetic Design," *Harvard Business Review,* November-December 1997, 103–113; Seth Godin, "If It's Broke, Fix It," *Fast Company,* October 2003, 131; Alan M. Webber, "Will Companies Ever Learn?" *Fast Company,* October 2000, 275–282; John F. Sherry, Jr., *Contemporary Marketing and Consumer Behavior: An Anthropological Sourcebook* (Thousand Parks, CA: Sage Publications, 1995), 23–30; Seth Godin, Purple Cow: Transform Your Business by Being Remarkable (New York, NY: Portfolio, 2003).

Chapter Four

1. George Bernard Shaw, retrieved 28 January 2004 from http://www.quoteland.com/author.asp?AUTHOR_ID=69; Kevin Cooney, Internet story on American businessman/Mexican fishing village, forwarded to the author 25 July 2003; John Perry Barlow, "A Taxonomy of Information," *Bulletin of the American Society for Information Science,* June/July 1994, 13–17; Claire McInerney, *Information Science–An Art and a Science,* 1997, retrieved 15 October 2003 from http://scils.rutgers.edu /~clairemc/infsci.html.

2. Gary Rivlin, "Leader of the Free World," *Wired,* retrieved 31 October 2003 from http://www.wired.com/wired/archive/11.11/linus_pr .html.

3. Dutch Boy paint sources:

- "Dutch Boy Paint®: A Background and History," retrieved 28 October 2003 from http://pressroom.dutchboy.com/press_releases/quart_dutchboy_backgrounder.htm.
- Robert Leaversuch, "Close-up on Technology—Paint Cans: All-Plastic Paint Cans Challenge Steel," retrieved 28 October 2003 from http://www.plasticstechnology.com/articles/2003 10cu1.html.
- Popular Science, "Best of What's New," retrieved 28 October 2003 from http://www.popsi.com/popsci/bown/article/0,16 106,388282,00.html.
- Barbara Perry, Ph.D., in presentation(s) with the author, 2003.

4. Albert Einstein, retrieved 10 February 2004 from www.prince ton.edu/~eszter/elist/elist-quotes.html.

5. David Boyle, *The Sum of Our Discontent: Why Numbers Make Us Irrational* (New York, NY: Thomson Texere, 2001).

6. Joan Didion, *The White Album* (New York, NY: Simon and Schuster, 1979); Christopher Locke, *Gonzo Marketing: Winning through the Worst Practices,* 1st ed. (New York: Perseus Publishing, 2001), 46; James P. Carse, *Finite and Infinite Games–A Vision of Life as Play and Possibility* (New York, NY: Ballantine Books, 1987); Clarissa Pinkola Estes, *Women Who Run with the Wolves* (New York, NY: Ballantine Books, 1996), 110–111; Gordon McKenzie, *Orbiting the Giant Hairball* (New York: Viking, 1996).

7. Chuck Williams, "How We Got Started (Williams Sonoma)," *Fortune Small Business,* September 2003, 31–37.

Chapter Five

1. Sophocles, *The Antigone* (London, England: G. Allen & Unwin, Ltd., 1941).

2. Yvon Chouinard, "Patagonia: The Next Hundred Years," in *Sacred Trusts: Essays on Stewardship and Responsibility,* ed. Michael Katakis (San Francisco, CA: Mercury House, 1993); Seth Godin, *Purple Cow: Transform Your Business by Being Remarkable* (New York, NY: Portfolio, 2003); Malcolm Gladwell, *The Tipping Point: How Little Things Can Make a Big Difference* (Boston, MA: Little Brown & Co., 2000); Edward Keller and Jon Berry, *The Influentials* (New York, NY: Free Press, 2003); Geoffrey A. Moore, *Crossing the Chasm: Marketing and Selling High-Tech Products to Mainstream Customers* (New York, NY: Harper Business, 1999);

Ryan Mathews and Watts Wacker, *The Deviant's Advantage: How Fringe Ideas Create Mass Markets* (New York, NY: Crown Business, 2002).

3. Everett M. Rogers, *Diffusion of Innovation* (New York, NY: Free Press, 2003).

4. A. Kimball Romney, Susan C. Weller, and William H. Batchelder, "Culture as Consensus: A Theory of Culture and Informant Accuracy," *American Anthropologist* 88, no. 2 (1986): 313–338.

5. Janelle Brown, "Their Little Secret, But for How Long?" *New York Times,* 7 March 2003.

6. Adam Sternbergh, "2003: The 3rd Annual Year in Ideas; Instantly Passé Trend," *New York Times,* 14 December 2003.

7. Focus group references:

- Foden Athol, "Customer-Focused Efforts Require Listening," *Marketing News,* 3 March 2003, Volume 37, Issue 5, page 56.
- Ric Casale, "It's Time to Retool Consumer Research," *Brandweek,* 3 November 2003, 24.
- Daniel Gross, "Lies, Damn Lies, and Focus Groups: Why Don't Consumers Tell the Truth about What They Want?" retrieved 13 October 2003 from http://slate.msn.com/toolbar.aspx?action=print&id=2089677.
- Dennis W. Rook, "Focus Groups Fail to Connect Theory, Current Practice," *Marketing News,* 15 September 2003, Volume 37, Issue 19, page 48.
- Todd Wasserman, "Sharpening the Focus," *Brandweek,* 3 November 2003, 28–32.
- Alison Steiner Wellner, "The New Science of Focus Groups," *American Demographics,* March 2003, Volume 25, Issue 2, page 29.
- Clive Thompson, "There's a Sucker Born in Every Medial Prefrontal Cortex," *New York Times Magazine,* 26 October 2003; 54–58, 85.
- Gerald Zaltman, "Marketing Knowledge: What Consumers Don't Know They Know," retrieved 17 January 2001 from http://www.marketingcafé.com/content/zaltman.htm.
- Gerald Zaltman, *How Customers Think: Essential Insights into the Mind of the Market* (Cambridge, MA: Harvard Business School Press, 2003), 17, 113, 122–124.

8. Rob Walker, "The Marketing of No Marketing: Pabst Blue Ribbon," *New York Times Magazine,* 22 June 2003, 42–45.

9. Naomi Klein, *No Space, No Choice, No Jobs, No Logo: Taking Aim at the Brand Bullies* (New York, NY: Picador USA, 2000); Diffusion of innovation references:

- Peter N. Golder and Gerard J. Tellis, "Beyond Diffusion: An Affordability Model of the Growth of New Consumer Durables," *Journal of Forecasting,* retrieved 6 February 2001 from http://www3.interscience.wiley.com/cgi-bin/abstract/10007 980.START.
- Peter N. Golder and Gerard J. Tellis, "Will It Ever Fly? Modeling the Takeoff of Really New Consumer Durables," *Marketing Science* 16, no. 3 (1997), retrieved 1 November 2001 from http://www.marketingscience.org/abstracts/vol16/no3/golerandtel lis.html.
- Kalle Lyytinen and Jan Damsgaard, "What's Wrong with the Diffusion of Innovation Theory: The Case of a Complex and Networked Technology," retrieved 6 February 2001 from http://www.cs.auc.dk/~damse/doitheory.html.
- Jennifer McFarland, "The Consumer Anthropologist," *Harvard Business School Working Knowledge,* 24 September 2001, retrieved from http://hbswk.hbs.edu/item.jhtml?id=2514&t= marketing.
- Geoffrey A. Moore, *Crossing the Chasm: Marketing and Selling High-Tech Products to Mainstream Customers* (New York, NY: Harper Business, 1999).
- Anthony W. Ulwick, "Turn Customer Input into Innovation," *Harvard Business Review,* January 2002, 91–97.
- Christophe Van den Bulte, "New Product Diffusion Acceleration: Measurement and Analysis," *Marketing Science* 19, no. 4 (2000).
- "Diffusion of Innovation Theory," retrieved 6 February 2001 from http://www.bu.edu/people/kaoki/cm380/lecture10 .htm.
- "Adoption, Resistance to, and Diffusion of Innovations," retrieved 6 February 2001 from http://courses.bus.ualberta.ca/ consumer-behavior/Lectures/98-99LectureNotes/Diffusion .htm.
- "New Products Take Six Years to Take Off," *Outlook,* April 1999, retrieved 6 February 2001 from http://www.coams.com /home/outlook.9904/newprodu.htm.

- Lisa Penaloza, "The Commodification of the American West: Marketers' Production of Cultural Meanings at the Trade Show," *Journal of Marketing* 64 (October 2000): 82–109.

Chapter Six

1. Winston Churchill, retrieved 14 March 2004 from http://www .brainyquote.com/quotes/quotes/s/sirwinston107050.html.

2. Ecotone definition retrieved 10 July 2003 from http://www.uw sp.edu/geo/projects/virtdept/ipvft/stop3.html.

3. Maslow references:

- Abraham Maslow, "A Theory of Human Motivation," *Psychological Review* #50, 370–396, (1943).
- Dr. C. George Boeree, "Personality Theories: Abraham Maslow," retrieved December 15, 2003 from http://www.ship.edu /~cgboeree/maslow.html.
- William G. Huitt, "Maslow's Hierarchy of Needs," retrieved 14 March 2004 from http://chiron.valdosta.edu/whuitt/col/reg sys/maslow.html.
- Abraham Maslow, *Motivation and Personality*, 2nd ed. (New York, NY: Harper & Row, 1970).

4. David Boyle, *The Sum of Our Discontent: Why Numbers Make Us Irrational* (New York, NY: Thomson Texere, 2001).

5. Randolph Fillmore, "Anthro-Journalism," The Center for Anthropology and Science Communications, retrieved 29 July 2001 from http:// www.scinecesitescom.com/CASC/ajrf.html.

6. Fritjof Capra, *The Turning Point: Science, Society, and the Rising Culture* (New York, NY: Simon and Schuster, 1982).

7. Charles Fishman, "The Wal-Mart You Don't Know," *Fast Company*, December 2003, 68, retrieved 20 December 2003 from http:// www.fastcompany.com/magazine/77/walmart.html.

8. Barbara Perry, in conversations with the author, 2000–2004.

Chapter Seven

1. Wilson Mizner, retrieved 18 March 2004 from http://www.quota tionspage.com/search.php3?homesearch=listen.

2. Burton Snowboards case study references:

- Cathy Horyn, "To Balance a Business, He Rides a Snowboard," *New York Times,* 24 August 2003.
- Jake Burton Carpenter interview, retrieved from http://snow board.mountainzone.com/interviews/2000/burton/html/.

3. Eric Fromm, *The Art of Listening* (New York: Continuum, 1998), 192.

4. Shunryu Suzuki, *Zen Mind, Beginner's Mind,* 1st ed. (New York, NY: Walker/Weatherhill, 1970).

5. Nathan Schwartz-Salant, *The Mystery of Human Relationships: Alchemy and the Transformation of the Self* (New York, NY: Routledge, 1998).

6. Rekha Balu, "Strategic Innovation: Hindustan Lever, Ltd.," *Fast Company,* June 2001, 120, retrieved 19 December 2003 from http://www .fastcompany.com/magazine/47/hindustan.html.

7. Procter & Gamble references:

- Fara Warner, "Don't Shout, Listen," *Fast Company,* August 2001, 130, retrieved 19 December 2003 from http://www.fast company.com/magazine/49/bestpractice.html.
- Randall Rothenberg, "John Quelch: The Thought Leader Interview," *Strategy + Business,* third quarter, 2000, 93–100.

8. Ibid.

9. Ibid.

10. Robert Kegan, *The Evolving Self: Problem and Process in Human Development* (Cambridge, MA: Harvard University Press, 1982).

11. Diane Ackerman, *A Natural History of the Senses,* 1st ed. (New York, NY: Random House, 1990).

12. "The Oneness of Life and Environment," retrieved 16 November 2003 from http://www.guernsey.net/~moorman/ESHO_FUNI.html.

13. Federico Garcia Lorca, *In Search of Duende* (New York, NY: New Directions, 1998).

14. Dinitia Smith, "Diagnosis Goes Low Tech," retrieved 30 October 2003 from http://www.npr.org/display_pages/features/feature_14808 63.html.

Chapter Eight

1. Antoine De Saint-Exupery, *Wind, Sand, and Sea,* retrieved 12 February 2004 from http://www.brainyquote.com/quotes/quotes/a/antoinedes154898.html.

2. John Guare, *Six Degrees of Separation: A Play,* 1st ed. (New York, NY: Random House, 1990).

3. Stanley Milgram, "The Small World Problem," *Psychology Today* 61 (1967) 60–67; "Six Degrees of Kevin Bacon," retrieved from http://www.theoracleofbacon.com.

4. Brian Hayes, "Computing Science Graph Theory in Practice, Part I: People Who Know People," *American Scientist,* retrieved 27 November 2001 from http://www.sigmaxi.org/amsci/issues/comsci00/compsci2000-01.html.

5. Duncan J. Watts, *Six Degrees: The Science of a Connected Age* (New York, NY: W.W. Norton, 2003).

6. Darby Saxbe, "Small World, After All: Two New Studies Test the 'Six Degrees of Separation' Hypothesis," *Psychology Today,* November/December 2003, 16,
Friendster references:

- Friendster, online at http://www.friendster.com.
- Michael Erard, "Decoding the New Cues in Online Society," *New York Times,* 27 November 2003.
- Jennifer Saranow, "Friend Frenzy," *Wall Street Journal Online,* 12 December 2003.
- Retrieved 17 December 2003 from http://online.wsj.com/article/0,,SB107029494248562500,00.html.
- Jon Gertner, "Social Networks," *New York Times,* 14 December 2003.

7. Dave Coleman, retrieved October 2003 from http://blogosphere.headmap.com/friendster/dav.html; Tinker Hatfield, in conversations with the author, 2000–2004.

8. Marshall McLuhan and Quentin Fiore, *The Medium Is the Message* (New York, NY: Random House, 1967); Marshall McLuhan, *Understanding Media: The Extensions of Man,* 1st ed. (New York, NY: McGraw-Hill, 1964); Carleen Hawn, "If He's So Smart . . ." *Fast Company,* January 2004, 68–74; Allison Arieff, "The Substance of Style," *Dwell,* November/December 2003, 124–128; Stephen H. Zades, "Creativity Regained," *Inc.,* September 2003, 61–68.

9. Lisa Bannon and Alessandra Galloni, "Brand Manager Deluxe: How LVMH's Arnault Matches Wild Designers, Iconic Labels to Commercialize Creativity," retrieved 13 October 2003 from http://online.wsj.com.

Chapter Nine

1. Gregory Bateson, *Mind and Nature: A Necessary Unity* (Glasgow, Scotland: Collins, 1979).

2. Gary A. Klein, *Intuition at Work: Why Developing Your Gut Instincts Will Make You Better at What You Do* (New York, NY: Currency/Doubleday, 2003)

Ken Gart, in conversations with the author, 2000–2004.

3. Thomas A. Stewart, "How to Think with Your Gut: How the Geniuses behind the Osbournes, the Mini, Federal Express, and Starbucks Followed Their Instincts and Reached Success," *Business 2.0,* November 2002, retrieved 19 May 2003 from http://www.business2.com/articles/mag/print/0,1643,44584,00.html.

4. Raymond Dreyfack, "Use That Sixth Sense—Instinct," *Industrial Management,* December 1967, 11–15.

5. Thomas A. Stewart, "How to Think with Your Gut," *op. cit.*

6. David Boyle, *The Sum of Our Discontent: Why Numbers Make Us Irrational* (New York, NY: Thomson Texere, 2001).

7. Gary Klein, *Sources of Power: How People Make Decisions* (Boston, MA: MIT Press, 1999).

8. Ibid.

9. Songbird case study references:
- Joseph Ogando, "Hear Today, Gone Tomorrow," *Design News* 57, no. 11 (2002): 54.
- "A Deafening Hush," *Community Pharmacy,* 2 April 2002, 27.

Chapter Ten

1. Lao-Tzu, retrieved 15 March 2004 from http://www.spiritwalk.org/laotzu.htm.

2. David Bohm, *On Dialogue,* (New York, NY: Routledge, 1996).

3. Ibid.

4. Paulo Freire, Myra Bergman Ramos (translator), and Donaldo P. Macedo (introduction), *Pedagogy of the Oppressed* (New York: Continuum, 2000).

5. Michael Jager interview, retrieved from http://www.jdk.com.

6. *Harvard Business Review*, 2004.

7. "Lovemarks: The Future beyond Brands (VW Beetle)," retrieved 20 October 2003 from http://www.lovemarks.com/lm/read.php?LID= 39.

Chapter Eleven

1. Brazilian proverb, source unknown.

2. David Abram, *The Spell of the Sensuous: Perception and Language in a More-Than-Human World*, 1st ed. (New York, NY: Pantheon Books, 1996)

Storytelling references:

- Stephen Denning, *The Springboard: How Storytelling Ignites Action in Knowledge-Era Organizations* (Burlington, MA: Butterworth-Heinemann, 2000).
- A.H. Almaas, *Essence with the Elixir of Enlightenment: The Diamond Approach to Inner Realization* (York Beach, ME: Red Wheel/Weiser, 1998), 135.
- Clarissa Pinkola Estes, *Women Who Run with the Wolves* (New York, NY: Ballantine Books, 1996), 15–20.

Conclusion

Scott Bowers, Oakley, vice president of Marketing Worldwide, in conversations with the author, 2003–2004.

Share the message!

Bulk discounts
Discounts start at only 10 copies and range from 30% to 55% off retail price based on quantity.

Custom publishing
Private label a cover with your organization's name and logo. Or, tailor information to your needs with a custom pamphlet that highlights specific chapters.

Ancillaries
Workshop outlines, videos, and other products are available on select titles.

Dynamic speakers
Engaging authors are available to share their expertise and insight at your event.

Call Dearborn Trade Special Sales at 1-800-621-9621, ext. 4444, or e-mail trade@dearborn.com.

Dearborn™
Trade Publishing
A **Kaplan Professional** Company